Becoming Americans

F
596.3
.06
K56
1982

Becoming Americans

Asian Sojourners,
Immigrants, and Refugees
in the Western United States

TRICIA KNOLL

COAST TO COAST BOOKS GOSHEN COLLEGE LIBRARY
GOSHEN, INDIANA PORTLAND, OREGON

Copyright © 1982 by Tricia Knoll.
Maps and graphs © 1982 by Coast to Coast Books.

Library of Congress Cataloging in Publication Data
Knoll, Tricia, 1947-
   Becoming Americans:
      Asian Sojourners, Immigrants, and Refugees in the Western
      United States.
   1. Asian Americans—West (U.S.)—History.
   2. Asian Americans—History.
   3. United States—Emigration and immigration.
   4. West (U.S.)—History.
I. Title
F596.3.06K56   1982   978'.00495   82-4539
ISBN 0-9602664-3-7 (hardcover)   AACR2
ISBN 0-9602664-4-5 (paperback)

Coast to Coast Books
2934 NE 16th Avenue
Portland, Oregon 97212

Printed in USA.

To Gillian, for becoming.

Foreword

Edwin O. Reischauer

The United States has often been called a nation of immigrants. The usual picture this cliché conjures up is of hordes of Southern and Eastern Europeans streaming across the Atlantic and entering the United States through New York, to join the descendants of European pioneers of earlier centuries and the involuntary black immigrants brought here as slaves. America once was a land of whites with a substratum of blacks. Naturalization was for long limited by law to members of these two races.

This situation, however, has significantly changed in recent decades. The greatest flow of people has of late been from the Caribbean area and Latin America. Asians, too, have recently become a noticeable proportion of the population. It is sometimes forgotten that indigenous Americans are from a branch of the Mongoloid people of East Asia, and that a significant proportion of Latin American immigrants have a strong strain of this same blood. Asian immigrants to the United States come overwhelmingly from the Mongoloid region of East Asia, not from South or West Asia. Thus, the United States has clearly changed from being a two-race society to a country made up of all three of the major racial types of humanity.

Although East Asians still form only a small minority of Americans, their recent rise in numbers has been spectacular, especially in the West Coast states and Hawaii. In the islands, in fact, they are the majority. The census of 1980 shows 3,500,000 people of Asian origin in the United States, roughly 1.5 percent of the total population. Their rate of increase has been astounding. After a high point of 243,000 East Asian immigrants between 1901 and 1910, immigration fell to only 9,000 in the 1930s. In 1970 East Asians still constituted only about three quarters of one percent of the population. But in the single decade of the 1970s, 1,312,000 entered, and their total number in this country more than doubled. Statistics for 1981 list another 213,000 arrivals.

As relatively late comers of different race and radically different cultural background from other Americans, East Asians have had a particularly difficult time in establishing themselves in their new country. From the start they were subjected to harsh discrimination. Much of this was enacted into laws, many of which were in force until after World War II. Despite these hardships, East Asians have made a solid place for themselves. One Chinese American has been a U.S. Senator, and as of the present writing there are three U.S. Senators and two Congressmen of Japanese origin. More important has been the success of East Asians as a whole. Most surveys show Asian Americans somewhat ahead of white Americans in average education and income and far above Latin Americans and blacks, the other two major ethnic minorities.

Tricia Knoll in *Becoming Americans* has not made a sociological study of Asian Americans but concentrates on the tragic, happy, and often noble stories of individual people who have come from East Asia to America, particularly to the western states, where most of them have always lived and discrimination against them in earlier years was most severe. She does not allow statistics to iron out human feelings into flat averages or reduce the suffering and joy of individuals to an insipid pudding of generalizations. She has divided her story of Asian American immigrants by their lands of origin. Each of them is sharply different from the others in language and culture, and each has produced a clearly distinct pattern of immigration, shaped by internal forces and by the history of its relations with the United States.

Except for native Americans, the earliest arrivals on our shores from across the Pacific were Chinese. Starting in 1848, they were lured by the fabled gold of California. When it ran out, many stayed to help build the railways of the West and perform menial labor which others disdained. The main Asian immigrants up until 1890, Chinese were the first to suffer discrimination and exclusion. Only after World War II did they again start to come to the United States in appreciable number.

Next to the Chinese in time were the Japanese, going at first to Hawaii and from the 1890s on to the West Coast. Taking the place of the Chinese as menial laborers, they also moved out onto the land, especially as truck farmers. They soon passed the Chinese in total numbers but were subjected to special discrimination and psychological pressure by the great Pacific War between their land of origin and the United States. The unquestioned loyalty to the United States and the magnificent combat record of the second generation Nisei in World War II played a major role in convincing their fellow Americans of the injustice of all racial discrimination and helped win equality for Asian immigrants with those from other parts of the world. Because of Japan's great prosperity in recent decades, emigration from Japan fell off markedly after 1960 as compared with that from other East Asian countries. Although the 1970 census showed the Japanese as still the largest Asian group in the United States, they had slipped to third place by 1980, behind the Chinese and Filipinos.

Koreans were counted for a while with the Japanese, their colonial rulers, but they are on the whole a late group of immigrants, surging from 5,000 in the 1950s, the decade encompassing the Korean War, to 270,000 in the 1970s. Their immigration, unlike that of the Chinese and Japanese but like that of the other Asian groups, stemmed largely from American military involvement in their homeland. They were, however, like the Chinese and Japanese and unlike the others in coming from a cultural background that placed great emphasis on formal education. They were, in fact, unique in that a high proportion of Korean immigrants came for purposes of higher education and already had bonds with mainstream American culture through Protestant Christianity. These factors help account for their rise at an even more rapid pace than the Chinese and Japanese to a relatively high status in American society.

Filipino immigration, like that of the Koreans, started with war, but goes back quite a bit further. It began with the American annexation of the Philippine Islands in 1898 and the use of Filipino mess boys by the American navy, but it did not become large scale until after World War II. Some 359,000 Filipinos entered the United States in the 1970s. With the large recent increase of immigrants, the Filipinos have not on the whole reached the levels in society of the Chinese, Japanese, and Koreans.

The remainder of the Asian Immigrants and the ones Ms. Knoll tells about in most detail are the refugees from the Vietnam War coming from the three former French colonial lands of Vietnam, Laos, and Kampuchea (Cambodia). In the census of 1970 they were lumped into a category of miscellaneous Asians, which altogether constituted only 7 percent of the Asian population in the United States. In the 1980 census, however, 322,000 Vietnamese, 141,000 Laotians, and 102,000 Kampucheans are listed, making up 16 percent of the Asian population. These form a far from homogeneous group, including a large number of the educated former leading families of South Vietnam, destitute boat people, who are in large part ethnic Chinese from Vietnam, and largely nonliterate mountain tribesmen, like the Hmong and Mien from Laos and Vietnam. Their experiences in this country are the most varied and certainly among the most poignant.

It is a very diverse account that Ms. Knoll records. There are great differences between the cultural backgrounds, reasons for emigration, and the conditions encountered in the United States among the various Asian immigrants. The subdivisions suggested by the subtitle of the book are especially revealing: "Sojourners, Immigrants, and Refugees." Like many Europeans, most of the early Chinese and Japanese immigrants saw themselves as sojourners, going abroad to an alien and hostile environment to seek their fortunes or possibly education and then returning home to profit from their years of hardship. For some, this is what actually happened, but more found themselves stranded in their new land. Gradually they shifted into being immigrants, and increasingly new people came to the United States with the thought of emigrating permanently. Then a series of wars involved the United States in the lands of East Asia, bringing waves of refugees to our shores. The Filipinos after the Spanish-American War and the Koreans after the Korean War may have come less as simple refugees than as people seeking new opportunities, but the Vietnam War let loose a flood of genuine refugees. Most of these too will in time make the shift from refugees to immigrants, putting down their roots in the new soil.

In all these different cases, from the lonely Chinese prospector of the 1850s to the bewildered Hmong tribesman of the 1980s, certain themes keep repeating themselves, echoing the experiences of European immigrants. There is the suffering and disappointment of the original emigrants, the discrimination and at times open persecution by a hostile ethnic majority, the painful clash of values between generations, and the eventual triumphs and satisfactions that made all the pain worth bearing, at least for some. It is a moving story Ms. Knoll tells and one that is becoming a significant, integral part of the history of the American people.

Edwin O. Reischauer
Belmont, Massachusetts
May 1982

Contents

Text

Appendices

Maps

Becoming Americans

Introduction

In the fall of 1980, I began talking with my publishers about Asian refugees living in Portland, Oregon. Through the media we sensed their struggles to find work and learn English. Like most Americans, however, we knew little about why the refugees were here or what they faced to survive.

As fall turned to winter and we learned more about the recent arrivals, we realized our ignorance of history as well as current events. Generations of Chinese and Japanese in America had mingled with immigrants from European nations, but what did we know of why they had left China and Japan? Thousands of Filipinos and Koreans came with vastly different backgrounds, but what did we know about their hopes and experiences?

After some preliminary research, we knew we wanted to tell the story of Asians in America. The account would begin with the Chinese—the first Asians to resettle here—and describe the experience of Japanese, Filipinos, and Koreans during the twelve decades before people began arriving from Vietnam, Laos, and Cambodia. The story would be grounded in Asian history to show how events in the Orient led to emigration or flight. The book would focus on the continental western states.

Why concentrate on the mainland West Coast? Thousands of Chinese, Japanese, and Filipinos worked on the sugar cane and pineapple plantations of Hawaii. Many stayed on the islands and helped build their current multiethnic society. Others came to the mainland as job opportunities and immigration laws permitted. Here they joined other Asians who had come directly to California, Oregon, or Washington—the states where most Asians first encountered America and where most Americans of Asian heritage live today.

Learning the story

This book is about experiences throughout 130 years in almost a dozen nations on both sides of the Pacific. The account is based upon reading in history, anthropology, literature, and current journalism; interviews with Asians of all national backgrounds; inspection of hundreds of photographs, both historic and contemporary; and study of census and immigration data. Each of these sources adds an important perspective, although each also has limitations.

There are rich historical materials about China and Japan and the experience of immigrants from those two nations. The Philippine Islands and Korea have received far less study, as have their emigrants. Even university research libraries have scant materials about Vietnam, Laos, and Cambodia—the nations of Southeast Asia once known collectively as Indochina.

Most historical writing about these nations or their peoples suffers from its political framework. Trends are dated with reference to reigns or wars. While rulers and conflicts are potent forces in the history of any nation, they tell only part of the story of how people lived. For other perspectives, I turned to novels, poems, autobiographies, and interviews—personal expressions by ordinary people of their lives in Asia and America. Those sources proved especially important with respect to recent arrivals.

Personal accounts, of course, bring their own set of problems. The meaning of a poem may be lost in metaphor or the significance of fiction be unclear to readers from other cultures. People writing autobiographies or giving interviews for publication may say only what they believe the host country wants to hear. All these sources, written and spoken, are filtered by the exchange of thoughts from one language into another. The interviewer may struggle to understand as hard as the speaker struggles to be understood, each losing information in the exchange.

To add another perspective to the personal accounts, several people worked with me to examine thousands of photographs from the holdings of historical societies, museums, agencies, and individuals. Since the 1930s, anthropologists have recognized the value of photographs as primary research sources. Scholars such as Margaret Mead and John Collier used cameras to gather ethnographic data. Historians, however, have been slow in learning how to glean information from visual images. Yet for the millions of people whose lives yield no written records, photographs are indispensable bridges to the past. Thus, photographs seemed an ideal way to enrich my understanding of the personal experiences of Asians in the United States. Historically, those experiences lie entirely within the era of the camera.

The personal expressions, photographs, and even history books and articles present subjective points of view. To get a better sense of immigration patterns, I turned to census and immigration data. These sources are useful, but bring with them still another set of problems. The census yields a poor count of people who move often, are poor, and avoid contact with anyone from government. Thousands of Asians in America have fit that description. Thousands still do. Thus Asians, along with blacks and several other minority groups, have been notoriously underrepresented in population figures. Adding to the confusion, the definition of ethnic group membership has occasionally changed from one census to the next, making comparisons difficult.

Immigration figures must also be used cautiously. The numbers come from government sources and represent only persons who entered officially. Moreover, the meaning of immigration data, like the meaning of census data, changes with historical circumstances. For many years Koreans were counted as Japanese because Japan controlled Korea. Filipinos were considered U.S. nationals before 1936, thus not counted as immigrants. Hawaii was not a state during the period it received most immigrants and the Royal Hawaiian Government skipped its own census in 1880. Recent refugees have come in so fast that immigration officials check their data with resettlement agencies.

Telling the story

Throughout this volume, Asians tell their own stories. Many excerpts are from unpublished collections of autobiographical accounts written as school assignments by refugee teenagers. The photographs are here too—126 of them dating from 1867 to 1982.

As my research and the collection of photos began to evolve into a book, my publishers and I realized the need for other visual aids. Maps appear near the beginning of each chapter. Charts and graphs are collected in an appendix to make it easy to compare data from one group or era to the next. Chronologies at the ends of chapters show in capsule form the sequence of events that affected each Asian nationality as its emigrants came to America.

What the story means

For three and a half centuries, people from a hundred nations have come to the New World to seek fortunes, start new lives, or escape persecution. Almost every nation has sent sojourners, immigrants, and refugees. Americans of Asian descent share this background with Americans of European and African ancestries.

No matter how long they have lived here, people of Asian ancestry often complain about persistent stereotypes. Advertising features Asians as low-paid workers in laundries and restaurants. Asian women suffer media images of ready-to-please geishas or sexpot Susies of Chinatown. Too many non-Asian Americans expect Asians to be polite, obedient, clever, humble, and timid.

It is true Asian cultures tend to hold aggressive behavior by individuals in low esteem. There are, however, sound reasons for caution in the historical experience of Asians in America. From 1870 through 1900, thousands of Chinese in America were shot by whites in episodes as brutal as any black lynching. Thousands more were herded from one hostile environment to the next in actions as hasty and harsh as the eviction of Indians from their lands. Very few white or black Americans protested these actions in politics, pulpits, or the press.

Anti-Chinese racism is vivid in the collective memory of almost a million Chinese Americans today. The events took place in the generations of grandparents and great grandparents. Furthermore, racist actions against Asians were not limited to Chinese. Filipinos were harassed, expelled, and sometimes killed as they sought new lives on U.S. soil. Japanese Americans were victims of one of the worst acts of racist politics ever to blot American history: the evacuation of 110,000 people to barren internment camps during World War II. For Americans of Filipine and Japanese heritage, these events took place in the generation of parents and grandparents.

Asians also know America's extraordinary military strength from deadly experience in their home countries. U.S. forces have often been allies. Just as often, however, G.I. Joe was the enemy. No nation populated by whites or blacks has felt U.S. power in the form of atomic bombs, defoliants, or napalm. Asian civilians as well as soldiers have suffered from all three. Most Asian Americans today were alive when these events took place.

Asians share these historical reasons for alert restraint during their everyday lives in America. On the other hand, these experiences Asians have in common should not obscure differences among them based upon factors such as nationality, age, language, and education. For generations, China retreated from Western ways while Japan welcomed them. The grandparents of preliterate mountain farmers in Laos and worldly urban merchants in Vietnam each migrated from China, but Hmong and ethnic Chinese are vastly different. Many Filipinos spoke Spanish and Vietnamese French long before either had to learn English. Korean and Chinese revolutionaries studied in U.S. universities while Vietnamese and Cambodians went to institutions in France. Japanese and Filipine intellectuals tended to stay home while Laotians got little education at all.

There are also profound differences among Asians in their reasons for coming to America and their experiences just before arrival. The early Chinese, Japanese, and Filipine immigrants were primarily healthy young men with families waiting for them to return with a share of America's wealth. Few got rich. Like gold seekers from our eastern states, many returned poor and embarrassed at their failure. Those who stayed, however, found in the United States an economy eager for muscle power and placing no premium on formal education.

Compare that experience to refugees from nations decimated by war. Strong young men have been killed by the thousands, leaving their widows, children, and elderly parents to migrate to safety. No extended families farm ancestral lands, assuring a haven in case of failure in the new world. In the United States they find few jobs not requiring skill in English and extensive formal education. For many refugee families, only the children can hope to share fully in the American promise.

Historians estimate that during the eighteenth and nineteenth centuries 10 percent of enslaved Africans shipped across the Atlantic died in passage. Estimates for deaths among people escaping Vietnam by boat during the last six years run as high as 40 percent. Between 1840 and 1910, famine and desperate emigration cut the population of Ireland almost in half. The Khmer Rouge wiped out almost half the population of Cambodia in less than four years. Jews by the millions have been persecuted and murdered for centuries in every occidental nation. Chinese by the millions have received the same treatment in the nations of the Orient as well as the United States, Mexico, Peru, and wherever else they went to settle. One writer compared the eviction of ethnic Chinese from Vietnam after 1975 to the Holocaust of World War II, claiming frail boats on the open sea were a cheap alternative to the gas chamber.

No group has a monopoly on suffering, and one group's agony does not diminish the others'. These comparisons do, however, point to the enormity of the Southeast Asian refugee plight. They also suggest reasons why recent refugees enjoy advantages in America unknown to earlier immigrants, whatever their nation of origin. Refugees of the 1970s and 1980s are protected by previously enacted civil rights legislation beyond the dreams of the most radical nineteenth century reformers. In response to worldwide pressure, U.S. agencies, some not even in existence forty years ago, provide food, clothing, shelter, and training in English. Families and churches, in the best tradition of lending a hand, help refugees start life over.

This history affects how people from Asian nations become Americans. Ethnic awareness is important to success in America, for ethnicity and politics are closely related. Power and position are often attained with the support of fellow ethnics acting almost as an extended family. Sometimes national ancestry lines are as important as party lines in securing the jobs, contracts, and other rewards inherent in politics.

Ethnicity in America is not just a matter of remembering a few dances, costumes, and recipes from the old country. It can be a matter of survival in the new. Languages, courtship patterns, family structures, eating habits, and much else significant to everyday life in the past may vanish in the face of American lifestyles. Often only fragile memories remain—hardly materials on which to build political power.

As the Statue of Liberty was en route from France to New York Harbor, exclusion leagues and mobs in the West fought Asian immigration. Leaders shrieked about threats of "Yellow Peril": Asians taking jobs from whites and undermining the American value system. In 1882, Congress passed legislation stopping Chinese immigration for over sixty years. That Chinese Exclusion Act became a model for laws restricting immigration from Japan and Korea until 1952.

Since 1970 almost 2 million Asians have entered the United States, evidence of how American immigration policy has changed. Now refugees from Southeast Asia knock at the Golden Door. Simultaneously victims and survivors of war and persecution, they sigh with relief that the door is open. Their treks through jungles blistering with enemies, voyages over seas swallowing almost half of all who dared, and long waits in refugee camps end with the hope of Liberty's promise.

America is the new beginning for immigrants and refugees. They accept the responsibilities of citizenship, establish communities to preserve their culture, and cooperate to build businesses and learn new trades. They relish the air of freedom. They too become Americans.

Tricia Knoll
Portland, Oregon
June 1982

ONE

(Thomas Cronise; Oregon Historical Society)

Exploring the Mountain of Gold

Chinese Americans

San Francisco, California, 1848: "The American brig *Eagle* arrived here from Canton, China on the 2nd of February, 1848, with two Chinamen and a Chinawoman, who were looked upon as curiosities by some of the growing town of San Francisco, who had never seen people of that nationality before."[1]

Detached and unemotional, this observer gives no hint of how Chinese would contribute to the history, economy, and culture of the American West. Nor does he foresee the hysteria their numbers would generate in less than thirty years. Though the onlooker knew gold strikes in Sutter's Mill had lured these Chinese laborers to America, he could not guess how soon wooden-soled sandals, padded cotton jackets, and long pigtails swinging from under straw hats would cease to be curiosities. Three years later 25,000 Chinese worked in California. By 1900 their number had swelled to a quarter million. They shared a dream that in *Gum San*, the Mountain of Gold, they would amass quick fortunes and return to waiting families.

Westerners referred to these men, and the rare woman who followed them, as "coolies"—workers willing to do hard manual labor for lower wages than anyone else. According to some sources, the term came from the Chinese phrase *ku li*, meaning "bitter strength."

Chinese expected to work long hours, six days a week, living frugally to save money. Most did not care that U.S. naturalization policy denied them citizenship because they were not "white." They came not as immigrants, but as sojourners intending to return to families who were the center of their lives and would arrange their marriages. Usually they brought neither wives nor brides-to-be. Most never planned to have children in America though birth on American soil would guarantee U.S. citizenship.

These sojourners made up the large-scale immigrations from China to America from 1848 to 1882. Most who came earlier remain shadowy figures of legend. Hui-shen, for example, was a Buddhist missionary who, in 441 A.D., discovered a land called *Fusang* far to the east—probably either Mexico or California.

For centuries after Hui-shen's voyages, Chinese had few reasons to travel outside China and many reasons not to. As the proud citizens of an ancient civilization, they called those who did not have the good fortune to be born Chinese "barbarians." Chinese were best served by having nothing to do with such foreigners. As late as the eighteenth century, the Manchu emperor declared that a man who left China could expect to have his head chopped off if he was caught.

Despite such threats, adventurers dared to disobey. In 1778 a group of 100 Chinese pioneers sailed with a British officer, John Meares, from Kwangtung Province in southern China to Nootka Sound on Vancouver Island, British Columbia. Mostly carpenters and skilled builders, they made the first ship built on the northwest Pacific Coast. History records little about their fates. British ignored them. To the Chinese government they were outlaws. Sketchy reports hint they explored from Puget Sound to Alaska. Tribes of Native Americans lining the Pacific Coast absorbed some.

In the interest of trade, some Chinese earned official permission to leave. Merchants who came to California prior to 1848 played a far more visible role than the early adventurers. They supplied settlements in California's gold fields with rice, sugar, tools, and textiles, prospering like other Chinese merchants already located in Southeast Asia. When the strikes of gold increased, they sent messages to China with their trading ships that there was work in America for the Chinese—and profit.

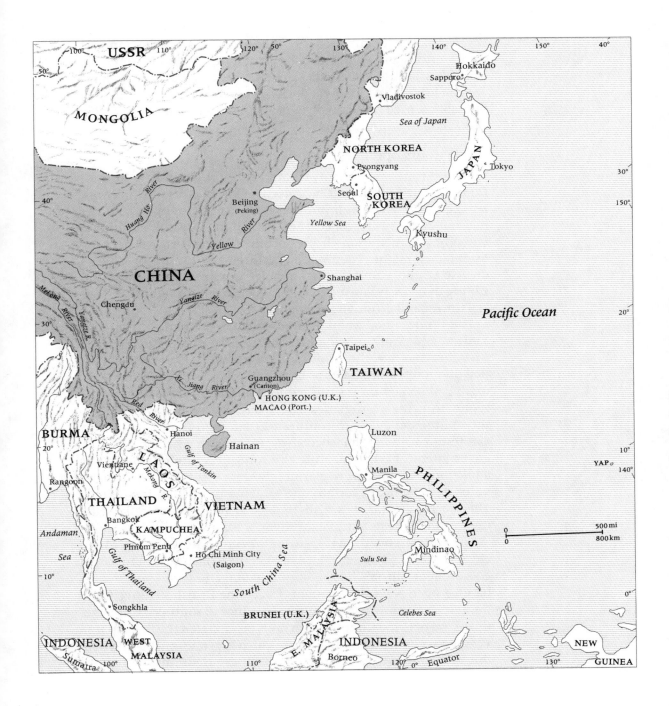

These messages attracted the laborers who had such an impact on America's coast and Hawaii's plantations. Proudly arrayed in silk robes and gold brocade jackets, the merchants may have watched those first laborers docking in San Francisco. If so, they probably sensed how rapidly a growing America and a changing China could profit together.

Trade doors open

Though Chinese merchants had traded throughout Asia for centuries, the trade doors to China itself had been closed to outsiders. By the 1840s Western influences had pried them open. Change had not come easily. Since 1664 the Ch'ing dynasty of Chinese emperors, Manchurians from northern China, had ruled China by military might. They never captured the loyalty of China's diverse ethnic, cultural, and language groups. By the 1800s the Ch'ing dynasty was struggling for its life against political and social unrest and economic problems.

The Chinese had known three kinds of "barbarians": pirates, traders, and Jesuit missionaries. In the mid-nineteenth century they met another: the British opium importer. Chinese had battled off pirates and traders as best they could, although they willingly had picked up scientific information and translation techniques from the missionaries. They were unable, however, to stop the opium smugglers in southern China who traded opium for Chinese tea, which had become treasured in England. Despite government efforts to capture the smugglers, the rate of opium addiction in China grew alarmingly. In 1839 the Manchu emperor decreed death for anyone growing or distributing opium. This decree included British traders arriving from India with opium-filled chests to trade for silver or tea.

The British government refused to cooperate with the Manchus. In 1839 Chinese officials held 350 British merchants and government officials hostage until 20,000 chests of opium were handed over. Next the Manchus forced the British to move from Canton, the capital of Kwangtung Province in southern China, to the island of Hong Kong. Both actions precipitated the first Opium War, between Britain and China, which raged until 1844. When the war ended, Britain controlled Chinese trade through Hong

Magazines in the United States reflected the public's fascination with Chinese. This engraving shows life on board the ship *Alaska*. (*Harper's Illustrated Weekly*, May 20, 1876)

Kong. China was no longer closed to Westerners. The "barbarians" had won.

The Manchu failure to stop the opium trade increased tensions in southern China. Workers no longer trusted the government. They believed only traditional Chinese family loyalties and respect for ancestors held China together. But China in the early nineteenth century was barely holding together. From a population of 150 million in 1651, China had expanded to nearly 300 million by 1850. Natural disaster, such as the flooding and changing course of the Yellow River in 1852, left thousands homeless. Famine and starvation followed years of bad weather.

The Manchu government could not cope with these massive problems. Government officials concentrated on bribes, payoffs, and promotions rather than duties. The outflow of silver from China to pay for opium made silver prices soar. Peasants could no longer scrape together enough copper coinage to buy silver to pay their taxes. When the rich hoarded silver, prices rose again. Bandits terrorized the poor in southern China. Rebels plotted to overthrow the northern Manchus. In a rebellion lasting more than ten years, probably more than 20 million died.

With the government failing, family organizations offered the only social stability. Family leaders solved disputes and arranged care for the elderly, sick, and disabled. They fretted that the majority of the rapidly growing population was so young—a surplus, unemployed labor force still needing food. Permanent emigration of families was not really an option because Chinese believed in living close to their ancestral grounds.

Laborers migrate

The opening of China to outside trade provided family elders with a solution: labor contracts sent youngest sons to work temporarily in other countries such as Cuba, Peru, Hawaii, Sumatra, Malaya, Australia, New Zealand, and Vietnam. Young men in Canton in southern China began to emigrate in such numbers that the government could not stop them. From 1840 to 1900, some 2.5 million Chinese left China. Of those millions, 300,000 came to the United States.

Gold in Sutter's Mill, California! Eager young men responded to calls from Chinese merchants in California in 1848. Wealth and work were powerful attractions. They signed documents written in English committing them to work many years in the mines. They accepted loans from Chinese labor contractors or shipowners for passage to California, agreeing to pay the money back with earnings yet to be made. Some, like 100 of the 500 passengers of the trading ship *Libertad* in 1854, died in dank cargo holds never designed to carry humans.

Handbills flooded China from 1848 on: *"There are laborers wanted in the land of Oregon, in the United States of America. They will supply good houses and plenty of food. They will pay $24 a month and treat you considerately when you arrive. There is no fear of slavery. All is nice. The money required for the voyage is $58. Persons having security can have it sold, or borrow money of me upon security."*[2]

At the other end, the U.S. government recognized the need for Chinese labor in the West. In 1868 the United States and China

Chinese miners, carrying all necessary equipment on their backs, often sought gold in places considered inaccessible or unproductive by others. (Nevada Historical Society)

signed the Burlingame Treaty, which allowed easy entrance of citizens of each country into the other country. Though it implied that citizens of either country would be treated as equals if they chose to immigrate, citizenship was never promised Chinese coming to America. The Burlingame Treaty remained in effect only as long as the United States needed Chinese laborers.

Chinese miners

Wherever new gold strikes were made, Chinese workers, their labor contractors, and merchants formed communities. From the hills of California to the rivers of Idaho and Utah, Chinese miners toiled, often doing work too tedious and tiring to interest non-Chinese. They led burros, moved gold pans, and operated hydraulic nozzles which flushed loads of soil to be examined for gold.

They picked through gravel piles for gold flecks overlooked by miners anxious for bigger hauls and hoarded grains of gold dust to send home.

An observer in 1890 described these miners: "... they soon flocked into the mining regions in swarms, well satisfied to work over the old abandoned claims left and deserted by others. They were welcomed by the mining communities with open arms, as it was soon discovered that the Chinese would not preempt or locate any new mining grounds, desiring only to buy at a fair price the old worked-out claims which had been abandoned ... and well did these disciples of Confucius merit the title of scavengers of the mining regions, for many of the old claims which had been abandoned as worthless, were not so in fact, as it was soon discovered that from many of them the Chinese were taking out large amounts of gold."[3]

The 1870 Census showed the large proportions of Chinese miners. In California 28 percent of the total mining population was Chinese. Other states were similar: Montana with 23 percent and Washington with 25 percent. Two were significantly higher: Idaho with 59 percent and Oregon with 61 percent.

Despite the Burlingame Treaty, Chinese miners were not treated equally with other miners scratching for gold, silver, coal, and borax. In 1854 California established a Foreign Miner's License Tax which rose steeply each year. As Chinese miners pushed north, Oregon, Washington, and British Columbia followed suit. Tax revenues were significant. For twenty years the Foreign Miner's Tax represented one-half of California's annual income from all sources.

Other legislation further discriminated against the Chinese. In most western states, statutes prohibited Chinese from testifying in court against whites. In 1860 California segregated schools. That state law stood until 1947. As Chinese moved out of mining into work in fishing, agriculture, and service industries, legislation to restrict their participation usually followed.

Despite legal difficulties, Chinese continued to move. They headed up the Columbia River Valley to Walla Walla, Spokane, Yakima, and Ellensburg. When gold strikes in Washington near Walla Walla and Fort Colville declined, they moved on to Idaho

Chinese physicians treated Chinese and non-Chinese in cities and rural communities. Their cures included herbal remedies and broths credited for healing everything from flu to blood poisoning. Lee Me Him practiced in Carbon, Wyoming, in the 1890s. (Wyoming State Archives)

and Montana. They drifted across Oregon, from Jacksonville to John Day to Baker.

Chinatowns

In each city the sojourners returned to segregated quarters known as Chinatowns which offered services to both Chinese and non-Chinese populations. Chinese sold mining supplies cheaper than white competitors. Delivery men hustled through crowded streets balancing goods on the ends of long poles slung over their shoulders. Guards lurked near thick doors that hid casinos where Chinese frequently lost their earnings at fantan, Chinese bingo, guessing games, or dominoes. On curbsides, barbers braided queues, the long pigtails Chinese men wore as part of the Manchu tradition. Dealers weighed and sold fish from baskets.

Everywhere space was at a premium. San Francisco landlords burrowed rambling underground passages, added balconies, and attached sheds and lean-tos to already crowded accommodations. Laborers scuttled down narrow, dark passageways to small compartments which had been partitioned and stacked with berths to provide cheap spaces for the men who crowded Chinatown in winter: workers from the salmon canneries in the North, fruit pickers, farmhands, and miners.

Distinctive sights, sounds, and smells characterized these bustling Chinatowns. Opium, which sold for 25¢ a 12-pipeful jar, scented the air until the drug became illegal in 1906. Music from clanging gongs, one-stringed fiddles, and banjos flooded into the streets from Chinese theaters. Productions starred men in women's roles, because there were so few women in Chinatown. Their sounds competed with the whine of knives sharpening, the calls of fruit and pork vendors, and the squawks of chickens in coops stacked outside grocery stores. The scent of incense burning on joss house altars decorated with paper prayers and candlesticks wafted through the streets.

New Years were celebrated in February as they had been in China—with tradition and jubilation. Households undertook cleaning sprees. Debtors paid bills to start over with a clean slate. Firecrackers exploded away bad spirits. People visited friends and relatives, leaving calling cards of red paper to wish them well.

Until the Japanese challenged them, the Chinese dominated every city's laundry business. All work was done by hand. Laundrymen worked eighteen hours a day, darting quickly from hot mangles to small metal irons for shirt collars and sleeves. Heated stoves dried piece laundry in upstairs rooms. Chinese succeeded in the laundry business because there was a steady demand in the frontier towns and the hand work took so long no one else wanted to do it. Commonly, when the weary men finished with the last shirts and sheets, they folded the laundry, smoothed out the ironing boards, and fell into sleep on the ironing tables until the first light of dawn awakened them to start the routine again.

Chinese men worshiped traditional deities in joss houses equipped with elaborate altars and scrolls. (Ernst Skarstedt, *Oregon och Washington*, 1890)

Chinese restaurants fed both Chinese and non-Chinese. They remain one of the most common Chinese enterprises to this day. A miner in 1852 described one of the earliest Cantonese-style restaurants: "They serve everything promptly, cleanly, hot and well-cooked; ... their own peculiar soups, curries, and ragouts which cannot be imitated elsewhere; and such are their quickness and civil attention, that they anticipate your wants and of course secure your patronage."[4] Favorite specialties were rice, soups, fish, fried pork, and chicken.

In the 1870s the gold rush fizzled. Easy riches disappeared. Some Chinese reworked the huge gravel piles left by hydraulic and dredge mining operations. Others leased mine claims, although they feared non-Chinese miners might drive them off if they were too successful. Many who had accumulated some wealth returned to China.

Dwindling finds dashed dreams of wealth. Mary Chan, a resident of Vancouver, British Columbia, tells a story typical of many Chinese families: *"My grandfather came over from Kwangtung in 1879 on a sailing ship. It took him several months to get here and he came right to Vancouver. He was coming to look for gold. You had to walk a long way along the river and then all you got was a bit of gold dust. He made just enough to eat. So then he went to work on the railroad. Many people died during the construction of that railroad. They lived in tents along the track and it was cold. Some people got arthritis. They were attacked by mosquitoes and black flies, and some people eventually went blind. And then, after it was finished, there was no other work. So he . . . raised pigs and chickens. He used white cloth to partition off his land."*[5]

In 1923 he returned to China, an unpopular decision with his family because living conditions in Asia were often more primitive than in Canada. Eventually some of the children this man took back with him to China, like Mary, returned to Canada.

Building railroads

The pattern developed of miner turning railroad worker. In 1863 Central Pacific began hiring mostly non-Chinese laborers. By 1865, however, only thirty-one miles of track had been laid, a far cry from joining the East Coast with the West. Charles Crocker, construction director of the Central Pacific, insisted Chinese be hired to lay track. When other company officials doubted the small Chinese could do the hard work, Crocker argued that if Chinese could build the Great Wall of China, they could probably build a railroad. The company pitted a Chinese crew against an Irish-American one in a week-long competition. The Chinese laid

More than 12,000 Chinese helped build the Central Pacific Railroad. To construct this 1,100-foot trestle over Secrettown Ravine sixty miles east of Sacramento, California, workers used only hand tools. They hauled diggings in wheelbarrows and one-horse dump carts. (Southern Pacific Railroad Company)

more track, straighter and neater, and settled all doubts.

Eventually 90 percent of the workers on the Central Pacific were Chinese. Albert Richardson, a correspondent from the *New York Tribune*, saw them toil: "They [the Chinese] were a great army laying siege to Nature in her strongest citadel. The rugged mountains looked like stupendous anthills. They swarmed with Celestials shoveling, wheeling, carting, drilling, and blasting rocks and earth."[6]

In 1869 the transcontinental railroad was finished; the Union Pacific met the Central Pacific. Few accounts of the driving of the last stake into a railroad tie acknowledged the Chinese, even though many lost their lives forcing those tracks eastward. One newspaper claimed 20,000 pounds of bones were collected from shallow graves lining the railroad tracks where Chinese workers had fallen. The bones were sent home to China for burial.

Families and tongs

After the transcontinental railroad was completed, those Chinese with money in their pockets returned to Chinatowns in hopes of finding new railroad jobs or went back to China. In major cities like San Francisco, Seattle, Vancouver, and Portland, large Chinatowns supported organizations to help them: family, district, or tong associations.

Family organizations had transplanted themselves easily from China. All Chinese believed that people with the same last name shared common ancestors. Though it was forbidden to marry someone with the same last name no matter how far back the relatives might have been related or how distantly, lineage was traced only through male bloodlines. Based on these strong loyalties, family organizations helped an unemployed member contract for new jobs.

District associations, called the Six Companies, formed in San Francisco as early as 1854. They reflected the six districts of southern China from which most of the laborers had come. Members of each association spoke the same dialect. The Six Companies unofficially governed Chinatowns: assisting in burial plans or sending remains to China, managing employment, and helping solve disputes. Later the Six Companies grew into the Chinese Consolidated Benevolent Association which is still represented in each Chinese American community.

The third kind of organization was the most notorious: the tongs. Tongs in America were rooted in the original secret societies of China that plotted to overthrow the emperor. A tong's membership consisted of families too small to be represented by a family organization. Tongs often fought family groups. Their methods were violent. Hatchetmen, known to the Chinese as *boo how doy*, enforced tong policy with knives, hatchets, and later, guns. Tong wars stemmed from jealousy over the scarce women available; gambling; smuggling and robbery disputes; and competition in business, including prostitution.

Tongs were national. The Hip Sings of Seattle, for example, shared loyalty with the Hip Sings of San Francisco, Portland, Spokane, and Tacoma. A young man tells why he joined a Seattle

Cramped living conditions in Chinatown encouraged vendors to crowd the streets. This peddler sold toys in Chinatown, San Francisco, at the turn of the century. (Arnold Genthe; California Historical Society)

tong to become a *boo how doy*: *"When I left China my mother had begged me tearfully not to mix in tong affairs. They had a bad opinion of the tongs in my native country, not understanding their value. But I had been living among tongmen, they were my friends, I left school partly because of ill health and partly because I had suffered deeply from an unhappy love affair. In this state of mind, it did not take much urging from friends to make me join the Hip Sings."* [7]

Tongs caused most violence in Chinese communities. In Portland, in 1890 the second largest community of Chinese in America, tongs fought openly. Starting with a fist fight between a Hop Sing and a Bow Leong, the war expanded to fifty men on each side swinging hatchets and knives. The Hop Sings ended the fight by bringing in two gunmen who killed five rivals. The dispute broke out periodically up and down the coast until 1917 when both tongs agreed to peace. Pressure from law enforcement and immigration officials forced the tongs to turn to less violent and criminal methods.

The district, family, and tong associations efficiently sprinkled Chinese all over the West from 1870 on in railroad work. Chinese laborers built the Oregon Central, Northern Pacific, Oregon and California, Seattle and Walla Walla, Canadian Pacific, and Central Pacific railroads.

Restrictions and riots

When railroad work ended, problems began. Cheap Chinese labor flooded markets where non-Chinese had been employed. A continual source of conflict was that Chinese willingly worked for less than non-Chinese.

Although it violated the spirit of the Burlingame Treaty, the first method used to reduce Chinese job competition was legal: laws to restrict the immigration of Chinese laborers. When President Chester Arthur signed the Chinese Exclusion Act of 1882, the intent was to halt the immigration of laborers for only ten years. At each renewal date, however, Congress extended the law. This exclusion act stated what immigration policy had long implied: Chinese immigrants could never be U.S. citizens. In 1888 the Scott Act prohibited any Chinese laborer not then in the United States from ever returning unless he had a wife or child here. While the laws allowed for the immigration of merchants and other highly skilled Chinese, they virtually ended the immigration of laborers, the bulk of the numbers coming to the United States from China. Repeal of these laws had to wait until 1947.

Justifications for exclusion came easily. Jobs were in short supply. Some claimed the Chinese sent too much gold home—that American wealth should stay in America.

Tongs reacted immediately to exclusion acts. They smuggled Chinese laborers to the Mexican and Canadian borders, landing them on isolated shores. From Vancouver and Victoria, British Columbia, Chinese came by foot or boat into the United States with forged papers that showed they had relatives here.

As mining grew less profitable and the completion of the railroads reduced opportunities for laborers, more Chinese made livings in cities. Many grew vegetables on the outskirts of town, then carried produce to markets in baskets slung from rake handles. (Oregon Historical Society)

State of Washington officials could not stop the illegal flow. Customs districts in Port Townsend and on the Olympic Peninsula were understaffed. Smugglers simply waited in Canada for rain and fog to hide their ships before moving south. The remote and forested San Juan Islands served as hiding spots when custom boats were sighted. Grim tales are told of non-Chinese captains who, fearing capture, killed boatloads of Chinese laborers. Northwest coves also served to conceal ships moving south to Ilwaco, Washington and Newport, Oregon.

Once laborers arrived in the United States from Mexico or British Columbia, government officials were almost helpless. Illegal immigrants walked as far as the Columbia River where they readily found jobs beside other Chinese in the fish canneries, a job market that would later attract Japanese and Filipino laborers. Until the Japanese started to replace them, almost 80 percent of the cannery workers in Alaska and the Northwest were Chinese. For $1.50 they cleaned 1,600 fish a day. They made cans by pounding them over an iron cylinder. In 1904 machines called "Iron Chinks" were introduced. Each machine replaced fifteen to twenty laborers, cutting the fish mechanically.

Chinese laborers paved the way in numerous job areas for Asians who came later to fill positions left empty by Chinese exclusion. By 1900 Japanese underbid Chinese in the canneries. Meanwhile Chinese branched out into shrimping in California. They established fishing colonies in Monterey, where they caught fish, dried seaweed for sale, and opened trade in abalone meat and shells. Years later Japanese fishermen would follow them into fishing trades along the California coast, particularly in tuna fisheries. As in mining, both groups were subject to taxes never levied against non-Asian fishermen.

Though exclusion acts restricted Chinese immigration and Chinese had diversified into occupations as varied as shirtmaker and vegetable grower, anti-Chinese feeling continued to ripple through the West. One observer said: "There are severe threats made against every Chinaman and every white person who hires them. I heard a man say that if he could find enough men of his mind, they would murder every Chinaman and every white person who had hired them."[8]

Anti-Chinese sentiment was widespread. In 1869 a Chinese crab fisherman in San Francisco was branded with a hot iron. In 1871 nineteen Chinese died in a Los Angeles riot. In 1885 in Rock Springs, Wyoming, townspeople murdered twenty-eight Chinese laborers because they voted against a mining strike.

One notorious incident of anti-Chinese violence took place in Tacoma, Washington, where many Chinese had moved after railroad work stopped. Tacoma's mayor, a German immigrant named J. Robert Weisbach, led anti-Chinese mobs after stirring them up to demand that Chinese leave Tacoma. He focused the discontent of labor unions against Chinese competition for jobs.

First Weisbach used the law. He passed a Cubic Air Ordinance modeled after laws in California which said each citizen needed

In the 1870s, Union Pacific began hiring Chinese to work on the railroads at half the pay of whites. Soon it extended the policy to Wyoming coal mines. In 1885 white miners killed twenty-eight Chinese in Rock Springs, Wyoming. Other Chinese came, with 250 federal soldiers to protect them and keep the mines open. (Lt. C. A. Booth, Seventh U.S. Infantry; Wyoming State Archives)

500 cubic feet of air, laws aimed at crowded Chinatowns. Often, when men were arrested for violations, jails were more crowded than the buildings had been in Chinatown.

Weisbach stirred up trouble. In September 1885 a mob of white men and Native Americans raided Chinese workers on a hops farm near Issaquah, Washington. They fired guns into tents, killed three Chinese, and drove the others out. Then masked men burned the houses of Chinese working in the Coal Creek mines near Tacoma. A month later the mayor went to a statewide labor convention where he urged forcing all Chinese to leave the state by November 1885. He told employers of Chinese to fire them. In reaction, Chinese left Tacoma for Oregon, British Columbia, and eastern Washington.

In October, Weisbach led a torchlit parade through Tacoma. Banners blazoned "Chinese must go." Though the governor of Washington urged moderation, Weisbach ignored him. Groups plotted to drive out the remaining Tacoma Chinese. By the end of October only 200 of the 700 Chinese residents remained.

On November 3, Weisbach acted. A cold rain blasted Tacoma. Foundry whistles signaled hundreds of men to flood the streets brandishing clubs and pistols. Massing near Chinatown, they pounded doors and threatened to slit the throats of any Chinese who stayed.

Not everyone supported Weisbach, but the nonviolent who might have spoken out faced a difficult decision. Weisbach threatened to post the names of anyone opposing him as targets for vengeance, a tactic which made it harder for the sheriff to recruit deputies to resist the mobs. Given the choice of following the mayor or those ministers who counseled speaking out for peace, most remained silent.

At the train station, Chinese paid fares to get away alive. As the train pulled out, Chinatown burned: homes, the joss house, and small stores. When fire crews rushed to extinguish the flames, they found hoses had been slashed.

Years later a student in a Chinese language school wrote about her fears for the Chinese community. Ming-tai Chen said: *"Why did we have to depart from our parents and loved ones and come to stay in a place far away from our homes? It is for no reason but to make a living. In order to make a living here, we have to endure all year around drudgery and all kinds of hardship. We are in a state of seeking shelter under another person's fence, at the threat of being driven away at any moment. We have to swallow down the insults hurled at us."* [9]

Relationships between Chinese and Native Americans were mixed. In Idaho, stories were told of Chinese lynched or driven from their homes into the mountains where they were accepted and lived peacefully in Native American tribes. In several places Native American and Chinese crews worked side by side on the railroad. Both groups perceived that they shared a respect for ancestors and family and the distrust of the white population.

A STATUE FOR *OUR* HARBOR.

Weekly magazines illustrated with steel engravings became popular during the 1870s and 1880s. Often their drawings revealed strong anti-Chinese feelings in the West. This vision of the supposed "Yellow Peril" is set in San Francisco Bay. (*The Wasp*, May 10, 1876)

Elsewhere they ran into conflicts. In 1875 a group of Native Americans murdered Chinese miners in Washington near the Methow River and Chelan Falls. Near Tacoma, when the Northern Pacific made an agreement with the Puyallup Indians in 1876 to use their lands for railroad tracks heading for the coal fields east of the reservation, the Puyallups forced the Northern Pacific to agree to give preference to native laborers. In fact, the Chinese got most of the jobs; once again they were willing to work for less.

For over forty years, beginning in 1900, Chinese immigrants who chose to stay—for reasons varying from owning businesses to having adjusted to life in America or having started families here—faced hard times. Workers initially drawn into agricultural jobs such as truck gardening fruit, flowers, and vegetables to urban markets faced competition from arriving Japanese immigrants. Exclusionists clamored for laws to forbid land ownership to aliens ineligible for citizenship. The first alien land law passed in 1906. By 1920 both Japanese and Chinese were disallowed as landowners, a restriction which, combined with declining Chinese populations, hastened the Chinese movement back to Chinatowns. Labor unions denied membership to Chinese.

From 1900 to 1930 the predominantly male Chinese population in the West drifted into middle age. Between 1872 and 1935, fourteen states passed laws prohibiting marriage between Asians and whites. The 1924 Immigration Act that restricted Japanese immigration to the United States also made it impossible for Chinese men to bring wives here. A kind of permanent Chinese bachelor society established itself. Denied wives, many men in Chinatown turned to gambling and prostitutes for diversion, both of which got them into trouble with authorities. Police cracked down on tong membership. Immigration officials regularly raided Chinatowns to examine immigration papers.

Changes in China

Chinese here kept close watch on events in their homeland. From 1898 on, Japanese intervention in the economic and political structure of Manchuria in northern China stirred conflict. Likewise, Chinese dissatisfaction with the Manchurian (Ch'ing) emperors continued to grow. In 1911 riots swept through China

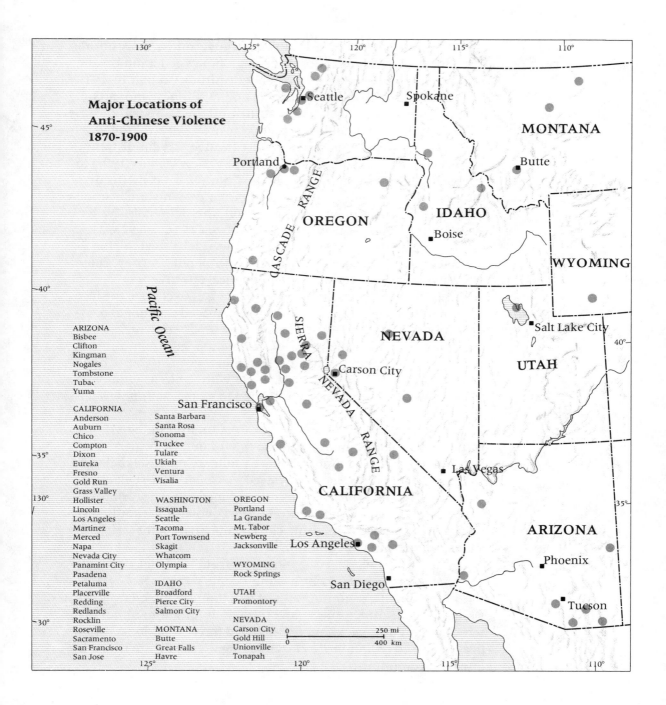

**Major Locations of
Anti-Chinese Violence
1870-1900**

45°

Pacific Ocean

40°

35°

130°

30°

130°   125°   120°   115°   110°

Seattle   Spokane

MONTANA

Portland   Butte

CASCADE RANGE   **OREGON**   **IDAHO**

Boise

WYOMING

Salt Lake City

SIERRA   **NEVADA**   **UTAH**

40°

San Francisco   Carson City

NEVADA RANGE

Las Vegas

CALIFORNIA   35°

ARIZONA

Los Angeles   Phoenix

WYOMING   San Diego   Tucson

ARIZONA
Bisbee
Clifton
Kingman
Nogales
Tombstone
Tubac
Yuma

CALIFORNIA
Anderson   Santa Barbara
Auburn   Santa Rosa
Chico   Sonoma
Compton   Truckee
Dixon   Tulare
Eureka   Ukiah
Fresno   Ventura
Gold Run   Visalia
Grass Valley
Hollister   WASHINGTON   OREGON
Lincoln   Issaquah   Portland
Los Angeles   Seattle   La Grande
Martinez   Tacoma   Mt. Tabor
Merced   Port Townsend Newberg
Napa   Skagit   Jacksonville
Nevada City   Whatcom
Panamint City Olympia   WYOMING
Pasadena   Rock Springs
Petaluma   IDAHO
Placerville   Broadford   UTAH
Redding   Pierce City   Promontory
Redlands   Salmon City
Rocklin   NEVADA
Roseville   MONTANA   Carson City
Sacramento   Butte   Gold Hill
San Francisco Great Falls   Unionville
San Jose   Havre   Tonapah

0   250 mi
0   400 km

31

aimed at the Manchu emperor. Regional governments, historically the most effective means of managing China's geographical and cultural diversity, declared independence from Peking. In 1913 the Manchu emperor left his throne, ending Chinese monarchy. Men in Chinatown celebrated by cutting off their queues.

No solid national government stood ready to control the vastness of China. China's provinces differed widely in administrative practices, culture, language, and geography. New leaders trying to establish a Western-style republic in China proved ineffective. Control fell to warlords. Chinese in America who understood these events sent money to Sun Yat-sen, the nationalist leader. Despite this support, the warlords ruled from 1916 to 1928. Men of strong personality whose armies ravaged local regions for financial support, they were generally unpopular. They ruled through military power rather than political effectiveness.

In the 1920s industrial modernization began to change the face of China. Urban labor forces in factories replaced traditional peasant economies. From 1901 to 1920, some 2,400 students, a category not kept out by the exclusion acts, attended American universities for business and technical training. From 1921 to 1940, the number grew to 5,500. They, along with students who went to Europe, Japan, and Russia, returned to China with new skills and ideas.

Educated, student-oriented groups finally defeated the warlords. The Kuomintang, a group first under the leadership of Sun Yat-sen, wanted to unify China by military means. Finally, in 1927, a faction of the Kuomintang led by Chiang Kai-shek established the Nationalist Party. This group wiped out the warlords as it tried to establish a strong central Chinese government. Chinese in America, denied American citizenship, shared the sense of China's developing nationalism.

Chiang Kai-shek faced opposition from another student-dominated movement. The Chinese People's Party, led by Mao Tse-tung, sought a communist social revolution. Both men agreed China needed strong central government, but their methods differed. Chiang Kai-shek favored military force. Mao looked to a peasant-based revolution, a class uprising to restructure China in line with communist principles.

Opium was introduced into Chinese culture by British traders. Although illegal in China, the drug was allowed in the United States until 1906. Chinese men smoked it to relieve respiratory illness as well as homesickness. (Library of Congress)

Under Chiang's leadership from 1927 to 1937, China faced numerous challenges. Other powerful countries such as Germany and the United States were too involved in their own struggles, primarily economic, to help. Chiang faced increasing aggression from Japan and Russia. He urgently needed to centralize government and combat opposition from students and peasants.

Depression and war

In America, Chinese suffered through the Depression with the American public. By 1929 unemployment in Chinatowns approached 50 percent. Joblessness, housing restrictions, and discriminatory local laws robbed *Gum San*, the Mountain of Gold, of most of its luster. From 1908 to 1943, 52,000 Chinese entered the United States. During that same period, 90,000 went home. One resident of a Chinatown describes how the Chinese who stayed tried to help each other: *"During the Depression, a lot of the lumberyards, shingle mills, and so on closed down, and there were no jobs anywhere. The Chinese Benevolent Association set up a soup kitchen in a building . . . If you had no money and no job, you could go for two meals a day. You got thin rice soup in the morning at nine, and once in the afternoon around four. And that was it, whether you were full or not. The Chinese Benevolent Association raised their own funds for this relief. There was no government help at all."* [10]

When Japan invaded Manchuria in 1937, China entered World War II. Chinese here formed the United China War Relief to send millions of dollars to China over an eight-year period. Because the United States was still committed to non-intervention in foreign affairs, a policy critics labeled isolationism, money from the Chinese in America was the only aid to reach China from here. Chinese and Koreans also organized pickets and boycotts of ships carrying iron from the United States to Japan. Meanwhile, Chiang Kai-shek fought a war of endurance against the Japanese, a strategy based on holding on until other nations could help.

When Japan bombed Pearl Harbor in 1941, Chinese and American relationships shifted. Suddenly they were allies against Japan. The American government urged Chiang Kai-shek and the communists to work together, little understanding the deeply rooted political differences dividing China. Though this alliance lasted until 1945, American money arrived too late to solve the problems of the Nationalist Party.

Chinese in America rallied to help relatives in China, as they had from the beginning. Most sent money. Chinese in Portland, Oregon, donated three planes for fighting the Japanese. Ironically, the planes were named *For the People*, *By the People*, and *Of the*

In February 1939, Chinese Americans gathered in Astoria, Oregon, to protest shipments of scrap iron to Japan. Longshoremen honored the picket lines for one day, then resumed loading ships. (Oregon Historical Society)

People. Chinese who were anxious not to be confused with Japanese immigrants wore buttons with crossed Chinese and American flags proclaiming, "I'm not Jap."

The U.S.-China alliance had an immediate impact on Chinese here. In 1943 the Chinese Exclusion Act was repealed in favor of quotas of 105 Chinese immigrants per year. Chinese were given the right to become naturalized citizens. The 1945 War Brides Act allowed Chinese women to enter the United States as wives of U.S. military men.

Restrictions relax

The 1940s witnessed the end of most legal discrimination. In 1947 the Supreme Court overruled state alien land laws, although some state laws prohibiting intermarriage between whites and Asians stood until 1967. After what must have seemed like a short breathing period for Chinese in America, the United States broke off diplomatic relations with China in 1949. In that year Mao

Tse-tung and his followers came to power, forming the People's Republic of China.

The 1950s marked some gains for Chinese here. Legislation in 1952 assured members of every race they could become citizens. In 1959 Hiram Fong was elected to the United States Senate from the new state of Hawaii. Chinese immigration expanded when the Refugee Relief Acts of 1953 and 1957 permitted refugees of the Chinese civil war and the Korean War to come to America.

Increased immigration from Taiwan and Hong Kong changed the ratio of Chinese men to women in America. In 1860 there were about 95 percent men to 5 percent women. As the decades passed, this ratio reached more of a balance, with approximately 52 percent men to 48 percent women by 1970.

One Chinese American describes the impact of this change: *"Before the war, Chinatown was very quiet, almost a no-man's land because the Chinese could seldom bring their families over. Most men came by themselves. They lived together in tongs and they started working each day as the sun rose and they stopped working when the sun set. You hardly ever found a man who had a day of leisure. But nowadays Chinatown is crowded with women all out shopping. It's at least 10 times more prosperous now."*[11]

After the relaxation of immigration quotas, the Chinese community witnessed a boom in the number of Chinese Americans born here. As became a pattern for most second and third generation Asians in America, some American-born Chinese experienced conflict with their elders. Few spoke Chinese fluently. By 1970 nearly a third chose to marry non-Chinese. At stake were the traditions and values that the foreign-born thought vital to preserving "Chineseness"—everything from arranged marriages to paying all bills before the New Year to the core of Chinese culture, respect for family. The choice of rebelling or conforming to their parents' values may lead to feelings of guilt and rejection. Faced with a society rewarding self-assertion, "doing your own thing," and "telling it like it is," younger Chinese Americans are confused when their parents stress being reserved and polite.

Being American-born has not always protected Chinese Americans from discrimination. Some have sensed they were treated differently in social settings than a white person would have been.

History books often ignore the contributions of those immigrants who, like this Chinese cowboy, do not fit our usual expectations. (Nevada Historical Society)

Statistics show that although Chinese American males enjoy lower unemployment rates and more education than the average American male, they make less money.

Many Chinese Americans chafe under media stereotypes. If they are not coolies with long braids, they are often portrayed as bespectacled scholars or evil villains like the Fu-manchus of movies. Though they experience few barriers in professions such as medicine and law, they have difficulty breaking into executive positions, sales, and highly paid skilled craft jobs.

One Chinese American, a community leader, was asked to compare the harassment of Chinese in America with that of black Americans. He said: *"We did [experience problems], but in a different way. The main reason for our maltreatment, we think, was because we were blind concerning American culture, and we were not well-educated people. So we made every effort to help our children in getting the best education possible. And we are still fighting in this way.''*[12]

In the 1960s Chinese Americans began to work with other Asian Americans and minority groups to redefine ethnic pride. Ethnic studies courses and periodicals started up that help build "Yellow Power."

For many Chinese in America this battle for education and self-identity has paid off. Now as many as six generations of people with Chinese ancestry have earned a flattering profile in American society. Few are on welfare rolls—exceptions being mainly some recent refugees. They tend to aid each other rather than rely on social services. More and more Chinese Americans have become solid members of the middle class which allows them to leave the Chinatowns for other parts of cities or the suburbs.

Like Japanese Americans, Chinese Americans are often called a kind of "super minority." Close to 30 percent of them are professionals in engineering, teaching, medicine, or white-collar jobs. Three Chinese Americans have won Nobel Prizes. Chinese Americans have good citizenship records and are involved in fewer crimes than the average American.

For the middle class who have left Chinatown, organizations based in Chinatown provide a continuing social connection. The Chinese Consolidated Benevolent Associations sponsor Chinese language schools and cultural events. They host lavish New Year's balls attended by governors and mayors.

Despite this solid middle class, other Chinese Americans resent the rosy picture of Chinatowns as quaint tourist and entertainment centers offering trinket and curio shops, restaurants, food outlets, and dishware stores. Studies reveal problems in Chinatowns in Boston, New York, and San Francisco that stem from their early role as places for laborers to procure inexpensive lodging near transportation facilities, harbors, and railroad terminals. Overcrowding is rampant. Garment industries employ Chinese workers in non-union shops that pay sweatshop wages. Crime rates and drug use are rising. Teenage gangs make life annoying or harrowing. Leaders in Chinatowns hesitate to apply for federal aid, fearing bad publicity will reduce walk-in traffic for meals and

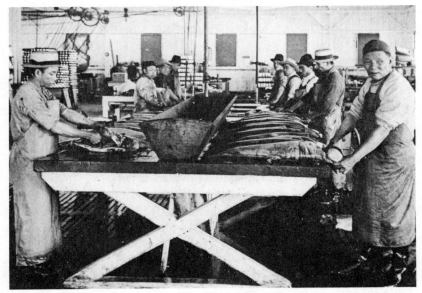

Thousands of Chinese processed salmon in canneries much like this one in Astoria, Oregon. Such work was so identified with the Chinese who performed it that when a machine was developed that ultimately replaced them, it became known as the "Iron Chink." (U.S. Department of Interior; National Maritime Museum)

browsing in shops. They do not want to call attention to ways Chinatowns now are ghettos: high infant mortality rates, poverty, housing shortages, high rents, and a general air of dilapidation.

Recent arrivals

President John Kennedy issued a directive in 1965 to allow Hong Kong refugees originally from mainland China to come to the United States. Immigration law revisions in 1965 further opened immigration to Chinese from Taiwan, Southeast Asia, and Latin America. Chinatowns began to overflow. Most of the new arrivals were well-educated and accustomed to urban living; they came from Hong Kong or Taiwan hoping for better housing or work opportunities. Refugees who escaped political unrest by dangerous trips by boat or on foot often waited months in refugee camps for admittance to the United States. To both immigrants and refugees Chinatown often looked better than the places from which they had come.

Newcomers slipped into niches in densely populated Chinatowns already feeling the pinch of inner city problems. In 1960, 217,000 people of Chinese ancestry lived in America. In 1970 there were 433,000; by 1980, 805,000. Of these, 90 percent concentrated in urban areas such as San Francisco, Honolulu, New York, and Los Angeles. Chinese in the 1960s and 1970s settled in cities that had been simply resting places for so many predecessors who panned gold, built railroads, or canned fish.

Newcomers find what those who came before them found: hard work is the key to survival whether it be in restaurants, retail trades, or small industry. Tommy Woo describes his family: *"My parents have a restaurant business in San Francisco. They are very hard working people. They start at eleven in the morning and work twelve hours a day. They've had the same restaurant for over ten years now, doing the same things over and over, serving the same people over and over, again and again. My parents didn't really want to open a restaurant, but, to them, they had no choice because they were immigrants and couldn't speak a word of English. They had had other jobs, of course, such as janitorial work washing the floor of big restaurants at Fisherman's Wharf, earning only fifty to seventy-five cents an hour. During that time, my sister couldn't go to school because she had to stay home and take care of me all day. So my parents opened a restaurant. The years have gone by; and, to me, my parents seem to be satisfied with their jobs. To enjoy is different than to be satisfied."*[13]

Out of San Francisco's Chinatown came a court decision that had a major impact on the fate of children from a broad spectrum of backgrounds—Spanish-speaking, Samoan, Native American, Japanese, Chinese, Filipino, and Southeast Asian. In 1970 some non-English speaking Chinese American students in San Francisco brought a class action suit against the San Francisco School Board charging they were not receiving the instruction they needed in English as a second language. The result was a Supreme Court decision that established the right of all non-English speaking children to get an education in English and their native tongue. This decision is the origin of bilingual education that has

From 1910 through 1940, Chinese immigrants waited anxiously on Angel Island in San Francisco Bay for permission to enter the country. (California Historical Society)

A contemporary Chinese American poet, Alan Lau, has written:

> *Here on an island of sun bleached rocks*
> *Where Chinese grandmothers sat on benches*
> *In the long afternoons waiting years   feet   inches*
> *For entrance to gold mountain*
> *The broken glass of windows lay on the floor*
> *Jagged tears eating dust.*
>
> *Green thriving bushes cover walls where inside*
> *Poems of despair*
> *Ten thousand washed out dreams*
> *Are scrawled in bitter blood*
> *And seagulls cut white patterns in blue sky.*

been important for Southeast Asian refugees coming to America.

Many of these Southeast Asian refugees are Chinese. They share with other Chinese Americans and recent immigrants from Hong Kong and Taiwan concern over the relative status of Taiwan and the People's Republic of China in the United Nations and American foreign policy. Most lament the communist takeovers of Vietnam, Cambodia, and Laos—takeovers that resulted in their exile. Many suffer the aftereffects of flight, detention in overcrowded camps, and the confusion of resettlement.

This refugee flight is the second chapter of Chinese immigration to the United States. These refugees and new arrivals learn the history of exclusion acts, of housing and educational segregation, and of land ownership and citizenship restrictions that confronted early Chinese. They do not fail to understand how much those early immigrants gave and the mark they have left on American history and culture. But they are also different people, and their trials and contributions will be different.

The refugees know the raw pain of fleeing their homeland rather than the confidence of laborers knowing there are jobs to be had. No families wait patiently at home for these refugees. Their families are fractured, held in camps, or dead in unknown waters and unforgiving jungles. There is a different gold shining in this recent run for *Gum San*—the desperate dream of escaping death to breathe freely.

Chronology

1848 Strike of gold at Sutter's Mill, California, draws Chinese immigrants to West Coast to mine gold.

1853 California levies Foreign Miner's Tax which forces Chinese to pay a tax not required from U.S. citizens. Other states follow.

1854 Law forbids Chinese testifying in court against whites.

1868 China and the United States sign the Burlingame Treaty agreeing to reciprocal trade, travel, and immigration. It does not provide for citizenship for Chinese in America.

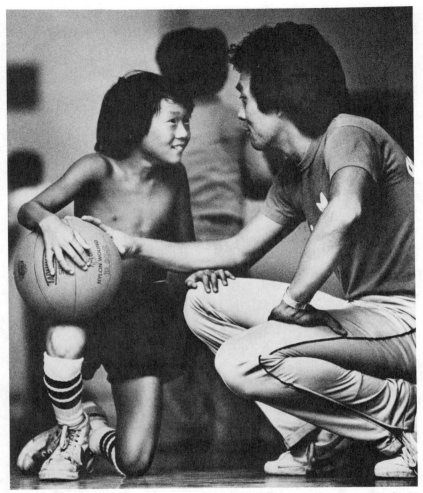

Coach Keith Lee works with a team sponsored by the Chinese American Citizens Alliance. (Brent Wojahn)

1869 Transcontinental railroad is completed. Chinese laborers built most of the western section.

1870 People born in Africa and people of African descent become eligible for U.S. citizenship. Asians do not.

1870 Cubic Air Ordinance in San Francisco says each person in a residence must have 500 cubic feet of air. The law aims at overcrowding in Chinatown.

1871 Anti-Chinese riots break out in Los Angeles and other cities.

1876 San Francisco passes ordinance requiring any Chinese arrested to submit to having his pigtail cut off.

1880 California fines employers hiring Chinese workers.

1882 U.S. Congress enacts Chinese Exclusion Act to halt Chinese immigration. It excludes Chinese from citizenship by naturalization, and slows Chinese immigration for 60 years. At this time 105,000 Chinese live in U.S.

1885 Chinese miners massacred in Rock Springs, Wyoming. Outbreaks against Chinese begin in state of Washington.

1900 Chinese population in America drops to 93,000 as Chinese return to China.

1920 Chinese population declines to 62,000.

1924 Immigration Act declares no one ineligible for citizenship may immigrate.

1929 Unemployment rates in Chinatown rise to 50 percent during Depression.

1937 Japan invades Manchuria. Chinese Americans protest.

1943 Chinese Exclusion Act is repealed. Quota of 105 per year set for Chinese immigration.

1945 Congress passes War Brides Act, allowing 6,000 Chinese women to enter U.S. as brides of men in U.S. military.

1948 Congress passes Displaced Persons Act to give permanent resident status to 3,500 Chinese visitors, seamen, and students caught here because of Chinese civil war. California repeals law banning interracial marriage.

1949 U.S. breaks off diplomatic ties with newly formed People's Republic of China.

1952 McCarran-Walter Act makes Chinese immigrants, many of whom have lived in the U.S. for decades, eligible for citizenship.

1953 Refugee Relief Act allows 3,000 Chinese into U.S. as refugees of Chinese civil war.

1960 Census finds 217,000 of Chinese ancestry living in U.S.

1962 President John Kennedy signs directive permitting refugees from mainland China to enter the U.S. as parolees from Hong Kong. By 1967, 15,000 refugees had entered under this provision.

1965 Public Law 89-236 permits Chinese from Hong Kong, Taiwan, Southeast Asia, and Latin America to immigrate to the U.S.

1970 Census figures for the last decade show a doubling of the population in the U.S. of Chinese ancestry to 433,000.

1972 President Richard Nixon's visit to the People's Republic of China reopens U.S.-China relations.

1973 Bilingual education required for non-English speaking students by a Supreme Court decision based on a case involving students in San Francisco's Chinatown.

1978 Mass exodus begins of Chinese from Vietnam and other parts of Southeast Asia because of persecution. (See Chronology of Overseas Chinese, page 276).

1980 U.S. Census lists 805,000 persons of Chinese ancestry in America, the largest Asian group in America.

GOSHEN COLLEGE LIBRARY
GOSHEN, INDIANA

TWO

(Thomas Cronise; Oregon Historical Society)

Issei, Nisei, Sansei

Japanese Americans

Strong winds and shipwreck made three Japanese sailors unwilling visitors to the western coast of America in 1834. Caught in a typhoon off Japan, they and the rest of the crew of a boat carrying rice and porcelain drifted after waves smashed their rudder. Prevailing winds nudged them east across the Pacific. One by one the sailors starved. Three survivors endured a final wreck on the rocks of Cape Flattery near the Olympic Peninsula in Washington.

Native Americans dragged the seamen ashore and delivered their strangely scripted message on rice paper to Fort Vancouver, Washington. There the tribe accepted ransom for the sailors from British officers stationed at the wilderness outpost. At Fort Vancouver, though the sailors studied English, they dreamed of returning to Japan.

After obtaining passage to London on a fur trading ship, the sailors switched to a vessel bound for Edo (now Tokyo), Japan. In the Edo harbor, however, the British ship was denied permission to enter Japanese waters even to return natives to their homeland. The Japanese wanderers traveled on to Macau, where they settled and taught their language to missionaries.

The sailors' story illustrates the firmness of Japan's closed door policy, which resisted Western attempts in the early 1800s to enter Japan for trade, missions, or any other reason. When finally opened by the threat of Western force, however, Japan chose a course different from China's rejection of "barbarian influence." The island nation eagerly sought Western ideas. Establishing consulates, the Japanese government had a greater influence on the fate of its citizens who eventually went abroad looking for work.

Though Japan had successfully remained closed to Russian and British explorers and traders through the early part of the nineteenth century, by 1850 pressure from American whaling and clipper ships to enter Edo intensified. Culminating years of diplomatic maneuvers, in 1853 American Navy Commodore Perry sailed into the same Edo harbor that had earlier denied the entrance of the British ship carrying returning Japanese citizens. Perry never used the massive gunpower prominent on his decks. Officers of the weaker Japanese Navy recognized Perry's superior weaponry threatened Japan as the Russian fishing fleets and British and Dutch traders had not. Without a shot fired, Perry's entrance to Edo changed the course of Japanese history, paving the way for a treaty in 1854 that opened selected Japanese ports to American ships and, consequently, Western ideas.

In the 1850s Japan, like China, was on the brink of rapid social change anyway. Though the emperor supposedly headed the government, real power over national policy rested in the hands of the Tokugawa shogun who commanded a network of vassals. These daimyos, or landowners, heavily taxed peasant farmers to raise funds to pay tribute to the shogun, leader of the Tokugawa clan. Samurai, a class of fiercely loyal warrior-soldiers, supported the daimyos by enforcing their rule.

Under the shogun, his daimyos, and the samurai, Japan prided itself on national security. It reacted to Perry's threat with a series of treaties that opened all Japan to foreign trade by 1858. Members of the Japanese ruling class vowed Japan would do whatever was necessary to ensure freedom from foreign control.

This vow tore traditional Japanese society apart. The shogun realized Japan could never successfully wage war against Western nations without industrializing. To accomplish that, he raised taxes. Daimyos, in turn, squeezed more money out of peasants already overburdened. When the daimyos realized that money could no longer be made readily in overtaxed agriculture, their

49

traditional source of revenue, they invested in industry. Samurai were loyal to daimyos who welcomed modernization. At the same time, samurai, whose code exalted fighting with swords, envisioned peasants armed with guns and foresaw the end of a way of life that had sustained their class for centuries.

Meiji restoration

While scholars formed the ruling class in China, feudal lords and warriors had always governed in Japan. Those samurai who feared foreign military superiority and recognized the futility of trying to oust "the barbarians" from Japan, believed Japan's only salvation was in learning from the West. They insisted Japan borrow technology and modernize as quickly as possible. Dissatisfied with the shogun's efforts, they banded together with factions of daimyos to overthrow him. By 1868 they had succeeded.

The year 1868 became Meiji One—the first year of the restoration of the Meiji line of emperors. The new emperor was only fourteen years old. Samurai did not care. They and the daimyos who created the new government intended the emperor only to have ceremonial powers. Japan's future was to stay firmly under samurai control.

To build Japan's military power, Meiji leaders promoted ship and railway building, iron smelting, and machine-oriented textile industries patterned after Western processes. Japan's need for raw materials grew. Understanding that colonizing other countries was the pattern for advanced European-style nations, Meiji leaders looked nearby. Japan reached into northern China, Korea, and southeastern Asia. After a war in 1895, Japan forced Russia to divide its interests in China. At home, Japan shifted from a preindustrial economy based upon feudal agriculture to an industrial one built on international diplomacy, trade, modern technology, and economic growth.

A new Meiji constitution resulted in problems that would plague leaders for fifty years. Military officers, legislators, and bureaucrats all had equal powers. No carefully defined system of checks and balances regulated the three groups to resolve policy conflicts among them.

Emphasis on assuming equality with Western nations sparked

Like cowboys in America, samurai in Japan are often portrayed as heroes. This ivory carving from the 1890s depicts a legend of murder and revenge dating from the twelfth century. (Alfred A. Monner; sculpture by Maruki, Carnegie Museum of Art)

other changes. In the 1850s Japan had 30 million citizens. By 1900 there were 46 million. The newly industrialized nation could not use this huge labor force. Peasant families left their rural farms for the cities, hoping to find factory jobs and willing to accept less pay than the city dwellers. Because Japanese law forbade unions or minimum wage guarantees, many city dwellers found themselves without work.

Immigration begins

From 1850 to 1900, however, many foreign countries needed laborers. Though Japan's concept of equality with Western nations ruled out a "coolie trade," sending displaced peasants and city people overseas for work was appealing. As early as Meiji One (1868), 148 contract laborers headed for the sugar cane fields of Hawaii. These laborers came from the cities and were unused to field work. Employers in Hawaii complained they lacked skill. Embarrassed and angry, the Japanese agent in Hawaii who oversaw the experiment ordered the laborers home.

From that time on, the Japanese government worked through its local consulates to examine conditions affecting Japanese workers abroad. These consulates were more effective in protecting Japanese citizens abroad from discrimination than Chinese nationalist associations had been in protecting Chinese. Japanese emigration proceeded slowly after the fiasco in Hawaii. Not until 1885 did Japan legalize emigration so large numbers of Japanese could come to the United States from Japan or Hawaii.

One Issei (a Japanese citizen born in Japan who came to the United States) described why he left Japan: *"I was surprised when I looked at the fellow villager who came back from America expanding his chest and flashing a gold watch chain across his belly. Listening to his story, which made it seem that in America there were a lot of money-trees, anybody would like to go there at least once, and it is quite natural that we poor villagers were amazed that a neighbor youth who went to America could send home 100 yen in a year. In addition, as the returnee was in a position to show a gold chain and such gentlemanly style, we believed his entire story."* [1]

The truth held few gold chains and money-trees. Japanese immigrants walked into a climate of anti-Asian feeling. Further,

In 1869 this Japanese band performed in San Francisco's Woodward Gardens. Why they came we do not know, but perhaps they were "goodwill ambassadors" from the new Japanese government formed in 1868. (Eadweard Muybridge; California Historical Society)

Japanese immigration fueled U.S. newspaper accounts of a new "Yellow Peril" threatening employment, housing, and American culture itself.

Japanese and Chinese were treated equally under American law—poorly. Banned from union membership, both accepted low-paying jobs. Segregation laws shoved both into small, over-crowded communities. After the 1906 earthquake leveled San Francisco, homeless Japanese drifted to the Little Tokyo in Los Angeles, which rivaled San Francisco's Chinatown for density. Little Tokyos, even in smaller California towns such as Fresno, Watsonville, and Salinas, offered services to Japanese laborers similar to those offered in Chinatowns: barbershops, boarding houses, hotels, and markets selling familiar foods. Life in these segregated communities did not encourage newcomers to learn English or interact with Americans.

Despite the proximity of Chinatowns and Little Tokyos, cultural conflicts and job competition made cooperation between the two Asian groups unlikely. Chinese resented Japanese aggression in Manchuria. Japanese underbid Chinese in areas where Chinese had always been employed: railroads, agriculture, canneries, and domestic service. The two groups did not speak the same language. Neither saw the struggle against second-class status in America as a mutual interest.

Other stumbling blocks to cooperation were evident. Japanese immigrants prided themselves on being from a more modern nation than China. They scorned the Chinese claim to a more advanced civilization. Japanese knew that on the average they were better educated than their Chinese counterparts.

Resentment and conflict

In spite of protests against their immigration, the number of Japanese in America ballooned from 25,000 in 1900 to over 70,000 by 1910. Most lived in California, and problems centered there. In 1900 trade unions in San Francisco protested the presence of 25,000 Japanese workers. California papers ran headlines decrying the "Yellow Invasion of California."

Events came to a head in 1906, the year of the largest Japanese immigration to the West Coast. The San Francisco School Board ruled that Chinese, Japanese, and Korean students must attend the Oriental school on Clay Steet in Chinatown because city schools were overcrowded following the 1906 earthquake. The school board further claimed local law supported segregation.

President Theodore Roosevelt's intervention in this action showed national interest conflicted with local anti-Asian sentiment. Aware of Japan's military aggressions in Manchuria and Korea, he decided not to antagonize the Japanese consulates that monitored the welfare of Japanese citizens in America.

Secretary of Commerce and Labor Metcalfe investigated the situation for Roosevelt and gave him what he needed to intervene. Metcalfe reported gangs attacked Japanese students on San Francisco's streets. He found newspaper accounts of "Mongol

Immigrant Japanese parents, Issei, and their American-born offspring, Nisei, posed for famed portraitist Cronise in 1907. Note they chose American-style dress. (Thomas Cronise; Oregon Historical Society)

hordes" overrunning the school system exaggerated: in 1906 ninety-three students of Japanese ancestry in San Francisco attended twenty-three different schools. Twenty-five children were Nisei (second generation Japanese in America who were U.S. citizens by birth). On Metcalfe's advice, Roosevelt forced the school board to retract its ruling.

California was not the only hot spot for the Japanese at the turn of the century. In 1907 anti-Japanese riots erupted in Vancouver, British Columbia, resembling earlier mob actions against Chinese. Promises of jobs and wealth from labor contractors had lured Japanese immigrants from Hawaii to Canada. In July 1907, 1,000 new immigrants flooded a town that only grudgingly had accepted a flow of 300 a month the year before. From January to September, 8,000 Japanese laborers entered the province looking for cannery and logging work.

Unions expressed concern over housing and job shortages. They resented the Japanese cultural tradition of loyalty to an employer, a tradition mirroring that of loyalty to the emperor and country. Loyalty meant Japanese laborers refused to strike when ordered to do so by unions.

The Asiatic Exclusion League, a lobby of union sympathizers, played on these feelings. On September 7, 1907, the league sponsored a parade of 5,000 people to march to Vancouver's city hall. Seating and standing room filled quickly. Thousands milled angrily outside. As others joined the waiting crowd, the street filled with nearly 30,000 people.

Inside, Canadians denounced Asian immigration. Canadian diplomatic policy aimed at avoiding hostilities with Japan was ignored. The assembly voted to ask for laws excluding Japanese from Canada, just as earlier U.S. legislation had excluded Chinese from the United States. In the street, tempers matched the steamy heat. A teenager threw a rock through the window of a shop owned by a Chinese, igniting a rush of vandalism. Merchants hid in the back of their stores.

The crowd next shoved down back streets. As it flowed toward the Japanese section of town, bricks flew. Windows shattered. Japanese merchants retaliated with rocks and bricks thrown from their roofs. Police arrived with clubs and barricades and forced the crowd back. Leaders of the Exclusion League left the meeting hall to urge citizens to forget violence and go home. Vancouver police patrolled the area for two days.

Many Japanese men in the United States worked on the crews that maintained the railroads. (Denver Public Library)

This mob action destroyed fifty-nine Japanese shops. No one died, but several Japanese were stabbed. Japanese shop owners announced they would arm themselves with knives and guns to protect their lives and property.

Official reaction was cautious. The government of British Columbia denied responsibility for the losses. The Canadian government hastened to assure the Japanese Consulate that damages would be paid. The consulate said it trusted the government to make good the loss and helped Japanese evaluate its extent. In time, the Canadian government did compensate Japanese merchants, to underscore that mob violence was not condoned or caused by government agencies.

Gentlemen's Agreement

Similar incidents all over the west coast of North America convinced both the U.S. and Canadian governments that steps had to be taken to control Japanese immigration. As a result, in 1907 President Roosevelt concluded the Gentlemen's Agreement between the United States and Japan to spare both governments the prospect of embarrassment by legislative action similar to the Chinese Exclusion Act of 1882. Japan agreed to stop issuing passports to Japanese laborers. Only children, wives, and parents of laborers, laborers who already owned land in the United States, laborers returning from visits to Japan, or professionals were allowed to immigrate. Roosevelt promised to block formal legislation restricting Japanese immigration. Japan then negotiated a similar agreement with Canada.

The impact of the Gentlemen's Agreement stands out in the population figures showing how many Japanese entered Hawaii and the Pacific Coast states between 1902 and 1910. From 1902 through 1908, the number arriving averaged over 16,000 a year. During the next two years, the total number was less than 6,000.[2]

The fact that the Gentlemen's Agreement did not restrict the immigration of Japanese women had a profound effect on the Japanese population here. Earlier Chinese exclusion acts had created a bachelor-oriented society for the Chinese, but by 1910 many Japanese men in the United States had saved enough money to start families. The Gentlemen's Agreement allowed them to bring wives from Japan.

Families and hard work

In most Asian cultures, marriage is not only a union between two individuals, but also an advantageous merger of family interests. Consequently, Japanese men in America sent messages to their families to begin the traditional procedure for finding a bride. Families requested the help of a go-between to arrange a marriage with a member of another family of good reputation. Only when the bride was selected and both families agreed did the disruption caused by the groom's residence in America interfere with the procedure. Usually the groom would not return to Japan for the

Picture brides came to America to meet men they were legally married to but had never met before. In 1919 the Japanese ship *Shunyo Maru* brought these women who waited for men on the pier to identify themselves as rightful husbands. (Riichi Ashizawa; University of California at Los Angeles Special Collections)

wedding. A member of his family stood in as proxy during the ceremony. Afterwards the bride sailed to America, where her spouse met her with only her picture to help him decide which woman getting off the ship was actually his "picture bride."

Japanese American families are full of stories of the disappointments of both spouses. A man would search for a photographer who would take the most flattering picture. He might rent clothing to disguise his laborer status. One middle-aged Nisei remembers hearing the story of how her mother rode silently in the seat of a jostling wagon, studying the agricultural land of her new country. When the wagon took a turn, she glimpsed a large white home with pillars. As her excitement grew, she turned shyly and asked whether that was their home. Her new husband shook his head and looked down at the horses. When they rounded the next turn, she saw her home—a rough cabin of handhewn logs with gaps where the chinking had fallen out. The wagon came to a dusty stop. For her to complain would shame her family. That day that Japanese bride experienced what thousands of other settler women did in the West, the realization that the land of opportunity was often harsh, dirty, and crude—a far cry from the civilized polish and tidiness of their family homes.

Exhausting work was the vehicle to success for young Issei couples. A typical story is that of the man who saved enough money from his pay of 35¢ a day as a laborer in Hawaii for his wife and daughter to join him on the mainland in 1906. Upon arrival he and his wife raised strawberries, work made even harder by thieves who waited to steal berries or profits. In the winters his daughter worked as a domestic for four dollars a month. In the summers she helped with the strawberry harvest. In turn, when she married, she and her husband opened a boarding house in Salinas, California, for other migrant workers, new arrivals anxious to save money. Eventually the young couple became labor contractors, acting as go-betweens for laborers and the farmers who needed them.

The story contains most of the elements of the Issei experience: work from dawn to dusk, settlement in rural areas, and working for others leading to family businesses. A woman managed the household chores on top of whatever wage-earning activities she found. Her day began at five, cooking for the family and hired help. After the regular working day, she did laundry, prepared more meals, and minded the home. At midnight, she could sleep.

Communication between Japanese in America and their families in Japan flowed steadily during the early years from 1890 to 1920. From America came word there was land: Japanese farmers could reclaim swamps or forests, and turn them into fields and orchards. Others told of their work in the canneries of Alaska, planting oysters in Washington, fishing, logging, farming, and in the services such as laundry, hotel, domestic, and restaurant. As more women joined the men, families wrote of births, businesses, and of deaths—a full cycle of life in a new country.

Immigrants kept abreast of events in Japan. They knew the

Oregon's fertile Willamette Valley attracted Japanese families to orchards and nurseries. As families prospered, some started small businesses. This group posed in Salem about 1917. (Oregon State Library)

Taisho emperor who took the throne in 1912 was not only ill physically, but also mentally. Still, he was accepted as a figurehead for the spiritual nationalism of Japan. Unlike the Chinese who were used to factionalized local governments representing different cultural groups, Japanese in America and Japan saw their nation as a kind of extended family. One owed loyalty to ancestors, family leaders in Japan, and the emperor.

Seeds of success

Despite these loyalties to home, many Issei realized they might stay in America. After they saved money from crops they grew as tenant farmers, they bought land. In 1900 thirty-nine Japanese worked 5,000 acres of land. By 1909 some 6,000 Japanese farmed 210,000 acres. They specialized in crops requiring intensive labor rather than large resources: strawberries, onions, flowers, asparagus, celery, and garden vegetables they sold out of carts in city markets. They converted land never before farmed, using musclepower rather than machinery. By 1920 Japanese farmers worked more than 50 percent of the California acreage dedicated to crops requiring hand labor.

Japanese agricultural impact grew. Aging Chinese farm workers were leaving rural areas. The number of Chinese also declined with decreasing immigration. Japanese moved in, working for lower wages than Chinese.

Japanese success did not go unnoticed. Farm lobbies and union interests hounded state legislatures for laws to restrict Japanese purchases of land. In 1913 California passed an alien land law that made it illegal for those ineligible for citizenship to own land. By 1920 thirteen other western states had passed alien land laws of their own, laws that stood until 1947. Again, pressure groups succeeded in forcing local laws to conform to their interests.

Issei had a hard time understanding why they could not buy the land they had cleared of rocks and timber, land that had once been considered marginal or too hard to reclaim. They sought ways to circumvent alien land acts. The answer lay in the Nisei. Being U.S. citizens by birth, Nisei could own land even if they were only toddlers. Throughout the western states, Issei adults farmed land owned on paper by their Nisei children.

Issei recognized the limits of how successfully they could adapt to American culture. Though they often dressed in Western clothing, they spoke little English whether they lived in cities or on farms. Groups of Japanese in the countryside tended to be just as cut off by language and culture from other Americans as they were in the more clearly segregated cities. Up until World War II, Issei retained control of their communities, providing services to men from the canning, logging, and fishing industries who moved in and out of the cities with the seasons. Issei established Buddhist and Protestant churches, hobby and youth clubs, language and cultural schools, and networks for social interaction that helped Nisei learn their traditions. But, Issei realized that as long as they were denied U.S. citizenship, they could never join the larger community surrounding them.

Issei wanted something different for Nisei. By Japanese tradition, Issei believed in equality with any people of the world. Thus it was natural to believe that if their children learned English and adopted Western customs, they would be respected American

In 1940 the Japanese Flower Market Association of California commissioned an album to include photographs of each member. Mr. Yuhei Oshima appears in one of these photographs, assembled to celebrate the 2600th anniversary of the Japanese Empire. (Takeji Manabe; Japanese American History Room, California First Bank)

citizens. At the same time, Issei believed in passing on their Japanese heritage to their children.

These beliefs sometimes caused conflict between Issei and Nisei. Some Nisei favored English over Japanese. Many Nisei quietly rebelled against Japanese customs, including loyalty to the emperor, belief in Buddhist doctrine, respect for elders, and Japanese concepts of formal etiquette. American law encouraged this break by treating Issei as non-citizens, shaming their Nisei children. Laws like the Cable Act of 1923 that took away citizenship from any American woman who married an alien not eligible for citizenship underscored this shame.

Meanwhile, in the rapidly growing western states the strong grabbed opportunities. Those with economic clout often determined civil laws and rights. Anti-Japanese lobbies were not satisfied with the Gentlemen's Agreement. They wanted no Japanese immigrants. In 1924 an immigration act passed Congress that said no one ineligible for citizenship could immigrate to the United States. This opened the door for another immigration; Filipinos, already U.S. nationals, filled positions left vacant by the sudden shut-off from Japan.

The 1924 Immigration Act had an immediate effect. From 1901 through 1924 more than 250,000 Japanese came to the United States mainland. Less than 7,000 came between 1925 and 1941.[3] Most of those later arrivals were students and professionals who found ways to stay when their visits ended.

Depression years

After the U.S. stock market crash in 1929, economic activity slowed, both in the United States and abroad, and unemployment soared. Some people grew richer. Many people suffered. U.S. immigration came to a standstill.

As they worked—in California's tuna fisheries, Alaska's canneries, the agricultural valleys, and businesses in cities and towns —Japanese in America learned that the military in Japan was gaining control of the government, an imbalance resulting from the original Meiji constitution. They observed Japan's rising nationalism as soldiers moved into Manchuria. They worried about relatives. In 1931 depression hit Japan, along with a major crop failure. Peasants chewed bark from trees and begged at railroad stations. Many incomes fell rapidly. Japanese here knew the hardships their relatives endured. Issei felt compassion. Japan was their homeland, even if it was not for their sons and daughters.

By 1940 the Immigration Act of 1924 had caused serious population warps in the Japanese American community. Cutting off immigration resulted in two age groups of people in America of Japanese ancestry—the young and the old. Issei, who reached late middle-age by 1940, were less than 35 percent of that population. Between them and their children, the Nisei, yawned an age gap with few people in their late twenties or mid-thirties, the very

A troupe of entertainers in San Francisco posed in 1907. (Riichi Ashizawa; University of California at Los Angeles Special Collections)

people who might have bridged the split between the two generations. The bulk of the population was under twenty-five and American-born. A normal population would contain more individuals in their thirties than in their fifties.

The year 1940 saw heightened tensions among Japanese in America. Japan signed a military pact with Germany and Italy. Chinese Americans, Koreans, and Chinese citizens in America clamored for a boycott of steel shipments from the United States to Japan. Then, when Japan entered Southeast Asia in July 1941, to protect sources of raw materials needed by Japanese industries, President Franklin Roosevelt cut oil exports to Japan by 90 percent. Because Japan had no domestic oil sources, leadership in Japan divided over whether to negotiate with the United States or go to war. Roosevelt continued negotiations based on Japan withdrawing from Southeast Asia in return for oil.

Pearl Harbor

On December 7, 1941, Japanese planes bombed Pearl Harbor in Hawaii. The United States declared war against Japan. Because

Japan was allied with Germany, Americans entered World War II on both the European and Pacific fronts.

To many Americans the news of Pearl Harbor is unforgettable. Seldom mentioned is the reaction of Japanese Americans. Paul Mayeda wrote this fictionalized account to capture the essence of Issei and Nisei fears: *"Grandfather put the radio on. I hated church music, it made me sick. I was playing with my egg when it happened. I didn't know how bad it was until Mother dropped the dishes. The radio sounded: 'This is not a test, this is the real thing. The Japanese have just bombed Pearl Harbor. I repeat, the Japanese have just bombed Pearl Harbor.' At that point everybody was frozen. I asked Mom what was wrong and she started to cry. I got so scared that I ran to Mom. She held me tight; Sister ran to her bedroom. Dad ran out in the rain saying, 'No, Noo, Nooo.' Brother ran after him and said, 'Dad.' They turned to each other and hugged each other. Grandfather looked at Grandma. She said something in Japanese; and I'll always remember this until I die, Grandfather took the samurai sword from the top of the fireplace and ran out the screen door yelling. He threw the sword in the air, then he knelt down . . .*

 then he knelt down . . .

  then he knelt down . . .

   then he knelt down and wept in the rain."[4]

Within days after Pearl Harbor, the FBI rounded up 2,000 Nisei leaders from Japanese American communities for questioning about involvement in war action against the United States. All Japanese Americans were forced to turn in cameras, binoculars, and short-wave radios to local police. U.S. military intelligence foresaw the possibility of direct attack against the West Coast and decided to determine to what extent, if any, people of Japanese ancestry might be spying or committing acts of sabotage. Strict curfews and the need for identification papers restricted the movements of all people of Japanese ancestry. West Coast states went on military alert. Patrols guarded beaches. Communities practiced blackouts for bombing raids, a routine barely concealing the fear of night attacks.

Statistics were used to justify every finger pointing at possible Japanese threats to American security. More than 85 percent of the Issei and Nisei lived on the West Coast. This was called a vicious plot to aid Japanese invasion—rather than an indication of

Despite his uniform and military honors, this U.S. Navy veteran of World War I was arrested and interned during World War II. (National Archives)

where there had been farmland and jobs when the immigrants arrived. Fanatics claimed that Japanese farms surrounding urban areas were strategically placed to disrupt major lines of communication, transportation, and public utilities. One rumor said strawberry farmers had chosen fields near Boeing Aircraft plants in Washington to spy on military technology, although the farmers had been there before the factory. Others said fishing fleets existed for spying purposes and that the primarily Japanese-owned San Diego tuna fleets were part of a military network.

Fact and fiction blurred. Under the threat of invasion of the mainland, Americans forgot that more than two-thirds of the people of Japanese ancestry were U.S. citizens. They discounted the fact many Issei had lived here for more than twenty years, time enough to raise families, invest money, and develop American loyalties. Representative John H. Tolan from California took responsibility from the House Committee of National Defense Migration to sort through the rumors. The hearings he held were intended to determine whether people of Japanese ancestry should be removed from the Western Defense Command, an area comprising the western halves of Washington and Oregon, all of California, and part of Arizona. While the investigation moved forward, prominent Americans, election rhetoricians, and the war-jittery press found the Japanese Americans guilty of sabotage, espionage, and treason.

Information provided the Tolan Committee proved neither Issei nor Nisei had aided the Japanese attack on Pearl Harbor. Friends of Japanese testified. American farmers said: "Since the war began our local Japanese have done everything to cooperate with our Government. . . . These people are farmers, they are not saboteurs . . . they know it is time to plant their crops—the earth is calling to them."[5] Another farmer went further: "Most of the Japanese aliens in the Yakima Valley have been there for at least twenty-five years. They are not citizens because they are not allowed to be citizens. They came here for the same reason all our ancestors came—to live where they might have freedom and pursue a richer, fuller life."[6]

Issei and Nisei also spoke for themselves, represented by the Japanese American Citizens League (JACL) formed in Seattle in 1930 to protect Nisei from discrimination. Responding to the persistent rumor of plans to evacuate all people of Japanese ancestry from the Western Defense Command and calls for voluntary migration out of the area, the JACL said: *"A large number of people have remarked that they will go where the Government orders them to go, willingly, if it will help the national defense effort. But the biggest problem in their minds is where to go."*[7]

The Japanese feared, with reason, that they would be unable to find a place to stay, kicked from town to town in the interior like the "Okies" of John Steinbeck's novel. Others feared the day when inhabitants of inland states, aroused by the steady influx of

When families moved into rough barracks at the camp in Minidoka, Idaho, they had no idea how long they would stay. Scrap lumber was used for building furniture and thin walls to divide the one room provided each family. (University of Washington Special Collections)

Japanese, would refuse to sell gasoline and food to them. And there was the possibility of mob action against them if they stopped in some town or village where they were not wanted.

On February 19, 1942, President Roosevelt signed Executive Order 9066 giving Secretary of War Stimson authority to establish military defense zones from which any person seen as a threat to the U.S. military effort could be excluded. The language was loose enough to have excluded Italian Americans and German Americans, although it was only used to exclude Japanese. It further authorized curfews, use of federal troops, and special housing for evacuees.

Internment

On March 2, 1942, the Tolan Committee was scheduled to submit its findings. Lt. General John L. Dewitt, the military commander appointed by Stimson to carry out evacuation, did not wait for that report. He began to execute his orders.

Any person with more than one-sixteenth Japanese ancestry had to leave the Western Defense zone. They had the option of voluntarily moving out of the zone or into temporary Assembly Centers outside major cities and agricultural towns with large Issei and Nisei populations. If they did not exercise this option, the military moved them.

As the JACL had predicted, voluntary migration worked inefficiently. Governors of all western states except Colorado refused to assure the War Relocation Authority (WRA) that any person of Japanese ancestry could safely relocate in their states.

The spring of 1942 blossomed with unrest. Japanese American leaders were interned. Farmers could not decide whether to plant crops. Banks proved reluctant to loan money for seed and supplies. Daisuke Kitagawa, a Japanese minister, described the normally green and busy White River Valley between Seattle and Tacoma: *This spring was entirely different. When I drove around the Valley, few people greeted me. The whole valley looked deserted. When I knocked at the kitchen door . . . I was greeted by voices filled with anxiety and fear.*[8]

In February and March some Issei and Nisei moved voluntarily out of the Western Defense Command. After March they moved into the Assembly Centers, makeshift detention camps in stables at race tracks or exposition halls at fairgrounds. Each family was given a number. Gawking crowds watched the families move in.

Whatever families could not carry in bundles they were told to leave behind. They got little for what they sold before boarding buses and trains for the Centers. Non-Japanese farmers reacted greedily, offering less than the farms and orchards were worth. After backbreaking years of establishing orchards where once there had been only forest, Japanese farmers were compelled to sell them at the height of productivity.

A Sansei (a third-generation Japanese American) describes her

Using ink on rice paper, an internee at Tule Lake, California, painted the camp in winter. (Suiko Mikami; First California Bank)

family's experience at the Assembly Center: *"Their first home after they became a number was the Tanforan Race Track. They were housed in one of the horse stalls. . . . Since the floor was filthy their next door neighbor decided to wash it with water which was a terrible mistake as they only dampened the manure under the hastily boarded floor and the smell was something else. [My mother] could hardly walk into their rear room for there were no windows."*[9]

Forced evacuation caused a crisis in leadership. Issei discovered American officials relied on Nisei who spoke English, while Nisei were uneasy with the leadership suddenly thrust upon them. Issei parents lamented the reversal internment caused in the tradition of respect for elders.

Contemporary Americans may wonder why Issei and Nisei went so quietly, standing obediently in long lines to fill buses and organizing families into efficient crews to move baggage and help the sick and elderly. Some Nisei insist they were trying to prove their loyalty through obedience. Others blame the heritage of cultural training to avoid trouble, to avoid being conspicuously different. Issei and Nisei knew the old Japanese proverb: "The nail that sticks out is the one that gets hit."

Compliance, however, did not dull their perceptions of what was happening. Never before in the United States had so many people—110,000, the majority of them American citizens—been deprived of the right to be presumed innocent until proven guilty. Imprisoned because of ancestry, Japanese Americans knew that neither German nor Italian Americans were being uprooted. The terms "Assembly Center" and "Relocation Center" did not fool them. The places were prison camps. The government's "protective custody" was internment.

By June 1942 the WRA had geared up to move the evacuees out of the Assembly Centers to permanent detention camps—the Relocation Centers. Located in rural areas, each held 10,000 people. Rough wood and coverings of tar paper barely blocked summer sun or winter wind. Barbed wire, searchlights, and armed sentries "protected" the residents. Families of eight lived in unpartitioned bedrooms twenty feet by twenty feet, sleeping on straw mattresses and using clothes for extra blankets. Medical supplies chronically ran short. Inmates waited in long lines for washing, toilets, and eating.

Although some families found the Relocation Centers drew them together, generally the regimentation had the opposite effect. A daughter of an Issei fisherman from Long Beach, California, who entered Manzanar at age eight says: *"My own family, after three years of mess hall living, collapsed as an integrated unit. Whatever dignity or feeling of filial strength we may have known before December, 1941, was lost. . . . Not only did we stop eating at home, there was no longer a home to eat in. The cubicles we had were too small for anything you might call 'living'. Mama couldn't cook meals there. It was impossible to find any privacy there. We slept there and spent most of our waking hours elsewhere."* [10]

A few Japanese Americans tested the orders creating these camps by refusing evacuation. They did not agree congressional and presidential war powers under the Constitution included the

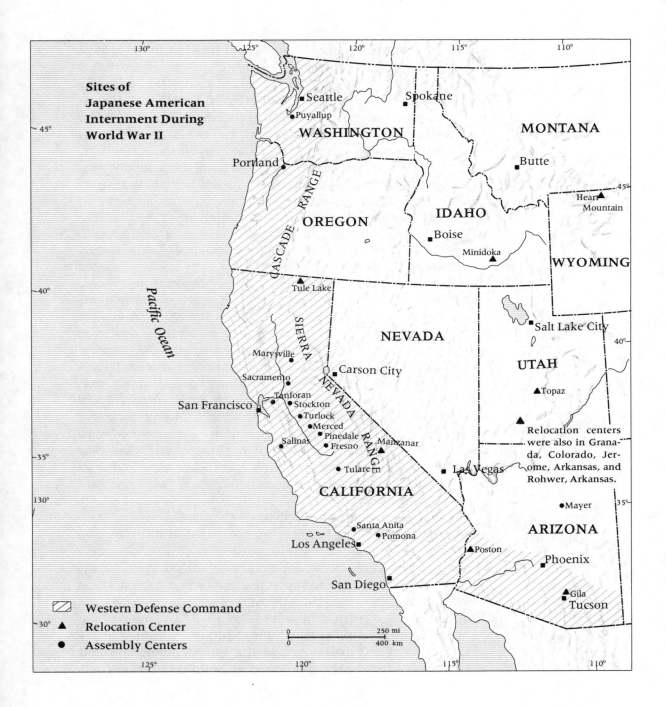

Sites of
Japanese American
Internment During
World War II

Pacific Ocean

WASHINGTON
- Seattle
- Puyallup
- Portland

MONTANA
- Butte

IDAHO
- Boise
- Minidoka

WYOMING
- Heart Mountain

OREGON

CASCADE RANGE

Tule Lake

NEVADA
- Carson City
- Las Vegas

SIERRA NEVADA RANGE

UTAH
- Salt Lake City
- Topaz

Relocation centers were also in Granada, Colorado, Jerome, Arkansas, and Rohwer, Arkansas.

CALIFORNIA
- Marysville
- Sacramento
- Tanforan
- Stockton
- San Francisco
- Turlock
- Merced
- Pinedale
- Salinas
- Fresno
- Manzanar
- Tulare
- Santa Anita
- Pomona
- Los Angeles
- San Diego

ARIZONA
- Mayer
- Poston
- Phoenix
- Gila
- Tucson

Western Defense Command
▲ Relocation Center
● Assembly Centers

250 mi
400 km

73

singling out of one group for forced incarceration for unproved purposes of "military necessity."

One of the first whose case was heard in the U.S. Supreme Court was Gordon Hirabayashi, a Nisei raised near Seattle. He was a senior at the University of Washington when Executive Order 9066 authorized curfews and internment. For him the order created a crisis in conscience: *"Like most people I was intending to comply with these orders. We are law abiding citizens, and this is our first reaction. I happened to be living in a dormitory about a half a block from the Japanese students club where I was a member. In this international dormitory I was the only person of Japanese ancestry at the time. The others became volunteer watchdogs for me. Whether we were at the library or on the avenue having coffee, about five minutes to eight several of the fellows would say, 'Hey, Gordon, five to eight.' I would get up and dash back. After about a week of this, I suddenly stopped part way home and asked why am I dashing home? The others are over there in the library or having coffee. What's so different? The only difference, of course, was the reason under which I became subject to the restrictions —Japanese ancestry. I could not accept that as a reason so I went back to where I was. I knew that if I couldn't conform to curfew, that this [evacuation to Assembly Centers] was even more objectionable. I was not making the beginning of a cause or setting a stage for a test case. It was something much more personal and relatively selfish. I was trying to keep myself together. Do I maintain my beliefs for what this country is supposed to stand for? Or do I learn to bend with the blows? Accept second-class citizenship? With those options, I really had no choices. I had to go through with being an American citizen which meant, strangely, that I had to take a negative stance."*[11]

The U.S. Supreme Court found in Hirabayashi's case that Congress and the President had the right to establish a curfew and require incarceration. It refused to rule on whether a curfew aimed only at people of Japanese ancestry was discriminatory. Two years passed before the Supreme Court changed any position concerning Japanese American detention.

During the long period from 1942 to 1944, Japanese in the camps were uneasy. Kibei (Nisei who had been educated in Japan) formed almost 10 percent of the camps' population and quarreled with those who advocated peaceful compliance. Issei

Horror stories about graveyard desecrations at home made the rounds of internment camps. Too often the stories were true. Robert Drinan, member of the Commission on Wartime Relocation and Internment, wrote that internment may have been caused by fear or racism or bad judgment or all three. "The time has come," he said, "to admit that the fear was unjustified, that the racism was inexcusable, and that the mistake must be rectified." (Oregon Historical Society)

feared they would never be able to go home. They heard of ruined businesses and farms. During 1942 disturbing reports surfaced of vandalism to graveyards where Japanese immigrants were buried, a shock to people who revered their ancestors. The 25,000 families in the camps had left nearly $200 million in property behind them. They were not sure they would ever see it or control it again.

As early as 1942 the WRA tried to determine who in the camps was loyal to the U.S. government and thus qualified for release to areas outside the military defense zones. Farm owners begged for laborers to help harvest crops for the armed services. Finally, many Nisei were released to harvest sugar beets.

Some Nisei joined the military to prove their loyalty. The 442nd Army Regiment, composed of Nisei, fought with valor on the front line in Italy and with the air invasion of Germany. President Harry Truman would later say to this Japanese American unit: "You fought not only the enemy, but you fought prejudice—and you won." Some 33,000 Japanese Americans served in the armed forces, earning 18,143 decorations for valor, 7 Presidential citations, and 9,486 Purple Hearts. Others served as nurses, language instructors, and translators in the Pacific. Those who remained in camps aided the war effort by weaving camouflage nets, donating blood, and buying war bonds. This support changed many Americans' minds about the Japanese American threat.

Before they proved their loyalty to the United States in action outside the camps, Nisei had to prove it by oath. To leave the camps, the WRA required every Nisei to answer yes to two questions: first, would the respondent serve in the U.S. Armed Forces; second, would the respondent renounce allegiance to the Japanese emperor. The questions sparked heated debate. Some Nisei urged NO votes to protest the involuntary detention of American citizens—and became known as the NO-NO boys. Others leaped to answer YES-YES to secure position in the military, return to college, or get jobs outside the Western Defense Command.

Parents were dismayed at the questions. Many Issei did not want their sons fighting against the home country, thinking of the ancestors buried in Japan. They would not declare loyalty while captive behind barbed wire. Also, they were citizens of only one nation, Japan, and if they agreed to fight for the United States, they were afraid they might lose that citizenship status or be forced to leave their children.

While loyalty issues continued to divide Issei and Nisei still in camps, the Supreme Court finally broke the trend begun in the Hirabayashi case. Mitsuye Endo had been fired from a California civil service job at the outbreak of the war because of her Japanese ancestry. In July 1942 she applied for permission to leave the camps. American born, she met every loyalty requirement and had a job and housing waiting for her. When her clearance was

During detainment, internees struggled to maintain the sense of a normal community. (Ansel Adams; Library of Congress)

delayed, she took the case to court. On December 18, 1944, the Supreme Court ruled citizens whose loyalty was not in question could not be held indefinitely against their will—though over

100,000 had been. Though the Endo case did not declare detention unconstitutional, it was the first step to closing the camps.

Postwar resettlement

By January 1945 the WRA cleared the way for resettlement of the 50,000 Issei and Nisei still in camps. Issei continued to fear reports of terrorist-style bombings of Issei land holdings, rifles fired through windows in the night, and telephone threats.

Those already back home faced other problems. Housing in Los Angeles and San Francisco was in short supply; black Americans had moved into Little Tokyos to work in shipbuilding and defense industries during the war. Orchards left in the care of tenants were withered from neglect or leveled by vandals. Household goods had disappeared from homes and storage depots. Barns and homes had been burned. Merchants refused to sell Japanese Americans the goods to start over again. Some banks froze their accounts.

Still, the pull to home was irresistible. One Sansei, Amy Eto, describes her mother's experience coming out of the camp: *"Mother's family had no house, property, or job in California to which to return, but it was 'home' where her parents had settled on arrival from Japan and where she was born and raised. The transplantation to the Midwest was an unhappy experience. The geographic area was unfamiliar, the climate severe in extremes, no old friends, only a few Japanese, and no Japanese community . . . all spelled out 'isolated and lonely.' So the family decided to return to California to old familiar faces and surroundings and to another new beginning."*[12]

The camps left scars on those who returned to the former military defense zone. Family loyalties had frequently broken down under arguments over loyalty questions and other frustrations. Property losses were severe.

One Nisei returned to the Manzanar Center in 1972, almost thirty years after she had left it. She recorded her reaction: *"I had nearly outgrown the shame and the guilt and the sense of unworthiness. This visit, this pilgrimage, made comprehensible, finally, the traces that remained and would always remain, like a needle. That hollow ache I had carried during the early months of internment had shrunk over the years to a tiny sliver of suspicion about the very person I was. It had grown*

During the early 1940s, nearly 5,000 Nisei volunteered for U.S. military service. Most were in the highly decorated 442nd Regimental Combat Team, whose motto was "Go for Broke." Three major actions in France and Italy cost the 442nd 750 men killed or missing and almost 3,000 wounded. (Visual Communications)

so small I'd forget it was there. Months might pass before something would remind me. When I first read, in the summer of 1972, about the pressure Japan's economy was putting on American business and how a union in New York City had printed up posters of an American flag with MADE IN JAPAN written across it, then that needle began to jab. I heard Mama's soft weary voice from 1945 say, 'it's all starting over.' I knew it wouldn't. Yet neither would I have been surprised to find the FBI at my door again. I would resist it much more than my parents did, but deep within me something had been prepared for that. Manzanar would always live in my nervous system, a needle with Mama's voice.''[13]

On August 14, 1945, Japan surrendered. Atomic bombs had leveled Hiroshima and Nagasaki. Tokyo was in shambles. Railroads did not run. There were no oil reserves. Over 2 million

Japanese homes lay in rubble. The average citizen had enough food to fight off starvation, but little will to live.

The United States occupied Japan under the direction of General Douglas MacArthur. War criminals were sentenced and the emperor's powers reduced. A new constitution created divided powers so the military could not again gain control.

At home Japanese Americans under JACL leadership lobbied for U.S. citizenship. In July 1948 President Truman signed the Evacuation Claims Act to help Japanese Americans regain some of their losses caused by relocation. Not only had the two and one-half year relocation cost the government $250 million, the Federal Reserve Bank estimated Issei and Nisei losses as high as $400 million. Issei and Nisei filed claims under the act asking for $132 million, far less than their estimated losses. In the end, the government paid $38 million, about 10¢ for every $1 Japanese Americans are thought to have lost. The last claim was settled in 1965, twenty years after the close of World War II.

For the Issei, as for others denied citizenship because of race, 1952 was an important year. The McCarran-Walter Act, 300 pages long, recodified and updated U.S. immigration and naturalization law. Of particular interest to the Issei and other Asian immigrants was the abolition of racial qualifications for citizenship. Every immigrant now had the right to apply for citizenship. This change furthered the promise heralded on the Statue of Liberty. Within days, elderly Issei flocked to federal offices to apply.

Since World War II, a new generation of Japanese Americans has matured: the Sansei, children of the Nisei. Most did not experience the camps but have heard about them. This mix of past and present, charged with observations of the psychological scars of the Issei and Nisei from forced imprisonment, makes Sansei wonder where they fit into American society. Sansei, and their Yonsei (fourth generation) children, inherit the shame and anger of internment. The 1960s and 1970s sparked a renewed sense of pride in ethnicity, cultural values, and traditions.

Issei to Nisei to Sansei

Sociologists have focused dozens of studies on the progression of Japanese American generations from Issei to Nisei to Sansei. The

Kime Young performed with a group of Japanese dancers in 1981 as part of a United Nations anniversary. (Brent Wojahn)

profiles that emerge of the Sansei provide a possible model for other Asian groups. Many Sansei have attained extremely high education and professional levels. They accept marriage with non-Japanese more easily than their parents, count many non-Japanese among their close friends, and show a shift in religious commitments from predominantly Buddhist to Christian. As time passes, these changes cause less conflict between generations.

Some suggest the changes show a breakdown in Japanese American culture. Yet studies of the Sansei reveal an avid Sansei interest in their origins.[14] More Sansei know exactly what city or locale their grandparents came from than do grandchildren of

European immigrants. Nearly all would like to be able to speak Japanese better than they do, although fewer than 20 percent can read a Japanese American newspaper.

Both Sansei and Nisei have made appreciable gains—enough that many Americans call Japanese in America a "super minority," just as they have Chinese Americans. There are no Japanese American ghettos. Japanese American merchants contribute to their communities as honored citizens. The average Japanese American family has more education and income than the national average. At the same time, both Nisei and Sansei have low rates of criminal involvement, mental illness, and juvenile delinquency. Sansei have successfully ventured into accounting, engineering, business, social services, law, and medicine—though they report stereotypes of Japanese Americans continue to affect them. Some choose non-traditional careers for Asians: construction, social work, politics, and law enforcement.

Despite their achievements, Japanese Americans stay vigilant as they accept leadership from the Issei, who are passing away. They remember the precedent in American law that makes it possible to evacuate any ethnic group from any area in time of military necessity. On a day-to-day level, they also seek to preserve their culture. West Coast cities abound with art shows, cultural classes in Japanese gardening, cookery, martial arts, and craft techniques, and Japanese Buddhist temples. Newspapers, specialty stores, and restaurants testify visibly to the impact of Japanese American culture on American society.

Among themselves Japanese Americans also debate the merits of the recent movement to redress their internment grievances. Many have testified before the Congressional Commission on Wartime Relocation and Internment of Civilians appointed in 1980. The commission studies the impact of the uprooting, its implications and historical background, and takes evidence refuting the idea of any military necessity for the internment of Issei and Nisei. Eventually it must decide if Japanese Americans should be compensated financially for the losses they endured. That issue often splits the Japanese American community. They unite in hoping the commission's work will help all Americans understand what life was like in those squalid tarpaper plywood shacks.

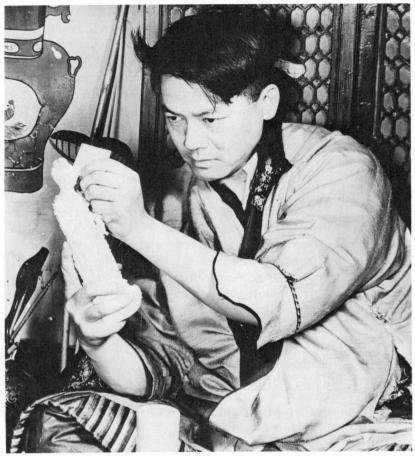

Ivory carver continued traditional craft technique in his new country.
Many forms of Asian artwork have widespread appeal. (History Room
and Archives, San Francisco Public Library)

Undeniably, the commission faces a difficult task. Forty years
later, the fire of fear and suspicion has smoldered into ashes. It is
hard to remember the pressures that made President Roosevelt
sign Executive Order 9066 before the Tolan Committee made its
report. But the precedent this act established—incarcerating all
members of a refugee or immigrant group whose homeland is in

battle with the United States—remains very much intact. Under Title II of the 1950 Internal Security Act six so-called emergency centers were created—for possible peacetime dissenters. Title II finally was repealed in 1970.

Some Sansei voice concern over increasing attention to competition from Japanese imports. Labor unions have too often meant trouble for Asian Americans. Sansei feel uneasy about foreign car bashings in auto factory towns. Cartoons comparing the unloading of stereos and cars in West Coast cities to Pearl Harbor make people of Japanese ancestry nervous in light of the reaction to the real Pearl Harbor. Japanese Americans are unwilling to become scapegoats for a slump in U.S. economic efficiency.

Justice Jackson in *Korematsu* v. *U.S.*, a court case testing the constitutionality of detention, called the precedent of incarceration of one ethnic minority a "loaded gun" in American law. To Japanese Americans this image is certainly apt, despite their success and reputation for accomplishment in the face of adversity. They urge others to share what they have learned about guns —disarming is harder than squeezing the trigger again.

Chronology

1869 First Japanese settlers arrive in Gold Hill, California.

1870 People born in Africa and people of African descent become eligible for U.S. citizenship. Asians do not.

1886 Japan lifts ban restricting emigration of Japanese.

1894 Saito, a Japanese man, applies for U.S. citizenship. Courts refuse because he is neither white nor black.

1900 25,000 Japanese live in America.

1907 President Theodore Roosevelt enters into Gentlemen's Agreement with Japan to limit Japanese immigration to mainland U.S. and Hawaii.

1913 Alien Land Law in California prohibits Japanese from owning land if they are not citizens.

1920 111,000 people of Japanese ancestry live in America.

1924 Immigration Act prohibits immigration to those ineligible for citizenship. Japanese are ineligible by a 1790 law.

1930 139,000 people of Japanese ancestry live in America.

1937 Japan invades Manchuria.

1941 December 7—Japanese planes attack Pearl Harbor, Hawaii. U.S. enters World War II.

1942 Executive Order 9066 authorizes the Army to remove any persons of Japanese ancestry from the Western Defense Command to detention camps.

1944 U.S. Supreme Court rules loyal citizens cannot be held in camps against their will—the first step toward camp closures.

1945 August 14—Japan surrenders.

1946 All internment camps are closed.

1948 Evacuation Claims Act authorizes payment of settlements to people of Japanese ancestry who suffered economic losses from internment: 10¢ is returned for every $1 lost.

1952 Issei become eligible for U.S. citizenship. 185 Japanese allowed into U.S. per year by quota system.

1980 President Jimmy Carter establishes 7-member Commission on Wartime Relocation and Internment of Civilians to study longlasting legal and social implications of the uprooting of Japanese-Americans during World War II.

1980 U.S. Census records 701,000 people of Japanese ancestry. Though they had been the largest Asian group in 1970, large Chinese and Filipino immigrations in the last decade slipped people of Japanese ancestry to the third largest group in 1980.

1981 President Ronald Reagan affirms his commitment to the Commission on Wartime Relocation and Internment by naming 2 more members to the commission. The commission collects data and holds hearings.

THREE

(Bill Ravanesi © 1981)

Proud Nationals

Filipino Americans

The Philippines, a lush cluster of 7,000 islands stretching from north to south along the South China Sea, bear the name of King Philip II of Spain—a clear symbol of Western influence. While the Philippines are geographically part of Southeast Asia, Filipinos are of Malay origin. Filipinos find a place in the history of Asians for two reasons. The American reaction to early Filipine immigrants paralleled that toward the early Chinese and Japanese immigrants who preceded them, and U.S. laws aimed at Asians were applied also to Filipinos.

In 1521 navigator Ferdinand Magellan discovered the fertile island chain and claimed it for Spain. Though Magellan lost his life to an angry chieftain who resisted Spanish exploration, Spanish traders and missionaries rushed to solidify the captain's claim. Thus began Western domination that would continue for more than four centuries.

The Spanish established Manila as a commercial port. Spanish textiles and firearms as well as Mexican silver were traded briskly through Chinese middlemen for Filipine gold, porcelain, and silk. Filipinos sailed on galleons over routes Spanish vowed to keep secret from competitors. Spanish missionaries converted thousands of Filipinos to Catholicism. Today 85 percent of Filipinos are Catholic. Catholicism more easily spread Spanish influence than in other areas of Asia, perhaps because Filipine religious traditions were less resistant than Buddhist and Confucian. Spanish came to be spoken as commonly as Tagalog and other native dialects. Filipine and Spanish intermarriage drew the bonds tighter.

Localized groups of Filipinos resisted the Spanish. Pirates attacked Spanish ships. Some tribes used guerrilla tactics to harass the Spanish, then fled to the northern mountains for safety. Resistance to foreign domination became a key to the political fervor of the islands.

While British forces pried open Canton's harbors for trade in the 1830s, Manila also became an open port, not just a stopover for the Spanish. European and Chinese ships flocked to Manila for sugar, coffee, coconuts, and cigar tobacco. Soon European-educated Filipine leaders spoke out for Philippine nationalism. By 1896 these nationalists led a full-scale war for independence.

That conflict opened Filipine immigration to the United States. While engaged in the war against the nationalists, Spain also entered into hostilities with the United States over Cuba. American warships defeated the Spanish fleet in the harbor of Manila in 1898, bringing the Spanish-American war to an end. As part of the settlement, President William McKinley announced the Philippines would become an American protectorate until the islands could establish a politically stable independence.

Strong Filipine nationalists claimed American domination was just another intolerable intervention, a trade of Spanish control for American. They began a guerrilla war. American soldiers, not acclimated to high humidity, heavy rains, and clouds of mosquitoes, were at an initial disadvantage. In 1902 superior American weaponry tipped the balance. As American markets drew larger and larger shares of Filipine exports, maintaining the Philippines as a protectorate whose tariffs the United States would govern made economic sense. The U.S. Congress renewed its promise to bestow independence on the Philippines at a later date. The defeated rebels had no choice but to acquiesce.

U.S. nationals

Protectorate status was a mixed blessing for Filipinos. Unlike Asians, Filipinos were nationals and so travelled to the United

USSR

MONGOLIA

CHINA

Hokkaido

Sapporo

Vladivostok

Sea of Japan

NORTH KOREA

Pyongyang

JAPAN

Tokyo

Beijing
(Peking)

Seoul

SOUTH
KOREA

Huang Ho
River

Yellow
River

Yellow Sea

Kyushu

Chengdu

Yangtze River

Shanghai

Pacific Ocean

Mekong River

Yangtze R.

Taipei

TAIWAN

Yz Jiang River

Guangzhou
(Canton)

HONG KONG (U.K.)
MACAO (Port.)

BURMA

Red River

Hanoi

Hainan

LAOS

Vientiane

Luzon

Manila

PHILIPPINES

YAP

Rangoon

Gulf of Tonkin

Mekong R.

THAILAND

VIETNAM

Bangkok

KAMPUCHEA

Phnom Penh

Ho Chi Minh City
(Saigon)

Andaman

Sea

Gulf of Thailand

South China Sea

Mindinao

Sulu Sea

0   500 mi
0   800 km

Songkhla

BRUNEI (U.K.)

Celebes Sea

NEW

INDONESIA   WEST
MALAYSIA

Sumatra

E. MALAYSIA

INDONESIA

Borneo

Equator

GUINEA

89

States without restriction. At the same time, Filipine nationals, like the Asian immigrants, had none of the rights of citizens. They could not vote, own land, or practice professions.

The first Filipinos to come to the mainland United States were students. At the prompting of the first U.S. civil governor, William Howard Taft, the colonial government sent some 300 young men to study in the United States between 1903 and 1910. After they finished their studies they were expected to return to the Philippines not only with skills in such fields as education, engineering, and medicine, but also to teach others about America. Although back home they were received with some jealousy, their success encouraged other, self-supporting students to follow. Once in the United States, many became disillusioned by their lack of rights.

Meanwhile, Hawaii, newly annexed to the United States, came under the 1907 Gentlemen's Agreement that shut off Japanese immigration to U.S. territory. Plantation owners were quick to see benefits for themselves. Pineapple and sugar growers needed more laborers. Filipinos could never be excluded from U.S. territory by law because of their status. The growers also hoped Filipinos would break Japanese worker strikes against low wages. While Japanese workers organized under the supervision of the Japanese Consulate, Filipinos had no consulate or other organization to protect them.

Status as nationals came at what seemed an opportune time to Filipine laborers. Ilocanos from the northwest part of Luzon wanted to escape the unstable employment conditions of the northern Philippines. Overcrowding on all the islands limited the size of landholdings, making farming increasingly difficult. Wages in the congested cities were even lower. The *Manila Times* summarized the appeal of America: "The migrating Filipino sees no opportunity for him in the Philippines. Advertise in a Manila paper and offer a job ... and you will get a thousand applicants. Make the same offer in any provincial town, and the response will be twice as great, comparatively. Is it any wonder, then, that the lure of pay four to ten times as great, in Hawaii or the United States, draws the Filipino like a magnet?"[1]

When labor contractors called, Filipinos signed up. They had no idea of the hard work, primitive living conditions, and low wages

President William Howard Taft called Filipinos "our little brown brothers." His kindly but condescending words described public reaction to these Igorrote tribesmen at the Alaska/Yukon Exhibition in Seattle in 1909. (F.H. Nowell; Historical Society of Seattle and King County)

in Hawaii. Between 1907 (the year of the Gentlemen's Agreement) and 1919 (the height of Japanese strike agitation in Hawaii), 22,000 Filipine young men went to Hawaii. With the onset of the Japanese workers' strike in 1920, the demand grew. Between 1920 and 1924, 17,000 Filipinos sailed for Hawaii.

Fewer went on to the mainland. California farmers seldom hired contractors to recruit Filipinos. Census figures indicate only 6,000 Filipinos lived on the mainland by 1924. Some came for education or to learn a trade. Few succeeded. Racism forced them into low-paying jobs that never covered education costs. The jobs open to them in agriculture kept them moving from farm to farm, hardly the lifestyle for a student.

The Immigration Act of 1924 that excluded Japanese increased the mainland need for Filipinos, but did nothing to stimulate high wages. Filipinos rushed to fill the labor gap opened by the cutoff of Japanese immigration, but again found only hard manual labor. From 1925 to 1929, 24,000 Filipinos entered California. Only 1,300 were women.

Eligible bachelors stumbled into the tangle of state antimiscegenation laws. These laws, declared unconstitutional in 1967, rested on race distinctions often difficult to make. In California, for example, until 1948 the law forbade intermarriage between whites and Asians. When a Filipino contested the refusal of a marriage license in the late 1920s, he won in the lower courts on the basis he was not "Mongolian." Los Angeles County appealed in 1933, and lost when the California Supreme Court decided the law did not include Filipinos. In 1935 the amended civil code included Filipinos under "Malay race."

Since Filipinos had intermarried with the Spanish and Chinese for several hundred years in the Philippines, it is hard to know how the term Malay could be reasonably applied. And it is not surprising that Filipine immigrants to the United States resented antimiscegenation laws.

Some Filipinos did marry women of Hungarian, Hawaiian, Spanish, Mexican, or Italian ancestry. In some cases these marriages probably were illegal, strictly speaking, but the law was not always enforced. Most Filipinos did not marry, however, remaining without family ties, on the move from town to town as harvests and availability of labor contracts dictated.

Willie Barientos, who came to Hawaii in 1924 before moving on to the mainland, is still angry about those lonely years: *"When we came here in 1925, the Filipino cannot marry a white. That's the law. This hurt me. We cannot marry. We cannot buy land, until we fight the war. That all hurt me. That's why I get old in my head and in my heart and in my hand. When I was young, I was strong. I have seen all those experiences in my life . . . I did not go to college and learn this. I know it."* [2] Barientos later helped organize the Delano farm workers in California who led the multi-ethnic United Farm Workers strike against grapegrowers in the Central Valley in 1966.

Between jobs, Filipine farm workers sought recreation where they could—at Chinese gambling casinos, dancehalls employing

Textbooks from America gave thousands of Filipine men visions of wealth and democracy across the Pacific. Many used Hawaii as a steppingstone, following Chinese and Japanese laborers into canneries and farm work on the mainland. (Hawaii State Archives)

white women, and cockfights. As Filipine populations in California grew, the men got a reputation for immorality, a charge leveled at most new immigrant groups including Mexicans, Italians, Portuguese, Chinese, and Irish. In fact, Filipinos continued the tradition of other immigrants, trying to live as cheaply as possible in crowded urban ghettos skirting Chinatowns and Little Tokyos. They accepted a lifestyle of rooming houses, bars, and poolrooms in the Little Manilas of Stockton, Los Angeles, and San Francisco, and the smaller stopover hotels in Portland and Seattle. City populations ebbed and flowed with the season. The Filipine population of Seattle numbered several thousand in the winter and a few hundred in the summer. Stockton's wintertime population of 1,000 swelled to 6,000 in the summer during planting season in the early 1930s.

Farms and canneries

By the early 1930s, 45,000 Filipinos toiled in "stoop labor," the backbreaking but delicate hand labor needed for crops that could not survive rougher handling. These farm workers, or *pinoy* as they called themselves, contracted to pick tomatoes, pack peas, cut asparagus, harvest grapes, lettuce, peaches, apricots, and berries, plant lettuce and celery, pick melons, hoe beets, and perform odd jobs on ranches. When one job ended, they hopped into beat-up cars and old trucks to move on to the next, where home was another made-over barn, run-down barrack, or patched-up shed.

One Filipino worked for a Japanese farmer whom he remembers fondly: *"After tomato picking, I moved to another ranch in Mountain View [California] and picked prunes. Aieee, that's the hard job again because I am on my knees. I said to myself if I work this kind of job, in three months I'm going to be old. But, what shall I do? I have to pick it. I need the money because I'm always thinking of my family. They need money. They are very poor. So after picking prunes, I make a little money and send it to them. I promised my mother I stay only three years in this country. If it is truly that easy to make money in this country, three years and I'll have the money to go back. This is not true. It is a lie. Well, in 1928 I got a little money to spend. It so happened that I entered a post office and received a letter that my mother passed away. I was about to send that little money I got to her, I felt disgusted, so I think to myself, I will stay."*[3]

Three generations of Filipino Americans. The number of Filipinos living in the United States rose rapidly from the early 1920s to the early 1930s, but antimiscegenation laws and low-paying jobs kept most from marrying or bringing family from the Philippines. (Bill Ravanesi © 1981)

In slack months *pinoy* headed into West Coast cities to meet labor contractors who often arranged jobs in Alaskan fish canneries for a percentage of wages. Contractors gave laborers pay, food, and shelter—expenses which came out of profits and which a contractor would try to minimize.

Abuses were rampant. Contractors cut corners wherever they could. Of the men in Alaska's canneries, 75 percent were Asians who worked for lower wages than other employees. Transported to remote canning centers, first by sailboat and later in the jammed steerage compartments of steamships, laborers were captive for the season and endured poor food and housing. Though in 1935 the canning industry halted the contractor system, cannery worker unions charge other abuses continue today.

Cannery work became the link making the migratory pattern of Filipine employment possible. Some canneries hired only Filipinos; others used only Chinese or Japanese. The work was routine and unskilled. First the men unloaded salmon from ships, tossing fish onto conveyors which carried them to docks. They fed fish by hand into the machines that cut the fish into pieces. Men known as "slimers" picked through the pieces to remove viscera. Another machine packed pieces into cans with plungers. Laborers wheeled cans to cookers which sterilized the fish and softened the bones. Men or machines applied labels.

Filipinos who came to the salmon canneries in Alaska probably fared better than those who stayed on the West Coast. Often cannery wages were higher than wages Filipinos could earn elsewhere. Many white workers found cannery work unattractive, so competition for these jobs was less. Also, no state law forbade intermarriage between Filipinos and Eskimos. Still, when Filipinos in Alaska sought unionization to improve working conditions, organized labor gave little or no help. In 1928 the American Federation of Labor voted to support a congressional bill that would exclude Filipine immigrants.

Few Filipinos became rich. A man considered himself lucky to arrive at his next job with anything in his pocket. Though wages had seemed high when they heard about them in the Philippines, the high cost of living gobbled them up. Families in the Philippines sometimes mortgaged farmland to raise money to send a son to

Photographer Dorothea Lange captured here the backbreaking nature of stoop labor. From their toil in the lettuce fields of California most Filipinos harvested only poverty and disdain. (Dorothea Lange; Library of Congress)

the United States, but he had to be extremely frugal to save enough to help them pay off the mortgage. Many remained in the United States rather than return home empty-handed.

A Filipine leader exiled in the United States during the Japanese occupation of the Philippines in World War II described a hand-to-mouth migratory existence: *"The tragedy of our life in America . . . is that it has been predicated on wishful thinking—'I want to go home.' We have been sentimental rather than realistic. 'Why should I plan, why should I take life seriously here, when this is only an interlude in my life? I am going home. It is where I am going to take root.' Birds of passage . . . do not plan. They drift aimlessly."*[4]

Those who disliked farm work found menial work in cities. Alfonso Engalla, who left Manila in 1927, describes arriving in San Francisco: *"We arrived in the early part of the evening. My brother, Mariano, met us on the pier, took us to a hotel on Kearney Street, a block away from Chinatown. So we spent our first night in the U.S. there. Next evening my brother and I and our friend Jimmy arrived in Stockton. . . . My brother landed us a job on the farm. I have never worked on a farm before and the cool morning of spring was a little too much for me. I wasn't able to get up very early and I couldn't even touch the water so as to wash my face and hands for breakfast. When my brother noticed that I wasn't cut out for farm work, he took me back to the city on the second day. The third day he told me that he got a job at a little restaurant. I told him to take it for himself and that I would find my own job but he told me that he purposely got it for me because I was not cut out to work on a farm. Being a younger brother, I was brought up to obey my elders, so I took the job obediently. I was employed as a waiter, dishwasher, vegetable man, and a custodian. In other words, I was an all-around man in a small restaurant."*[5] City jobs available to Filipinos like Engalla were low-paying. Men survived as houseboys, gardeners, cooks, elevator boys, cannery workers, and sometimes as movie extras.

Neither farm workers nor city dwellers escaped harassment. Many Filipinos were mistaken for and suffered the same discrimination as other Asians and Chicanos. Hotels refused service. Men were not allowed in white barber shops, swimming pools, restaurants, or movie houses.

Beginning in the 1920s, Filipinos met the same anti-Asian outbreaks that resulted in exclusion laws for Chinese and Japanese. Near Yakima, Washington, in September 1928, 150 white men stopped two buses of Filipine workers headed for apple orchards and told them to turn back. They threatened the Filipinos' lives for taking their jobs. Filipinos packed peas and lettuce in the White River Valley south of Seattle until white farm workers attacked and kidnapped several of them in May 1930.

In Exeter, California, in the fall of 1929, white migrant workers demanded all Filipinos harvesting figs be fired. They smashed automobiles owned by Filipinos. In January 1930 in Watsonville,

Filipinos lacked the regional and family organizations of the Chinese and the consulates of the Japanese to organize them. From dozens of remote islands, the men finally found unity through the American labor movement. In 1965, some thirty years after this photo was taken, Filipinos merged with Mexican American union members to form the United Farm Workers. (Visual Communications)

California, white farm workers protested the hiring of Filipinos to plant lettuce. Then, when a club for Filipinos hired white women under rigid standards to be dance partners for the men, local residents mobbed the club. Mobs attacked Filipinos at a nearby ranch, firing random shots into bunkhouses and killing one laborer. Gangs of youths stoned Filipine cars. Persons wanting Filipine exclusion tossed bombs into the Filipino Federation of America hall in nearby Stockton.

These Depression era incidents reflect the experiences of many Filipinos. Mob action broke out wherever Filipinos worked: in Salinas and San Bernardino in California; in the Hood River Valley in Oregon; and in Idaho and Utah. Job competition fueled the attacks; racism ignited them.

Though Japanese exclusion laws opened opportunities for Filipine laborers, the Great Depression, the dustbowls of the Southwest, and the pressure of homeless, jobless Americans shut them off. A self-described Filipino American "pioneer" who came to the United States eager to study agriculture says: *"When I finished high school, I was going to Oregon State University. I went and looked at the campus. Then the Depression came. It was hard for me to find a job. I found a job in the fraternity house, waiting tables for room and board. I was not able to continue my studies. When the Depression was over, I thought I was too old. I said I would rather work. At that time we were not able—even with how educated we were—the only jobs to do were odd jobs: cooks, waiters, janitors, busboys, and farm work, but there were no white collar jobs. I took the civil service examination—I had everything but they found out I was not a citizen, they disqualified me."* [6]

U.S. citizens

Citizenship seemed an impossible dream. As nationals, Filipinos were in limbo. No consulates protected them. The U.S. government refused to grant Philippine independence or U.S. citizenship to resident Filipinos.

The only route to citizenship lay in 1925 legislation to give citizenship to Filipine men after three years service in the military. By 1929, 5 percent of the U.S. Navy was Filipino though regulations banned access to any rating other than mess attendant. This experience opened some jobs for Filipinos in the merchant marine or

Those *compadres* who survived the first desperate decades in the United States call themselves *manongs*: older brothers. (Bill Ravanesi © 1981)

in service occupations such as hospital attendant, butler, or waiter. Today many Filipinos still enter the U.S. Armed Services as a first step to citizenship.

During the 1930s life became progressively drearier. Job shortages slashed immigration. In 1940 only a few hundred more Filipinos lived on the mainland than in 1930. Americans complained Filipinos stole their jobs. The Filipino Federation of Labor tried to protect Filipine interests. Still, whites owned most of the land. Minorities—Asians, Mexicans, and blacks—worked the fields.

Carlos Bulosan told the story of Filipino American life from firsthand experience. In 1930, at the age of 17, he left the central Philippines for Seattle. Quickly he adopted the survival strategies of other Filipine migrant laborers. He hopped freight trains and slept in bus stations. He washed fish heads in a San Pedro, California, cannery, picked peas in Salinas, and kept moving—covering California, as well as Oregon, Washington, and Alaska. Bulosan wrote of his experiences. The places he knew—hotel rooms, bunkhouses, poolrooms, Mexican restaurants, and Chinese gambling casinos—come alive through the dialogue of the people he loved: impoverished laborers, trade union organizers, card dealers, derelicts, and occasionally, a woman. He balanced his writing craft with practicality. Believing strongly in trade unions as a solution to the poverty and humiliation of Filipine laborers, he helped organize the United Cannery and Packing House Workers of America.

In 1938 Bulosan summed up his understanding of fellow Filipino Americans: *"Do you know what a Filipino feels in America? I mean one who is aware of the intricate forces of chaos? He is the loneliest thing on earth. There is much to be appreciated all around him, beauty, wealth, power, grandeur. But is he part of these luxuries? He looks, poor man, through the fingers of his eyes. He is enchained, damnably to his race, his heritage. He is betrayed, my friend."*[7] Bulosan's stories emphasize the shattering irony of Filipine residence in America: Americans treated Filipinos as inferiors while Filipinos, believing in the basic principles of American equality, regarded all Americans as equals.

As another Filipino said of his painful awakening: *"My school teachers at home were idealistic Americans who told me of America's promises of liberty and equality under the law, but forgot to mention the economic discrimination and racial complexes with which you interpret your rainbow-hued promises."*[8]

Carlos Bulosan, like many other laborers, followed the crops during the Great Depression. Unlike other laborers, Bulosan earned money from his writing: essays, editorials, short stories, poems, plays. (University of Washington Special Collections)

If it had been legally possible for Congress to exclude Filipine nationals as it had Chinese and Japanese aliens, it might have. In 1935 President Franklin Roosevelt signed a Repatriation Act that would pay expenses of Filipinos wanting to return to the Philippines. Lobbyists screamed for exclusion acts from 1929 on. By 1935 Congress passed a quota system allowing only fifty Filipinos into the United States per year. Filpinos took the hint. Many returned to the Philippines.

The political climate changed somewhat in 1935, when the United States declared the Philippines to be a commonwealth. This was the first step to the independence that was promised in ten years. Filipinos here and abroad rejoiced.

The outbreak of World War II dimmed their hope of an independent future. On December 8, 1941, Japan invaded the Philippines. Connie Noblejas described her family's life in the early part of the war: *"Soon it became very strict; everyone was now being told what and what not to do; and many of the provinces had already been occupied by Japanese soldiers. A few days later, Japanese planes were flying overhead, dropping bombs they carried. Now the people began fleeing from one place to another. Some were so scared that they just kept on running, following the direction of flowing people. Two of them were my mom and sister. My mom at that time never even thought of where her own mom and sister were. But the worst thing of all was that she had been separated from my dad. My dad went to hide somewhere else while my mom ran in the opposite direction for safety. She said while she was running with my sister in her arms all that was in her mind was how she can save the two of them. Not even thinking whether my dad was hit, lying in a street gutter somewhere. Tears rolled down her cheeks that were pale from not eating."* [9]

Filipinos in America lost contact with relatives in the Philippines until the end of the war in 1945. Filipinos listened with sorrow and fear to radio accounts of battles raging throughout the Philippines. Nearly a third of the Filipinos in American joined the U.S. military to fight Japan. Many were decorated for bravery.

Filipinos also watched as Japanese and citizens of Japanese ancestry were herded into detention camps. One Filipino American recalls his feelings: *"When Japan bombed Pearl Harbor, Manila, and all parts of the Philippines, I was entirely against the Japanese too. My*

The patrons of Tommy's Cafe in the 1950s reveal the multiracial background of Seattle's international district. (Elmer Ogawa; University of Washington Special Collections)

feeling was 100% against them, but when those Japanese in the war showed their patriotism in favor of this country, I changed my mind. They should not have been taken. Like the Italians and the Germans. All those born here are citizens. They should not have been suspected as spies.'' [10]

The United States regained the Philippines in 1944 and restored the commonwealth. In 1946 the Republic of the Philippines was proclaimed, although many economic and military ties with the United States remained.

Americans recognized Filipine contributions in the war. Stories of daring Filipine guerrillas fighting Japanese occupation warmed public opinion. With Philippine independence, citizenship was offered Filipinos living in America and the immigration quota was raised—but only to 100 immigrants a year. Filipine pioneers in this country since the 1920s finally had the opportunity to marry the women who were allowed to come. Many of the men were in their forties and fifties.

Work in agriculture did not end with World War II. The 1960 Census showed Filipinos were still largely employed in unskilled labor. In 1959 the AFL-CIO formed the Agricultural Workers Organizing Committee (AWOC) whose membership was mostly Filipine. At the same time, Cesar Chavez formed the National Farm Workers Association, drawing membership from both Filipine and Chicano workers. In 1965 AWOC struck thirty-three grape-growers in Delano, California. Chavez' organization joined eight days later. In 1966 the two groups merged into the United Farm Workers Organizing Committee (UFWOC) that continued the struggle to improve wages and working conditions.

In spite of the forces relegating Filipinos to stoop labor and other low-paying positions and denying them entrance into trade unions, many Filipine pioneers are grateful to the United States. If circumstances did not allow them to complete their education, many point out the Depression had the same effect on other Americans. A president of a Filipino American Association says: *"We had a hard life, but we maintained a good life for the younger generation. Now we tell the younger generation to maintain that kind of life. Try to live according to the dictates of the law. To us who came here as pioneers, we tried to maintain that standard. We want the younger generation to preserve their pride, the hospitality from the old country. I don't regret our grandchildren don't know much about Filipine culture. They were born American. We don't expect to go to the Philippines to live for good in the future. The weather, the food, the water is different. The food is strange to me after 54 years of living here. It's like going to a different culture and starting to learn their way of life and culture again."*[11] When citizenship was offered to Filipinos in America, he was one of the first to apply.

Gratitude and humility are tones of the first generation. Due to the early immigrants' late marriages, the second generation is just coming into its own as homeowners, parents, and wage earners. Many smile as they tell how their fathers developed *compadres*, or close friends, up and down the coast whom they feel comfortable visiting on a moment's notice. But the second generation suffers from a muddy sense of their own identity. One member of

Rosita De Leion, Delores Gonzales, and Mariane Sison were part of the Seattle Filipine Festival Court in the 1950s. During the decade from 1950 to 1960, Filipine immigration quadrupled from what it had been during the two prior decades. (Elmer Ogawa; University of Washington Special Collections)

the second generation, aware that his Spanish surname creates confusion, says: *"Filipinos are confused with Chicanos and everyone else. No one ever mistakes anyone for a Filipino."*

In spite of the first generation's affirmation of the goals of the so-called melting pot, the second generation has found it difficult to sort out how they fit in. Greg Oliveros says: *"I'm still trying to find myself ethnically. . . . We have no model. I have no Bill Russell to look to. It's similar to an adult looking into a mirror for the first time. They're frightened. We have no recognition in terms of celebrated people. We have no political power. We have no Sony Corporation. We don't have anything to grab onto because the first generation never gave us anything. I have no sense of oral tradition. I've never really had a conversation with my brother and father that described for me in a very specific way what it was really like over there. My mother told me that she got up at five in the morning. She'd run down to the wharf and my grandfather would give her a fish to take home. On the way to school she'd sell the fish. That's about it. I don't see evidence of cultural heritage on a commercial level. There's no art. We don't have the dandy restaurants the majority can identify with. We have nothing. If you look at all the Asian groups, there's something out there they can attach themselves to, that says they're ok, or that they've succeeded and that they're part of the successful American dream. I can't say that.''* [12]

Recent immigration

Immigration law as revised in 1952 allowed the second wave of Filipine immigration. From 1952 to 1965 roughly 2,500 Filipinos a year entered the United States. After 1965 immigration legislation increased quotas that figure steadily rose. By 1970, 30,000 Filipinos a year came seeking homes in cities: Los Angeles, Chicago, Honolulu, and New York.

Recent arrivals tend to be either professional people or students coming for training in areas like medicine, engineering, or technical careers. Though professionals suffer from local certification requirements that make finding jobs in their area difficult, Filipinos gradually step into occupations as diverse as nurse, dentist, banker, and travel agent. Individual Filipinos arriving since World War II have researched marine agriculture, worked on the U.S. space program, served as judges, coached Olympic teams, and gained political office—far cries from the stoop labor jobs which were all that were open to Filipinos before World War II.

Like Issei and first generation Chinese Americans who studied developments at home, first generation Filipino Americans, both early and late arrivals, pay close attention to political and economic conditions in the Philippines which encourage the "brain drain" to the United States. Philippine President Marcos, elected first in 1965, and his government have been charged with corruption, denial of human liberties, and social injustices. Crime and poverty soar in the Philippines. Inflation was over 30 percent in 1979. These conditions foster the desire to emigrate.

Filipino Americans suggest the postwar history of Filipinos in the United States is not all sunshine either. Underemployment is

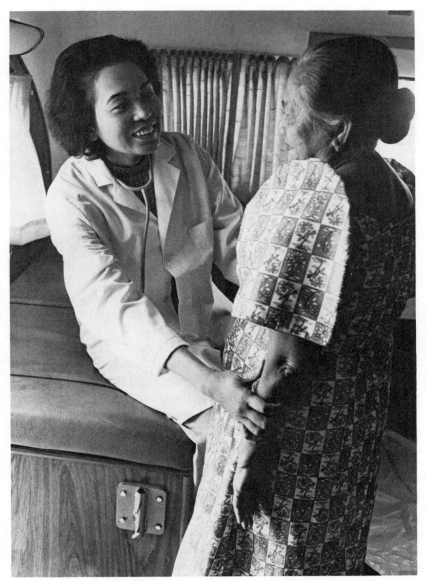

Since 1970 more than 1.5 million immigrants have come from Asia. In the 1970s, 359,000 Filipinos came; 41,000 arrived in 1981. While most earlier arrivals ended up as laborers, Filipine immigrants today are frequently well-educated professionals. (Visual Communications)

prevalent; medical aides accept jobs as janitors in hospitals. Filipino Americans are victims of the same stereotypes as both Chicanos and Asians, a confusion making individuals uncertain about their ethnic images.

Some Filipinos also say issues exist in the Filipino American community that divide them now just as the migrant nature of their work did decades ago. Filipino American pioneers complain that the new, more professional arrivals ignore older, less advantaged senior citizens—a complaint echoed by pioneers in Korean American communities. Other leaders say frequent intermarriage dilutes the culture.

A quiet voice

Perhaps no complaint is more common among Filipine and Asian immigrants than that their history is largely ignored in standard textbooks, films, and art. Yet Chinese and Japanese, by their sheer numbers and visible organizations, have forged a place in American consciousness. Not so Filipinos, whose numbers were relatively few until after 1965 and whose cultural tradition does not include the formation of large organizations.

European Americans study aspects of Asian culture such as wok cookery, the meditation of the tea ceremony, and the martial arts; Filipine culture remains unexplored. And while there is a growing political participation by and recognition of Asian minorities, Filipinos largely remain unheard.

Of the Filipino Americans who came with so much hope of succeeding and assimilating into American culture, comparatively little is recorded. Unlike books on Chinese Americans and Japanese Americans that span rows on library shelves, the chronicles of Filipinos in America remain the untold narratives of farm workers who harvested grapes in the sizzling California sun, mess attendants who cooked for America's soldiers, and nurses who tended the sick. Historians solicit oral narratives from elderly Chinese and Japanese, but new accounts of ethnic history in America often overlook Filipinos.

Some Filipine pioneers claim their anonymity testifies to willingness to merge in American society. Others are beginning to seek recognition—to lift themselves from the role of an invisible

The first generation of Filipine immigrants was predominantly male. In 1930 there were 14 men for every woman. They married late in life when immigration laws finally allowed more women to arrive. Third generation Filipino Americans are often quite young. Francis Estrada shares the strong family orientation of his elders. (T. Brian Collins)

minority. Many search to identify heroes and political representatives, break through the tangle of misidentifications that plague them, and struggle to understand the exhausting labor of the first generation, now grandfathers.

The large numbers arriving here from 1970 to 1980 have made Filipinos America's second largest group of Asian ancestry. They remain underrepresented culturally, politically, and economically. The void underscores a statement made by Carlos Bulosan about why he recorded the experiences of Filipino Americans from 1930 to 1950 in his book *America is in the Heart*. As he wrote before his death in 1956: *"What impelled me to write? The answer is —my grand dream of equality among men and freedom for all. To give a literate voice to the voiceless one hundred thousand Filipinos in the United States, Hawaii, and Alaska."* [13]

Less than thirty years later that number has grown to more than 775,000. Yet their voice remains far quieter than their numbers and contributions deserve.

Chronology

1521 Ferdinand Magellan claims the Philippines for Spain.

1898 The Philippine Islands become a protectorate of the U.S. under the Treaty of Paris ending the Spanish-American War.

1902 U.S. smashes the rebellion of Filipine militants seeking independence.

1907 Gentlemen's Agreement between the U.S. and Japan restricts Japanese immigration, thereby opening jobs in Hawaii to be filled by Filipinos.

1924 Immigration Act halts the flow of Japanese laborers to both Hawaii and the mainland. Filipinos arrive to work on farms.

1927 Filipino Federation of Labor is founded in Los Angeles to protect migrant workers from the abuses of labor contractors and farm owners.

1929-1930 Anti-Filipino riots and murders occur up and down the West Coast. The Depression intensifies competition for jobs between minority farm workers and whites.

1930 Census figures show Filipine population jumps from 6,000 in 1920 to 45,000 in 1930.

1934 Tydings-McDuffie Act promises independence to the Philippines in 10 years. It also creates a quota of 50 Filipine immigrants per year.

1935 President Franklin Roosevelt signs an act of Congress which offers to pay the way back to the Philippines for Filipinos choosing to go. Only 2,000 Filipinos leave.

1941 Japan invades the Philippines. A third of the Filipine men in the U.S. sign up to fight in the American military.

1946 Japanese occupation of the Philippines ends. Philippines become independent. U.S. citizenship is offered to all Filipinos, not just servicemen.

1952 Filipinos become subject to new quota system, but approximately 2,000 Filipinos per year enter the U.S. up until 1965.

1959 AFL-CIO Agricultural Workers organize to represent farmworkers, many of whom are Filipinos.

1965 Immigration Act increases Filipine immigration to above 20,000 per year.

1970 Census shows 337,000 people of Filipine ancestry in America.

1980 U.S. Census reports 775,000 people of Filipine ancestry live in America. This makes the Filipine population the second largest Asian group in the U.S. after people of Chinese ancestry.

FOUR

(Visual Communications)

Silent Immigrants

Korean Americans

One Korean compares his country to a shrimp eyed hungrily by whales. Another repeats the Korean proverb that tall mountains cast long, treacherous shadows to describe the double threats of China and Japan in Korean history. No matter what terms Koreans use, a frustrating history of division, foreign domination, and internal conflict is clear. These political realities loom in the minds of Koreans settling in America.

No place in Asia illustrates better than Korea how geography influences destiny. Russia, China, and nearby Japan surround Korea. The peninsula thus occupies a strategic central position, making it vulnerable to occupation by one or more of the three during times of conflict. The rugged mountain range in the north that separates the Korean peninsula from mainland Asia probably helped prevent surrounding nations from swallowing up the rich and complex Korean culture. At the same time, separation of mineral deposits in the northern mountains from agricultural output in the southern lowlands set the stage for internal conflict over control of important economic resources.

The Scilla Kingdom, 676-935 A.D., united the peninsula and drove out the Chinese. However, Chinese trade continued to greatly influence economics and Chinese scholarship, as in a number of other Asian countries, shaped politics. When Korea emerged as an entity during the Koryo period, 936-1392 A.D., political structures followed Chinese models. Government officials with scholarly backgrounds attained the highest status. Later, in the seventeenth century, Korea became a backdrop for the violent conflicts between the Manchurians and the southern Chinese for control of China. Although a battleground for foreigners, Korea established an isolationist reputation stronger than China's, earning it the title of Hermit Kingdom. When western forces asserted themselves in Asia in the nineteenth century, Korea continued to follow an isolationist policy rather than modernization in the Japanese style.

Japan also influenced Korea, indirectly and directly. Recognizing Korea's strategic position, Japan invaded the peninsula first in 1592. This and later invasions embittered Koreans, enhancing the Chinese-inspired goal of total isolation. The Japanese shattered this goal in 1876 when the Meiji government forced a treaty that placed the Japanese in a dominant position within Korea. Chafing under Japanese occupation, organized nationalist groups that opposed the occupiers continued until Japanese forces left at the end of World War II.

Christian influence

Christianity also eroded Korean isolation despite intense early resistance to missionary efforts. In 1784 a Korean who had accepted Catholicism in China returned with prayer books and crosses. Korean leaders perceived that missionary teachings of one God as spiritual leader conflicted with traditional Confucian values of ancestor reverence. The Christian concept of equality of all people threatened hierarchical loyalties to fathers, teachers, and kings. By the mid-1830s, many missionaries and their Korean followers had been executed.

The mood changed after 1882. That year Korea and the United States signed a treaty agreeing to peaceful relationships and open trade. In 1884 a Presbyterian missionary arrived in Seoul. He earned the gratitude of the king by furnishing medical treatment to the king's nephew who had been wounded in a court skirmish over political power. Backed by official tolerance, Protestantism spread, particularly in the north where famine and distance from

USSR

MONGOLIA

Hokkaido

Sapporo

Vladivostok

Sea of Japan

NORTH KOREA

Pyongyang

JAPAN

Tokyo

Seoul

SOUTH KOREA

Beijing (Peking)

Huang Ho River

River

Yellow Sea

Kyushu

CHINA

Yellow River

Chengdu

Yangtze River

Mekong River

Yangtze R.

Shanghai

Pacific Ocean

Taipei

TAIWAN

Guangzhou (Canton)

Xi Jiang River

HONG KONG (U.K.)
MACAO (Port.)

BURMA

Hanoi

Red River

Hainan

Gulf of Tonkin

Luzon

Vientiane

LAOS

Manila

PHILIPPINES

YAP

Rangoon

THAILAND

Mekong R.

VIETNAM

Bangkok

KAMPUCHEA

Andaman Sea

Phnom Penh

Ho Chi Minh City (Saigon)

South China Sea

Mindinao

Sulu Sea

Gulf of Thailand

Songkhla

BRUNEI (U.K.)

Celebes Sea

INDONESIA

WEST MALAYSIA

E. MALAYSIA

INDONESIA

NEW

Sumatra

Borneo

Equator

GUINEA

500 mi
800 km

court influence created a more flexible social structure—ripe for Christian teachings of equality and brotherhood. Also, dissatisfaction with official policy was acute in the north because the southern leaders controlled all food production and distribution. Christian teachings probably served to emphasize inequalities in official policy. A redemptive saviour seemed more appealing than a discriminatory king.

Besides suffering internal division, Korea at the end of the nineteenth century was caught squarely in the middle of clashes between Japan and Russia. Korea became part of the battlefield of the Russo-Japanese war over Manchuria: Japan sent samurai, displaced by modernization, into the peninsula in 1904. The war ended in 1905 when Japan sank all but three of thirty-five Russian ships in the Korean Straits. Peace settlements established Korea as a protectorate of Japan much as the Philippines was of the United States.

Eager immigrants

The combination of Japanese presence and Christian influence offered several incentives to young Koreans to follow Japanese laborers to Hawaii. Because of Korea's protectorate status, Hawaiian labor contractors could recruit Koreans, who received work papers through the auspices of Japanese agents. Presbyterian and Methodist missionaries urged new converts to take advantage of these offers, promising Christianity could be practiced freely in Hawaii—that believers would share the economic and social benefits of a Christian world. Contractors underscored the missionaries' words with their own promises of high wages, educational advantages, and free transportation.

As if encouraging words were not enough, other events in Korea made the message irresistible. In 1901 a drought spread famine over northwestern Korea, where Christian influence was strongest. The Korean government realized the exodus of laborers to Hawaii would reduce the effect of rice shortages. Korean soldiers who lost their jobs upon Japanese occupation became another source of eager immigrants. All over Korea the poor agreed to go wherever the contractors would take them.

History repeated itself. The first stopover for laborers was sugar

A Korean port, most probably Inch'on in the 1880s, during a time of increasing trade with the United States. (Denny Family Collection, Oregon Historical Society)

or pineapple plantations in Hawaii. Owners greeted them warmly, seeing the Korean presence as another way to break the protest movement building among Japanese workers. A trickle of ninety-three Koreans to Hawaii in 1902 swelled to 11,000 by 1905. Work conditions were unpleasant, as they had been for other Asian sojourners. After ten hours stooping in sweltering fields, men walked wearily "home" to makeshift barracks with no privacy. Finally, in protest, Japan halted Korean emigration to Hawaii in 1905 by exercising its right as an occupying nation to oversee the welfare of Korean citizens.

Japan rode a wave of national pride in its rapid modernization from 1905 to 1930. It attempted the same miracle in Korea through a series of repressive controls. This generated a wave of Korean immigration to the United States. Earlier emigration had slowed with the Gentlemen's Agreement between the United States and Japan in 1907 that included Korean laborers since Korea was a protectorate of Japan. This agreement did not, however, exclude students. Thus, small groups of scholars were able to leave Korea to escape Japanese control of education, politics, and industrial militarization.

Life in America

Though Korean immigration in those early years was much smaller than that of Chinese and Japanese, Koreans in America retained a sense of community. Nationalistic opposition to Japan spawned patriotic societies, Korean brotherhoods, and cultural groups. Where Koreans settled, small newspapers with political themes often started up, although they flourished only briefly. Koreans decided acting collectively was the best way to compete with Chinese and Japanese. In rural areas from 1910 to 1924 Koreans formed farming cooperatives that competed with more established Japanese vegetable farmers in the San Joaquin Valley of southern California; Oregon; Montana; and Colorado.

Christianity also bound Koreans together. In 1905 a Korean Methodist church opened in San Francisco. A year later a Korean Presbyterian church was founded in Los Angeles. Both Christian training and small numbers encouraged Koreans to learn English faster than other Asian groups. Their need to interact with American culture was greater.

After the Gentlemen's Agreement, wives of already resident Korean men could come to the United States. From 1910 to 1924, picture brides could also immigrate. Some 1,000 did, repeating the experience of their Japanese counterparts. The promise of wedding and travel expenses was sometimes all a bride needed to decide to come. Her own village most often offered only poverty or starvation. As the practice increased, go-betweens in Korea deducted from half to three-fourths of the groom's bridal payment, leaving the apprehensive girl just enough money for steamship fare.

In America picture brides handled disappointment according to their temperaments. One refused to marry a man twenty years older than the man of her dreams. Others married out of a sense of

The few Koreans living in the United States before 1950 sometimes mixed with other groups to express political opinions. Here Koreans in Los Angeles march with people from Puerto Rico in support of President Franklin Roosevelt. (Visual Communications)

loyalty and started families—the foundations of Korean communities both in Hawaii and on the mainland. When the 1924 Immigration Act ended both Japanese and Korean immigration, it also halted the arrival of picture brides.

On the mainland, students formed the most visible group of Koreans from 1908 to 1924. Young and predominantly Christian, they led demonstrations against Japanese occupation of Korea, mirroring the protest of students in their homeland. Generally they clustered near college campuses in San Francisco and Los Angeles. Some established boarding houses for other arriving bachelors. Many studied Korean history and language in Korean organizations throughout California and Hawaii. The Japanese banned both studies in Korea. Though they were educated, skilled, and vocal, these young men were unable to obtain work for which they were qualified. Their efforts focused on drawing American attention to the plight of their occupied nation through rallies, fundraising, and lobbying.

The intensity of these nationalist feelings shows up in an early protest centered around Durham White Stevens, a pro-Japanese American working in the Korean diplomatic service because of his solid Japanese connections. In San Francisco in 1908 Stevens made a speech deriding both Korean peasants and officials. Korean nationalists then living in California were shocked and clamored for a meeting with Stevens.

Stevens agreed. The session quickly got out of hand. Korean delegates smashed Stevens with chairs as tempers flared. Stevens ran, but three bullets stopped him. In court the nationalist assassin revealed the fervor of the movement: *"I was born on March 30, 1875, Pyeng Yang, Korea, and became a baptized Christian in my early days. When I saw my country fall into the hands of Japanese aggressors, I was filled with sorrow, but unable to do much to help. I applied for the status of an immigrant and came to Hawaii hoping to learn something in order to help my country. As a traitor to Korea, Stevens should die for his betrayal, since, through his deception, he made the Japanese occupation of Korea possible. I wish that I could have killed the traitor for my people. What is life? It is not enough to die, but one ought to know how to die. To die for having shot a traitor is glory, because I did it for my people."* [1]

In response to this incident, Japan tightened requirements for obtaining student visas to squelch student protest movements. Few Koreans, however, were assassins. Men such as Syngman Rhee, who eventually became the Korean head of state after World War II, gave speeches and met with government leaders in the United States to gain support for the Korean nationalists.

As Japan moved into the 1930s, nationalist sentiments among Koreans in America intensified. Word came of Japanese exploitation of Korea's mineral resources. Japan banned the Korean language from schools and public use in favor of Japanese and told Koreans to adopt Japanese names. Koreans were moved to Japan to provide cheap labor in Japanese factories. In Korean cities, the

A Korean family in California in the 1920s. The U.S. Korean population did not grow much until the 1960s. More settled in Los Angeles than any other city: 150,000 by 1980. (Visual Communications)

Japanese controlled every aspect of law enforcement, industry, education, and justice.

Both circumstances and personalities encouraged Koreans in America to maintain their sense of unity. By 1945, some 3,000 Koreans on the mainland and 6,500 in Hawaii were subject to anti-Asian sentiments aimed at other groups. Forced to live on the fringes of Little Tokyos and Chinatowns, Koreans bristled when mistaken for the Japanese whom they regarded as competitors here and oppressors abroad. Though some Koreans worked in the agricultural valleys, most opted to stay in city neighborhoods not readily identifiable as Korean except for the Korean religious and political organizations.

In 1940 Korean-owned businesses dotted Los Angeles: thirty fruit and vegetable stands, nine groceries, eight laundries, six trucking companies, five wholesalers, five restaurants, three drugstores, two hat shops, one employment agency, and one rooming house.[2] Other Koreans worked as janitors, busboys, and cooks—jobs common to all early Asian immigrants.

Syngman Rhee encouraged these urban residents to maintain Korean culture rather than intermarry, as some Filipinos had done. He asked all Koreans in America to prepare to fight for a free Korea and to collect money to train forces.

Effects of war

Given this history, it is not surprising many Koreans in America were initially delighted by anti-Japanese sentiments that boiled over after the Japanese bombed Pearl Harbor. Some formed voluntary military organizations to fight Japanese in Manchuria or joined Chinese protests against scrap iron shipments to Japan. Ironically, in Hawaii Koreans were subject to the same curfews as Japanese because Japan occupied and was allied with Korea. Nowhere, however, were Koreans in America detained in camps.

The defeat of Japan fanned hopes for Korean independence. However, Japanese surrender terms in Korea, drafted by the United States and unchallenged by the USSR, divided Korea at the 38th parallel. Japanese forces north of the 38th parallel surrendered to the Soviet commanders, those south of the 38th to the U.S. commander.

The division, intended as temporary, continued after the surrender and the two zones became known as North Korea and South Korea. Korea's strategic geographical position affected the outcome once more. In 1946 a United Nations resolution called for general elections in Korea under the observation of a Temporary Commission on Korea. The USSR refused the temporary commission entry into North Korea. South Korea did hold elections under UN supervision. In 1948 the Republic of Korea came into existence; Syngman Rhee, long-time nationalist-in-exile, became president.

No elections were ever held in the north. Russians continued to occupy North Korea just as the United States occupied the south in an arrangement that was supposed to be temporary. In June 1950, North Korea invaded South Korea. At a United Nations

When World War II came to a close, Koreans in America celebrated the end of Japanese dominance in Korea. (Visual Communications)

conference, members agreed to send aid to South Korea. Fourteen nations sent ground troops. Within months the fighting stalemated near the demilitarized zone across the center of Korea, although the armistice did not come until mid-1953.

The Korean War was bloody and frustrating. The United States provided half the ground forces and most of the air and naval power for South Korea. Death and casualty figures were staggering: an estimated 142,000 Americans, 300,000 South Koreans, 520,000 North Koreans, 900,000 Chinese, and 380,000 UN soldiers other than Americans died in the fighting.

The war created refugees. Metropolitan areas in the south swelled. Job opportunities declined. Increasing numbers of professionals sought to fill the quotas under the Asia-Pacific Triangle provisions of the 1952 Immigration Act to find better jobs, comfortable housing, and a stable political climate in the United States. The quota limit for Korea, exclusive of special exemptions, was easily filled from 1951 until 1965 by students hoping for a brighter future and war orphans placed for adoption in the United States. Changes in the immigration law in 1965, primarily the elimination of rigid quotas, broadened immigration opportunities for both professionals and students.

The largest number of Korean immigrants from the Korean War to 1975 were war brides—a phenomenon not limited to that war. American soldiers in occupied Japan after World War II married 50,000 Japanese women. Twenty-eight thousand Korean women returned with American soldiers from 1947 to 1975. In the 1960s and 1970s, such intermarriages were common throughout Southeast Asia. Regardless of nationality, brides of U.S. service men are not subject to quota restrictions.

Intermarriage

Profiles of the "standard" intermarriage emerged from sociological studies. Early in American history, state laws discouraged marriage between races. In 1906 it became illegal in California for any white to marry a "Mongol," a law in force until 1948. The U.S. Supreme Court did not strike down all state antimiscegenation laws until 1967, long after large numbers of Japanese and Korean war brides had already entered the United States.

During the late nineteenth century, Koreans got to know Americans mainly through educational rather than commercial institutions. Korean Americans have used education to overcome racism and build economic security. (Visual Communications)

Though the laws were not uniformly enforced and not all Americans supported them to begin with, they were on the books. Also, most Asian cultures, with the exception of Filipine, disapproved of intermarriage. That these marriages took place in spite of cultural barriers indicates how completely war breaks down social norms. In Japan, the Philippines, Korea, and Vietnam, so many men died that marriage-age women far outnumbered prospective husbands. The same forces of war broke up families and disrupted regular prospects of employment. Refugees lost roots and belief in the stability of their culture.

The U.S. military presence, predominantly male, filled gaps in the fractured social structure. The military created jobs. Legitimate employment was available in clerical, sales, or service-oriented positions. Though Asian families might not approve of daughters and sisters working for the military instead of in their traditional role of tending family offspring, they often had no say. Unemployment was too high to object to how a family member earned a paycheck. A woman's job threw her into an unfamiliar culture that condoned unchaperoned dating. As she gained more independence via her work, she was tempted to turn her back on her family's suspicions. Many chose to date American soldiers.

The decision to marry, on either side, was not simple. Soldiers report that when they told friends or commanding officers, they were besieged with pictures of sisters and girlfriends at home on the assumption they had forgotten what they had left behind. Parents responded warmly at times, but all too often they thought their son had made a mistake. Women he knew at home might assume he had decided to find a maid rather than marry a wife —or that his Asian fiancée was pregnant. The Asian woman saw her family turn away from her, making derogatory remarks about the color of the soldier's skin or what their babies would look like. Asian families expressed little more tolerance for children of mixed marriages than do many American families.

The marriage announcement was only the beginning of the couples' problems. Immigration law required security checks, physical exams, and documentation difficult to acquire where war had disrupted government agencies. Military chaplains discouraged the marriages on the grounds that the divorce rate among war brides and their soldier grooms exceeded that of the average population.

For women who remained married, a series of challenges and emotional responses seem typical. Arriving in America unable to speak English well, a bride often found she was not well-accepted by members of her own ethnic group who assumed that if she preferred to marry someone of a different background, either white or black, she no longer needed their support. Her husband's parents might not welcome her. Those parents who warmly greeted their new daughters-in-law faced language and cultural obstacles confronting anyone making contacts between cultures.

Ethnic awareness builds through efforts to preserve both language and literature. (Visual Communications)

For the woman unable to find joy in her new role, prospects were dim. Silently she suffered from the shame of hurting her family or from intense bouts of loneliness. If her husband was insensitive to her anguish, he placed additional strains on the marriage. If her husband realized the nature of cultural loneliness and what adjustments she had to make, then the marriage had a chance to thrive.

Children of war

The histories of mixed-race babies born during the Korean War and of their mothers are as poignant as those of the war brides. Fathered by members of the United Nations forces in Korea— Turks, Greeks, Scandinavians, Americans, and many others— mixed-race babies were mocked and ridiculed in Korean society. Though soldiers promised to return to marry the Korean mothers and claim their children, many did not. Some women waited ten years, patiently longing for lovers to prove faithful. Meanwhile, such mothers were outcasts from their families. No social services existed to counsel them in war-torn Korea. Despairing, a mother might abandon her child on a doorstep.

The Holt Foundation, an international adoption program, acted in 1956 to give these women an option. Through the foundation they could offer their children for adoption in the United States. Dr. David Kim, now Director of Holt International Children's Services, describes those mothers' dilemmas: *"It was heartrending, those women and those children. I don't want to ever see it again. The mother would cut off her limbs to help those children. Sometimes one woman would come to us with her baby while she was still breastfeeding. She would leave the baby, but later she would come back because her breasts were too full and hurt so badly. Sometimes she took the baby away with her. Then later they might come back, usually when the child reached school age. To enter school in Korea children have to have a family registration. It's more than an American birth certificate. It's based on the nuclear family and records births, deaths, weddings—even criminal acts—going back three generations. You can trace a family's history with those registrations back 300 years. Koreans show them when they apply for jobs, for anything. If the child was not born in wedlock, the child cannot be listed—or every family member would have to show a*

Esther Kim and her young friend arrived from Korea in June 1953. (California Historical Society)

family registration with an illegitimate child. This is a very important thing to Koreans. The mother wrings her hands and sobs, 'What have I done?' If the child went on to school, they were called names for being of mixed blood. This child could not bear it. He might refuse to go to school.

Then the mother would come and say, 'I waited too long. You must take my child to his father's country.' She would say that softly to the child so they could part. 'You are going to your father's country.' Then she wept. She bit her tongue to hold back her tears. Next she ran away crying after she gave us the papers she had signed.''[3]

No wonder Dr. Kim does not remember those years with joy. In 1962, 74,000 children waited in Korean orphanages for adoption. Years later the Holt Foundation performed similar services in Vietnam until the fall of Saigon. Now, while work continues in finding foster homes and adoptive homes for children from India, Nicaragua, and Bangladesh, Holt publishes newsletters describing how Korean children who found homes in America are graduating from college, raising families, and starting businesses.

Open doors

The 1965 changes in U.S. immigration policy increased quotas and dramatically increased the number of Koreans entering America. From 1961 to 1964, 10,000 were admitted, a great number of whom were women and children. From 1965 to 1970, 24,000 entered, including large numbers of professionals. Statisticians discovered the majority of late-arriving Korean immigrants were between the ages of 20 and 44 and more educated than any other ethnic minority immigrating to America. Before 1970 the bulk of the new immigrants followed the pattern for Asian immigration by settling on the West Coast.

Beginning in 1970 the U.S. Census listed Korean immigrants separately in its tallies rather than in the broader category of "other Asian." This allowed for more accurate recordkeeping and gave some recognition to the increasing numbers here. Not only did Korean immigration pick up substantially after the Korean War, but approximately 62,000 Koreans were admitted to the United States between 1960 and 1970 on temporary visas. Many sought to change their status to permanent resident or immigrant as they finished educations here.

The 1970s saw a phenomenal growth in the Korean population in America. Between 1970 and 1975, 122,000 Koreans sought homes here, giving better education and job opportunities as the reason. The 1980 Census recorded a Korean population of

During the 1950s, as the Korean War drew to a close, the U.S. military worked with civilian agencies to bring thousands of orphans into western states. (Gordon Peters; California Historical Society)

354,000—five times the number in 1970. People of Korean ancestry became America's fourth largest Asian population.

Political conditions in South Korea encouraged this emigration. Under Park Chung-hee's leadership from 1961 to 1979, South Korea suffered from a government that minimized human rights.

The Korean Central Intelligence Agency increased surveillance on dissidents, particularly students, who disagreed with government attempts to normalize relations with Japan. Koreans became less satisfied with martial law, censorship, and the threat of riots. In 1972 a revised constitution granted Park the power to serve as president indefinitely, a mandate to rule with a clenched fist, which he did until his assassination in 1979.

What is known of Korean immigrants to the United States since 1970 comes primarily from academic sources.[4] Compared to the Southeast Asian refugees, Koreans in America have earned little attention in the media beyond the portrayal of martial arts expertise. One reason may be that, unlike other Asian groups such as the Chinese and Japanese, later-arriving Koreans have dispersed more throughout the United States.

Koreatown

The obvious exception is Koreatown, a five-square-mile area in the Olympic area of Los Angeles. Near the heart of the city, it has drawn a large number, perhaps 150,000, Koreans. A variety of organizations service the established and recently-arrived Korean populations there: alumni clubs, trade associations, and seventy-two Korean churches, which are mostly Protestant. Unemployment runs above the national average despite the educational background of the residents of Koreatown. Though 72 percent held professional or managerial level jobs before coming to the United States, due to language problems involved in obtaining U.S. professional licenses, they have not been able to find work for which they are qualified. For some, such as the 300 Korea-trained pharmacists in southern California, the frustrations run even deeper: they may not even take the exams because they were not educated in this country.

One solution to unemployment in Koreatown is similar to that discovered by the Chinese and Japanese: self-employment. Almost 300 Korean businesses cater largely to Koreans and employ other Koreans. They include hamburger stands, barbershops, grocery stores, food-related businesses, maintenance companies, and professional services.

This Koreatown pattern is one Southeast Asian refugees may

Numerous signs in Korean near a Los Angeles street reflect the large number of Korean Americans in that city in 1982. (T. Brian Collins)

follow. The major difference between the two groups is that Korean businesses often flourish with money brought from overseas. In contrast, Southeast Asian refugees tend to work first at subsistence jobs. They save money as they go, pooling with family members, as the Chinese and Japanese once did, to make initial cash outlays necessary to start businesses or acquire loans.

Other than their visibility in Los Angeles and Honolulu, Koreans tend to be overlooked in magazines and newspapers, echoing the experience of Filipinos. The reasons, however, differ. Until 1970, Korean immigration was small. Even in Los Angeles and Honolulu the variety and number of political groups and religious denominations worked against the establishment of community-wide organizations to represent Koreans to the community at large. Korean populations have not fostered groups like the Chinese Benevolent Associations or the Japanese Americans Citizen League. In addition, war brides and orphans have weak ties with the mainstream of Korean American ethnic history because of their assimilation into non-Korean families.

Memories and the future

The best source of feelings, reactions, and opinions about Korean American ethnicity is the memories of Korean Americans. For example, Dr. Sammy Lee's father arrived in Hawaii in 1905 and in California in 1907. Because he was bilingual and could translate for Korean and American workers, railroad workers financed his way to the mainland. Dr. Lee remembers his parents: *"Our parents motivated us to be contributing citizens. I know they told me a good American was a good Korean who brought forth all of the good ethnic qualities into this great American melting pot."*[5]

The pattern emerges again. Asian American children retain respect for their parents. Though Dr. Lee's habits differ from those of the first immigrants, he takes pride in his ancestry. When asked what is most important to him in his ethnic background, he says: *"I loved my parents and would have done nothing to shame them or my ancestral heritage. Somewhere or somehow I had the thought that if I made it big in sports I did not want the general public to think I wanted to lose my identity because I was a part of the American sporting scene."*

Dr. Lee did make it big in sports. In 1952 he became the first diver in Olympic history to win the high diving medal twice in a row. Since then he has been elected to the Diving Hall of Fame. His reaction to his success underscores his sense of mixed identity, the successful American proud to be an Asian American: *"I cried when I became the first American-born Asian to win a gold medal for my country, the U.S.A. I wanted to prove it could be done because I was an American-born Korean. When I won it the second time, I was elated to prove to the world it was not an accident."*

Not an accident. These words sum up the massive contributions Asians have made and continue to make as Asian Americans or Americans—depending on the identity each individual chooses. For more than 100 years, Chinese, Japanese, Filipinos, and Koreans have proved themselves through their perseverance and accomplishments.

Their experience suggests a path for other newcomers. Survive at first through the strength of your muscles if that is what it takes. Recognize the power of education. Create employment when you can. Where families survive, honor family loyalties; cooperate in

The Jackson Community Council in Seattle represented a wide range of ethnic and racial interests. These council members in the late 1950s looked toward the future of Seattle's International District. (Elmer Ogawa; University of Washington Special Collections)

extended families and community groups. This has been the pattern for generations of Asian immigrants, an honorable blend of Asian and American cultures.

Chronology

1876 Japan forces Korea open to foreign trade.

1883-1903 Approximately 100 students and diplomats from Korea enter U.S. for training.

1903-1904 7,000 Koreans go to Hawaii to work in sugar cane and pineapple fields.

1905 Japan controls Korea as part of the settlement of the Russo-Japanese War and halts Korean immigration to Hawaii.

1906 Korean children are included in the decree by the San Francisco School Board that all persons of Asian ancestry must attend segregated schools in Chinatown.

1907 Gentlemen's Agreement between the U.S. and Japan includes ban on further Korean immigration to the U.S. as laborers.

1909 Korean National Association forms in San Francisco to encourage Koreans in America to oppose the intervention of Japan in Korea. Students flee Korea to come to the U.S.

1919 Koreans in America protest Japanese occupation of Korea.

1924-1948 Korean immigration to the U.S. slowed to 20 non-laborers per year.

1937 Japan pressures Korea to support Japanese military effort in Manchuria.

1942 Japan drafts Koreans to fight in World War II.

1945 When Japan surrenders in 1945, temporary partition of Korea established at 38th parallel. Japanese forces north of 38th surrender to Soviet commanders; those south surrender to U.S. Two zones formed: North Korea and South Korea.

1948 U.S. Immigration and Naturalization Service begins counting Koreans separately from "Other Asians." 39 immigrants enter U.S. from Korea. That rate continues until 1952.

1950 North Korea invades South Korea. United Nations countries send air and ground troops to support South Korea.

1952 Korean-born immigrants eligible for U.S. citizenship.

1954 Geneva Conference on settlement of Korean War ends without success. "Temporary" partition remains.

1960 Census shows 11,000 Korean-born residents in U.S.

1962 Korea allows easier emigration. Professionals leave for better job and educational opportunites in U.S. Arrivals from Korea climb to over 2,000 per year. Many are on student visas.

1965 Change in U.S. immigration law allows Korean immigration to go over 3,000 per year. It reaches 8,900 annually by 1970.

1970 Decade of large Korean immigration begins. Census shows 69,000 people of Korean ancestry in U.S.

1980 U.S. Census lists 354,000 persons of Korean ancestry in America. People of Korean ancestry make up the fourth largest Asian group in America.

FIVE

(John Isaac; United Nations)

Seekers of Refuge

United States Refugee Administration

The United Nations estimates 2,000 people per day try to escape their home countries. In 1980 refugee populations reached 15.9 million—from Southeast Asia and countries such as Cuba, Haiti, Afghanistan, Uganda, the Soviet Union, and Ethiopia. These statistics put the more than 550,000 refugees from Southeast Asia who have resettled in America since 1975 into perspective. They represent only a fraction of the worldwide refugee crisis.

The United States plays an enormous role in this crisis. Since 1945 this country has provided a new home to nearly 2 million refugees. U.S. government assistance to refugees in 1980 alone topped $1 billion. Assistance also came from individual donations, church congregations, and voluntary agencies.

The Congressional Refugee Act of 1980 limited admission of refugees to 50,000 a year through 1982. Then it gave the president the power, after consulting with Congress, to increase that number. President Jimmy Carter exercised that power in 1980 to allow 156,000 refugees into the United States from Southeast Asia alone. Although forty nations, including Canada, China, Australia, and France, have worked together, their admissions barely put a dent in the numbers of people needing resettlement. Worldwide monetary outpourings and other assistance have not ended starvation and disease caused by refugee flight.

Throughout the world, first asylum nations, nations that initially receive refugees, stagger under the refugee load. Headlines flared in late 1978 when Malaysian naval ships surrounded boats fleeing Southeast Asia and towed them into international waters, where most sank. In June 1979, Malaysia's prime minister said his government would shoot newly arrived refugees unless world aid increased. Malaysian newspapers accused world powers of quibbling and procrastinating while Vietnamese Chinese drowned and their bodies bobbed to shore. In May 1980, crewmen on a Singapore warship, using boat hooks, beat Vietnamese refugees who had abandoned a sinking ship and threw children overboard to keep them from boarding.

Thailand, Malaysia, the Philippines, and Singapore cannot handle influxes of refugees without the promise of second asylum nations to offer resettlement as quickly as possible—and not just for desirable skilled and educated refugees but also the handicapped, aged, and sick. With their own populations growing at an alarming rate, both citizens and governments in first asylum nations resent refugee arrivals.

Resettlement efforts

The Office of the United Nations High Commissioner for Refugees (UNHCR) administers refugee aid and resettlement around the world. This agency sets policy and coordinates the relief efforts of member nations and voluntary agencies. Through UNHCR, second asylum nations process resettlement requests.

Created in 1951, UNHCR was designed to meet the growing demand to resettle refugees which had begun with the Russian Revolution in 1917, when 1.5 million sought asylum abroad. Until 1951 resettlement was under the aegis of the League of Nations or other UN commissions. Since World War II these international commissions have helped refugees from Eastern Europe, Jews desiring to go to Palestine, war orphans, Palestinians displaced by the birth of Israel in 1948, Chinese fleeing after the 1949 revolution, homeless Koreans, and refugees from South Africa, Cuba, and recently, Southeast Asia.

National governments compose the next layer of refugee bureaucracy. The 1980 Refugee Act formalized the U.S. position on

REFUGEE CAMPS

▲ Kampuchean
● Lao
⬢ Vietnamese

CHINA

Lao Cai

NANNING

Red River

Dien Bien Phu

HANOI

HAIPHONG

BURMA

Chieng Khong

Mekong River

Luang Prabang
(Royal Capital)

Tonkin
Annam

Gulf of Tonkin

Phayao

Nan

Xieng Khouang

Vinh

Hainan

Chiang Mai

Ban Nam Yao

Sayaboury

VIENTIANE
(Administrative Capital)

Uttaradit

Ban Vinai

Nong Khai

17th Parallel

RANGOON

Hue

Moulmein

THAILAND
(SIAM)

Da Nang

Si Khiu

Ubon

Tavoy

Surin

Sa Kaeo

Khao I Dang

Mekong River

Andaman Sea

BANGKOK

Kamput

Angkor

KAMPUCHEA
(CAMBODIA)

Tonle Sap

Laemsing

Khao Larn

Annam
Cochin China

Ban Mai Rut

PHNOM PENH

HO CHI MINH CITY
(Saigon)

Gulf of Thailand

Kampot

Mekong Delta

South China Sea

⬢ Pulau Bidong, Songkhla,
and twelve other Vietnam-
ese refugee camps are in Malaysia and Indonesia.

0   150mi
0   240km

LAOS

VIETNAM

refugees, substituting specific procedures for hit-or-miss reactions to crisis. The act helps refugees become self-sufficient as quickly as possible, recognizing that the elderly, unaccompanied minors, and some single parents require more cash assistance and medical aid than those with job skills.

The federal government of the United States plays many roles in refugee resettlement. It determines the criteria for entrance. High priorities include reuniting families, recognizing past service to the United States, helping in hardship cases, and assisting escape from communist countries. Congress further limits how many refugees are accepted annually and administers repaying state and local governments for cash assistance and medical programs benefiting refugees.

The federal government is now reducing cash support for refugees, money appropriated separately from ongoing social service and welfare costs for the larger American public. Where refugees once enjoyed a guaranteed three years of cash and medical assistance, beginning in 1982 this aid will be considerably less. Sponsoring agencies fight the idea that cash assistance is an end in itself, claiming it prolongs the lethargy long residence in refugee camps began. They favor separating medical and cash benefits so a refugee who finds a low-paying job with poor medical benefits is not inclined to drop the job in order to retain needed medical services. Most people involved in refugee resettlement would like to see cash assistance used as a tool while job and language training are offered to those who are employable.

Meanwhile, unemployment in some refugee groups runs as high as 50 percent. One-parent families, the disabled, those over sixty-five, and hardship cases will continue to receive supplemental security income. Service providers fear for many others.

In mid-1981 a Hmong refugee unable to find work hung himself because the state threatened to cut off his cash assistance. His family later told Adult and Family Service workers he killed himself so his wife, head of a single-parent family upon his death, could receive continuing support. Though his case is unusual, it points to the desperation refugees feel when they cannot get jobs and support runs out.

Cash assistance. Special educational and medical benefits.

Two Hmong children play in the Ban Nam Yao refugee camp in Thailand. Some Hmong, Mien, Lao, and members of other ethnic groups have been in Thai camps since 1975. (John Isaac; United Nations)

Crowded low-income housing. These cause many Americans to claim refugees unfairly benefit from the public purse. Letters pour into assistance offices reporting cases where refugees buy expensive cars or stereos with public money. Those who defend these purchases claim refugees are like other minorities; they want to fit into the American mainstream and choose the most obvious cultural symbols in their efforts. Frequently these purchases do not belong to an individual, but are made in the spirit of the extended family loyalties of Southeast Asians. Four to five families pitch in to buy one car.

Refugees understand assistance dependency affects their status in American communities, but jobs for predominantly nonliterate or poorly skilled arrivals are rare. Though refugee leaders realize economic self-sufficiency is the only route to success, 75 percent of the refugees arriving after 1978 are nonliterate in their own language. The best educated and most highly skilled fled first. Few speak English. Only recently has the government developed strong sanctions to deter refugees from turning down low-income jobs in favor of cash assistance.

Cash assistance points out a major difference between early Asian immigrants and recent refugees. Refugee entrance to the United States was not selective for those who could perform work here as it was for earlier laborers. Refugees came because their desperate plight stirred compassion. Though early immigrants were mostly men between the ages of fifteen and thirty, refugee arrivals include families of ten children who get by on minimum wage earnings of one or more members of the family. Various family members suffer aftereffects of severe starvation or other medical problems. War-wounded, handicapped, and aged come too. In addition, the more recently refugees have arrived, the greater the chance they have been affected by communist persecution or regimentation, inadequate nutrition, lack of organized schooling, disease, the uncertainty and boredom of camps, and psychological traumas.

Some experts say the refugee economic situation will improve. A study of the pattern of Vietnamese employment from 1975 to 1978, done by HEW, concluded that refugee employment rates for those eligible rose from 68.2 percent to 95.8 percent.[1] Skeptics respond that the government study ignored a large group of "non-eligibles" to overstate refugee successes. Since 1978 employment rates have reflected the rising national rate of unemployment and relaxed educational standards used to select refugee admissions from the camps.

A study done in 1976 on immigrants from various countries —not refugees—shows that after three to six years the average immigrant family earns as much as the average American family and pays as much in taxes.[2] As time goes on, immigrant families earn more than average American ones. More family members may work. Refugee workers look forward to the day when refugees pay more in taxes than they collect in public services.

In 1978 and 1979, nearly 280,000 refugees from China and Southeast Asia flooded Hong Kong. Refugee camps in all asylum nations generated hostility among permanent residents who resented overcrowding and refugee services paid for by taxpayers. (Hong Kong Christian Service)

Besides aid, government agencies also must coordinate providing information to refugees. The implication for the various agencies serving refugees is staggering. Health care and driver training manuals are translated into five or six Southeast Asian languages. The problem recurs in tax and citizenship brochures, notices of social or legal events, and public transportation guides.

VOLAGs and sponsors

The nitty-gritty work of deciding where a Southeast Asian family initially settles, however, belongs to a creation of the refugee crisis: the VOLAG. VOLAG is an acronym, dating back to the 1940s, for a voluntary agency that resettles refugees with a sponsor under a contract grant from the U.S. Department of State. A refugee must have a sponsor before entering the United States.

Many VOLAGs are church-affiliated: U.S. Catholic Conference, Lutheran Immigration and Refugee Service, HIAS (a worldwide

Jewish migration agency that does some work with Southeast Asians), World Relief Services (evangelical churches), and Church World Services (a variety of churches neither evangelical nor Lutheran). Others are nonsectarian: International Rescue Committee and American Council for Nationalities Service. The Tolstoy Foundation, created to help Russian refugees earlier this century, now assists other refugees. Each VOLAG maintains offices near where refugees resettle to help sponsors in orientation, obtain housing and employment counseling for refugees, and oversee the initial phases of resettlement.

The affiliation of VOLAGs with church congregations as sponsors leads some Americans to charge churches use sponsorship to boost church memberships through high-pressure missionary work. Both refugees and social service workers report occasional abuse of sponsorship status. Sponsoring agencies respond that all sponsors are encouraged to respect differing religious and cultural beliefs. Agencies stress that refugees have a complete system of worship; to challenge Buddhist and other beliefs makes a refugee feel more isolated and cut off from his traditions.

Whether a sponsor is an individual or a church congregation, financial commitments are required. Though sponsors do not pay travel expenses to the city of sponsorship, they do cover initial rent payments. They arrange for the refugee family's food, clothing, housewares, and bedding.

Finding housing gives sponsors the first realization of what faces arriving refugees. In cities with housing shortages, some landlords hesitate to rent to refugees. Sponsors debate whether it is better to tell a landlord they are renting for refugees or let the news come out later. The first choice gives a landlord a chance to make up excuses. Despite laws against discrimination, it is hard to bring the landlord to justice. The second alternative may lead to unpleasant confrontations later.

Housing choices are based on refugee preferences whenever possible. Refugees want to live close to family or other members of their ethnic group. Where landlords cooperate, this works. In Houston, Texas, a landlord agreed to create a Khmer Village (Khmer are from Kampuchea, formerly Cambodia) out of his twenty-three two-bedroom brick cottages. In Portland, Oregon,

This boy spent several years with 5,200 other Kampuchean refugees in the Ban Mai Rut camp near Klong Yai, Thailand. Like other unaccompanied minors resettling in the United States, he will need foster care, language training, and perhaps psychological counseling. Nearly 2,500 children under the age of 18 have come by themselves to the United States from Southeast Asia. (John Isaac; United Nations)

an apartment complex called Halsey Square has catered to successive groups of refugees: early Vietnamese arrivals, then Hmong from Laos, and now Mien from Laos. In Seattle, Washington, trouble between refugees and other resident minority groups in Mt. Baker Village led the city to decide not to put any more refugees there. In Denver, Colorado, Chicanos who mistakenly thought Vietnamese in their housing project had fought against the United States chased out eighteen families after a battle of brick and bottle throwing.

To be fair to landlords, some refugees have not had the help they required to live easily in American housing. One family huddled for three weeks on the cold floor because sponsors had not explained the furnace. Another family lit a fire on the kitchen floor for the same reason. American plumbing is not familiar to all Southeast Asians; children have trouble adapting to the new hardware. Housing authorities insist children should sleep in separate rooms from parents, though many Southeast Asian families are used to being closer. In Hong Kong refugee camps, each family was given one double bunk where they were expected to rest, pass time, sleep, eat, change diapers, and store their possessions.

Sponsors help refugees find work, enroll in job training programs, or learn English. Refugees need help obtaining social security numbers, getting medical screening, and enrolling children in school. Sponsors explain how to work appliances and ride mass transit systems. They plan tours of local banks, stores, post offices, and markets where refugees can buy food they are accustomed to. They teach how American currency works and how rent, utility, and tax bills are paid. Sponsors explain laws—that driver's licenses are not automatically issued when the fee is paid as they were in Cambodia.

A Vietnamese minister active in resettlement describes sponsorship: *"Sponsorship is like helping a broken car. That car needs some people to push it and when the car is running then you don't need to push it. And the refugees, they don't want to just sit there and get assistance from the church. When they come here, they try to study the language and find a job. They want to make it on their own. So the church has to be able to sense that time and let the refugees help themselves."*[3]

Relationships between sponsors and refugees vary as widely as

Hmong women in the Ban Thong refugee camp in Thailand wear embroidered skirts which may take a year to complete. (Lois Calloway)

the individuals involved. Increasingly, working refugees sponsor their own relatives where in the past individual Americans or congregations acted as sponsors. Some see sponsorship as a moral commitment, as a way to help others. Some enjoy teaching. Others relish the friendships that grow.

Clustering in the West

A recent study shows that per population densities, western states accept the greatest share of sponsorship responsibility.[4] States absorbing the most refugees per million residents are Hawaii, California, Oregon, Washington, Utah, Minnesota, New Mexico, Oklahoma, Iowa, and Nevada—all west of the Mississippi.

The prominence of the West in sponsorship is explained in several ways.[5] Large Asian American populations ensure refugee needs receive media attention. Refugees are drawn to developing communities of their own ethnic background. Other less obvious factors correlate with high sponsorship rates: the number of educated women in a state, recent statehood, and high voter turnout.

Where either unemployment or income level is extremely high, sponsorship levels drop off.

When a refugee family decides to move from the place of initial resettlement to another American town, sponsorship responsibilities terminate. While sponsors frequently feel they have failed, often these moves simply mean refugees feel independent. Climate, availability of jobs or social services, family reunification, or a larger community of refugees of the same ethnic background all spark refugee movement.

This movement is so common that state and federal agencies call it "secondary migration." Generally the movement is westward. One Hmong left Boise, Idaho, where he had first settled because of sponsorship by an American friend. In Boise he never saw other people with jet black hair. Wherever he turned, he glimpsed only non-Asian faces. As months went by, he grew despondent. He spent much time dwelling on the thought of suicide. Finally he expressed his gratitude to his sponsor and drove to Portland, where a large Hmong community existed. Within days, his psychological aches diminished.

Despite the initial government policy in 1975 of dispersing refugees throughout the United States, clustering is the rule. California is the obvious center with close to 35 percent of the Southeast Asians living there by the middle of 1981. They concentrate in five counties: Los Angeles, Orange, San Diego, San Francisco, and Santa Clara. Large numbers also resettle in Houston and the District of Columbia. Other cities with large populations, in descending order, are New Orleans, Seattle-Tacoma, Portland, Dallas, Chicago, Minneapolis, Denver, and Philadelphia.

Secondary migration patterns differ from group to group. An official at the federal Office of Refugee Resettlement sums up his experience keeping population statistics: "The Hmong, for instance, who are now coming in greater numbers are settling largely in the north central states (and Rhode Island) .... To my knowledge the Vietnamese fishermen are not leaving Texas and the Gulf Coast despite trouble there. That is the only occupation they know and they are good at it. They can make a marginal business pay whereas an American fisherman cannot. They have moved from the more tension laden spots but not from the coast.

It's cold, but it's still a playful bath at the Ban Vinai refugee camp in Thailand. (Galen Beery)

To my knowledge the Hmong in Minnesota are not moving out. They have been treated well there and have a firm Hmong community and plenty of farmland, so I have seen no evidence they

are heading to LA. The ones coming to LA are new refugees joining their families there."[6]

Secondary migration plays havoc with the predictions of government agencies about the number of residents needing special
services. School districts feel the impact as refugee numbers swell
and decline rapidly when clan or family groups decide to move.

Government agencies do their best to measure refugee populations. At first the task is not too difficult. U.S. Center for Disease
Control health screening is one measure. The Department of State
monitors the initial assignment of refugees to VOLAGs. The only
government measure that follows a moving family is the requirement for all aliens to register with the Immigration and Naturalization Service every January. Of the Southeast Asians in the
United States, 85 to 90 percent comply with this requirement,
though it is not strictly enforced.

Mutual Assistance Associations

Repeatedly the question pops up about what refugees do to help
themselves. The MAAs, another acronym of resettlement jargon
meaning Mutual Assistance Association, are their first vehicle.
Sustained by federal and private grants and refugee contributions,
the MAAs function much like tongs and family organizations did
for earlier Asians. Southeast Asians too respect family loyalties,
but here their families are often scattered. Or, they may not know
who still lives, who is in a camp. Networks of support that worked
in smaller villages have evaporated. By electing officers and planning strategy, community members now throw their support behind the MAAs, though in some communities strong clan groups
also emerge.

MAAs are based on ethnic identification: Hmong, Lao, Lao Thai
Dam, Mien, Vietnamese, Khmer, or Chinese. Some include reli-
gious affiliations. Vietnamese have chosen to belong to Buddhist,
Catholic, or Protestant associations.

Refugees regret the multiplicity of MAAs may splinter refugees
from each other. Ideologies, language, religion, and war experiences already divide them. Factionalism here does not serve their
interests. Consequently, in many communities refugees create
forums to deal with problems they have in common. These Refu-

Fou Seng Saechao and his family file to change their status from parolees to permanent residents—only one step away from becoming U.S. citizens. Refugee workers recognize that the family is Mien, from Laos, by the "Sae" prefix to the last name. (Tim Jewett)

gee Forums invite VOLAGs, MAAs, and state and federal agencies to discuss issues like police protection, job training, English as Second Language classes, and cash assistance. Cultural barriers between Vietnamese, Kampucheans, and Laotians break down as they meet to solve common problems.

MAAs offer priceless services to their communities. A Vietnamese clergyman sums up what MAAs can and should do: *"Unlike the development of ethnic enclaves of Chinese and Japanese immigrants in the early 20th century, which evolved out of the necessity to survive and succeed in a generally hostile and discriminatory society, the most and well accepted important function of Indochinese community organizations consists in the creation among the refuges of a new sense of self-confidence and a firm belief in strengthening of cultural preservation."*[7]

Cultural events sponsored by MAAs often revolve around the most important Southeast Asian holiday, the New Year, which is celebrated on different dates, often months apart, by the various ethnic groups. Feasting, entertainment, cultural shows, and native dress can bring a smile to the face of the loneliest refugee. If Chinese, Japanese, and Korean communities are any indication, Southeast Asian communities will develop newspapers and radio shows and sponsor athletic teams, student associations, and fraternal social clubs as well as provide orientation.

Refugee associations can help individuals open businesses. Members pool savings and make loans to those wanting to buy small shops. Grocery, gift, and department stores sprout up beside restaurants catering to Southeast Asians. Refugees pursue strength through cooperation. In Los Angeles 850 businesses formed a Vietnamese Chamber of Commerce. In the San Francisco Bay Area, 350 businesses followed suit and provide business counseling, attract investors, and educate members on American tax law, marketing strategies, and loan applications.

MAAs encourage refugees to maximize their skills. Hmong and Mien associations, for instance, organize cottage industries based on traditional needlework, jewelry, and handicrafts. Other self-help programs establish self-contracting service corporations which draw on a refugee community's labor pool as earlier Asian contracting services did.

In 1980 a Hmong accountant formed a Lao-Hmong Credit Union in Orange County, California, to organize money pooling. Then he set up a Lao-Hmong Security Agency to train former military employees as security guards. A former army major from Kampuchea started with a series of small investments to create a chain of doughnut shops. He leases them to Kampuchean refugees whom he has sponsored.

MAAs encourage self-help. They recognize federal assistance is not permanent; refugees must not feel the U.S. government owes them a living. Employed refugees volunteer time to help others find jobs. MAAs search for those who can speak English and will work as liaisons with the larger community. They hope Americans will stop labeling all Southeast Asians as "dependent refugees" and see them as new Americans bent on self-sufficiency.

Women have a harder time adjusting to their new life in the United States than men. Heavily influenced by traditional taboos, separated from family and friends, and isolated with small children in unfamiliar homes, adult women learn the customs and language very slowly. (Cathy Cheney)

Obviously refugees face some difficulties job hunting. Refugee status can extend the time needed for security clearance or restrict opportunities for employment with the military or federal government. A study in Washington's King County (Seattle and environs) suggests refugees are the first laid off when seniority rules are applied, a problem plaguing other minority groups.[8] MAAs insist language skill deficiencies contribute to all these problems.

English classes assume tremendous importance. Literacy rates among refugee groups varied substantially in their home countries. In Vietnam an estimated 85 percent of the citizens were literate, in Laos 30 percent, and in Cambodia a little over 30 percent. Learning English is complicated when a refugee has never learned to read his own language.

English is also based on meaning structures that do not occur in any Southeast Asian language. These languages do not employ inflexional endings to show the difference between jump and jumped or boy and boys. Other words indicate tense or number. In addition, Southeast Asians have never used articles, infinitives, or different subject and object pronouns. In Lao one letter always represents one sound; no confusion arises between words like though and rough. Vietnamese is tonal. Each word contains at least one vowel whose musical pitch, or tone, is indicated by a small mark over or under the vowel. Depending on what mark covers the vowel in the Vietnamese word *ma*, the meaning can be ghost, check, then, tomb, horse, or young rice plant.

Cultural adjustment

Everywhere refugees turn they experience culture shock—the feeling of being slapped in the face by the new, the unfamiliar, perhaps even the immoral or bizarre. Though refugees come from an enormous spread of ethnic, educational, religious and occupational backgrounds, they are equally embarrassed and pained by cultural differences.

On a day-to-day level, cultural differences may be as simple as when two Southeast Asian girls hold hands in public. Members of their own culture see nothing unusual. When this happens in the cafeteria of an American high school, Americans may misunderstand. A Vietnamese girl confides she will no longer speak Vietnamese in public. Rude Americans ridicule the "sing-song" sound of the language. Because Southeast Asians value social harmony, they occasionally lie rather than upset an American who asks a distressing question. Or, they may smile. Though white lies are accepted in American culture, the Asian is seen as being shifty or dishonest rather than as seeking to spare unpleasantness.

Cultural differences can cause more extreme hardships. Many Kampucheans never used banks. Recently a family lost substantial savings in the form of jewelry they had left locked in a parked car. Police crime prevention programs are crippled when their

The public library offered this Hmong refugee a glimpse of automotive history. To buy a car, frequently three or four refugee families must pool their resources. (Kurt Foss)

audiences represent six or seven cultural groups whose people speak different languages. Many Southeast Asians harbor a heart-felt mistrust of police: agents of death, oppression, and injustice in their own countries. In 1981 when police officers investigated a situation where a Southeast Asian man was clearly drunk, his sobbing wife begged officers not to kill him.

Some Americans also undergo culture shock. In 1980 a group of Southeast Asian children took a hike with their newcomers' class in Portland, Oregon's Forest Park—a lush rain forest. Photographs in local papers showed the children breaking twigs for spearing fish in the creeks. One child promised to protect his teacher from tigers lurking on the trail ahead, a legitimate response in the culture and physical environment he grew up in. Americans were surprised, then charmed. The same confusion did not seem so charming when eleven Southeast Asians (Kampucheans and Laotians) foraged in San Francisco's Golden Gate Park in late 1980 for available food: flowers, berries, edible shrubs, and park "wildlife"—dogs, pigeons, squirrels, and ducks. Police arrested the eleven. The incident prompted widespread comment and numerous jokes. City officials dropped charges and explained that hunting in a city park is illegal in the United States.

The rapid adjustment refugee children make to American society disturbs their parents. Arguing with parents and teenage dating become heavy burdens to parents and grandparents who promote traditions from the home country. Parents fear their children will find divorce acceptable or that when they become elderly, their children will not want to care for them as they would have in Southeast Asia.

A Vietnamese professor suggests each refugee has three alternatives when presented with a new culture.[9] First he may react conservatively, resenting all changes. This is often the posture of the elderly, to abhor permissive sex, divorce, nursing homes for the elderly, and "bratty" children. The second alternative is to assimilate. This means turning away from the old culture, rejecting its assumptions, and struggling to fit into the new. When a situation arises where an individual sees he may not be able to cast off all the old ways, assimilation can lead to inner conflict. Emotional stability lies in the third alternative: bi-culturalism. An individual realizes the possibility of blending the old and the new. Bi-cultural individuals solve conflicts between the old and the new in personal ways.

As refugees resettle, physical and emotional problems emerge. Food deprivation in young children has led to some behavioral and developmental problems. Refugees still mourn for relatives who have died before their eyes—horrible deaths from starvation, clubbing, or being stuffed down a well shaft. Worries nag

Southeast Asian refugees, like Asians who preceded them, find jobs in agriculture requiring intensive hand labor. This Laotian woman is picking raspberries. (T. Brian Collins)

those who do not know the fate of relatives left behind. Some have nightmares, while others, particularly Kampucheans who know that as many as half of their people have died, suffer a kind of "survival guilt," wondering why they survived when so many others did not.

None of this is new. As early as World War I studies showed psychological problems associated with resettlement. After World War II Armenians, Russians, and Jews resettled in New York showed the same profiles of depression, fear, anxiety, grief, reliving old memories, crying in the night, weight loss, and headaches as Southeast Asians experience now.

Few remedies exist. Kampucheans by tradition do not share intense emotions outside the closest family circle. Few Southeast Asians are comfortable with psychiatry. So few Buddhist monks survived to come to America that the most traditional comfort, religion, is not widely available.

With apprehension, some refugees try the sleeping pills and tranquilizers our culture offers. The results are mixed. Southeast Asians suspect that Western-style drugs do not work on a people of a different build. They change the dosage. Where medical problems complicate psychological ones, they try what they believe in before turning to Western doctors.

Most Southeast Asians see no conflict in combining medical systems, many of which ignore Western medical practice. Herbal medicines and folk remedies retain their appeal. Other Southeast Asians believe disease results from an imbalance in supernatural forces: charms or ceremonies administered by a shaman or monk can return balance to the spirit world. In some areas a belief in yin and yang medicines thrives based on opposing forces, of hot and cold, male and female, that must be balanced for health.

Western health practitioners were ill-prepared to deal with "coining," a widespread Southeast Asian practice of rubbing an area of the body with a coin or piece of metal until the area bruises. At that point, coining has successfully driven out illness. More than one Southeast Asian parent has been accused of child abuse. The accusation is shocking to people whose children are seldom even lightly spanked in rebuke.

Slowly Western doctors learn tolerance. Translated and illustrated books advise the doctor not to attack the refugee's beliefs. In this way they stand a better chance of administering to top priority problems: the need for immunizations against mumps, polio, diphtheria, and whooping cough, lingering outbreaks of malaria and tuberculosis, dental problems aggravated by malnutrition and other conditions brought on by residency in the overcrowded refugee camps.

Refugees experience their full share of stress. Marital conflicts arise when new employment and homecare patterns shift the roles of men and women. Generational problems occur as they did among earlier immigrants. Remedies include training Southeast Asians for counseling and health care positions and building sensitivity to the cause of refugee depression.

Americans too need to learn about Southeast Asians. It is not

The physical difficulties of adjusting to life in the camps did not prepare the refugee for less easily defined difficulties of adjusting to American culture. This Laotian no doubt remembers a far different way of life. (H. Gloaguen; UNHCR)

enough to look at history by how it appears from Spokane, Washington, or Anaheim, California. Refugees see it from war-torn, famine-stricken Southeast Asia. Traditions peculiar or abhorrent at first sight take on a new meaning in their historical and cultural context. That Hmong and Mien grew opium as a cash crop may be disturbing. Yet Americans must understand that traders encouraged opium growing as a money-maker, and then traded the opium to willing buyers. Hmong and Mien bought medicine, food, and other supplies as well as made jewelry with their payment from traders.

For many Americans, including Vietnam veterans, the memory of the Vietnam War or the media coverage of it—jungle guerrilla warfare, bombing, and death—taints any view of Southeast Asia. Few Americans defend all the decisions to involve America in

Vietnam, the bombing of Cambodia, and military incursions into Laos; the wounds of division in the United States over the Vietnam War have only begun to heal. Vietnam veterans complain they have never received the recognition they deserve as veteran-survivors of a costly war or compensation for their psychological and physical traumas. New political hotspots around the globe are referred to as "potential Vietnams." The connotation is never a positive one.

These memories affect refugees seeking resettlement. In 1975 the governments of Cambodia and Laos fell. The government of South Vietnam had already fallen. A Gallup poll indicated 55 percent of the American public opposed bringing Vietnamese refugees here. It appeared new arrivals from Asia would find less than enthusiastic welcome.

On their side, refugees hope to leave behind what one Vietnamese pastor called "the land of murder" for the "land of freedom." They anticipate change and its trials. As one Lao man said, *"It's easier to move the mountains than get used to American culture."* He wonders how Lao teenagers will do twenty or thirty years from now. The teenagers are not sure either. The hope of success glimmers in learning English, becoming "American" as fast as possible. They want good jobs so they can buy a car and house, and make "the land of freedom" feel like home.

Most refugees accept the risk they took though homesickness often keeps pace with gratitude to America. They want to work; they want to compete. The success of other Asian Americans in law, athletics, the sciences, medicine, agriculture, commerce, and politics suggests a place for these new arrivals in the diversity of American society.

Adjustment to a different culture, preservation of a rich cultural heritage, and the struggle to become economically self-sufficient are the history Southeast Asians in America now live. The resolution of dilemmas these demands present, by refugees and the generations that follow, is the first measure of their achievement in America, the beginning of the history later to be written.

Chanthou Sam escaped Cambodia (Kampuchea) with her family in 1975 when she was twelve years old. When she arrived in the United States, she did not speak English. In 1981 her fellow high school students elected her Rose Festival Princess in Portland, Oregon, in recognition of her scholastic achievement and warm friendliness. She hopes to become an accountant, but she understands that her goals differ from what is expected of her. She says, *"A Cambodian woman is supposed to sit at home, cook, and clean house. I want to be somebody. I want my own job, house, and car before I marry. I want to be independent. It is very hard to be caught in the clash of cultures."* (Edmund Keene)

Chronology of legislation as it affects Southeast Asian refugees

1875-1945 Refugees seeking asylum in the U.S. were treated no differently than immigrants. Immigrants from Asia were subject to specific exclusion acts. Later, as those acts were repealed in the 1940s, Asian immigrants were subject to small quotas.

1946 The United Nations establishes an International Refugee Organization to distinguish between refugees and immigrants. The UN worked with member nations to aid more than 1 million Europeans uprooted during World War II, including Jews wishing to go to Palestine and Eastern Europeans who chose not to return to their homelands.

1948 U.S. Congress passes Displaced Persons Act, allowing Chinese displaced by civil war in China to remain in the U.S. as permanent residents. The number admitted is charged off against future Chinese quotas.

1951 United Nations creates Office of the UN High Commissioner for Refugees (UNHCR). Member nations encouraged to help meet the growing demand for resettlement of refugees. A refugee is defined as a person outside his country of nationality or habitual residence from a well-founded fear of persecution because of race, religion, nationality, social memberships, or political opinions and who is unwilling to return because of this fear.

1952 McCarran-Walter Act institutes concept of parolee for all refugees. A parolee does not have permanent resident status. His entrance is based upon emergency procedures taken by the Attorney General. He may apply for permanent resident, or immigrant, status after living here for two years (later changed to one year). From 1956-1958, 30,000 Hungarian refugees were admitted to the United States under parolee status. The same procedure admitted Cuban and Southeast Asian refugees later.

1953 United States goes outside the quota system by passing the Refugee Relief Act to offer nonquota immigrant visas to Chinese and Eastern European refugees.

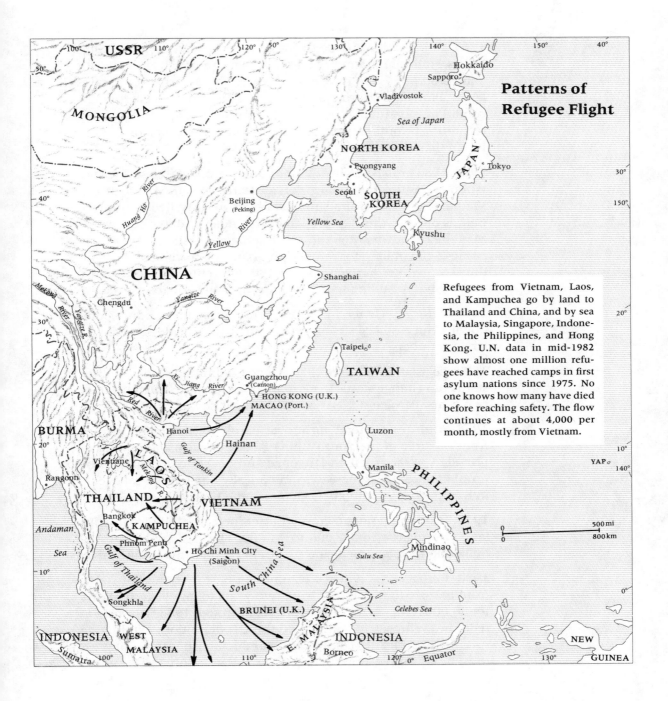

Patterns of Refugee Flight

Refugees from Vietnam, Laos, and Kampuchea go by land to Thailand and China, and by sea to Malaysia, Singapore, Indonesia, the Philippines, and Hong Kong. U.N. data in mid-1982 show almost one million refugees have reached camps in first asylum nations since 1975. No one knows how many have died before reaching safety. The flow continues at about 4,000 per month, mostly from Vietnam.

1965 Immigration Act defines a series of preferences for immigrants after eliminating restrictive Asian quotas. It provides for admission of 17,400 refugees per year. The Attorney General is again allowed to parole additional refugees on an emergency, conditional basis. This act describes refugees as persons fleeing communist-dominated areas of the Middle East, a narrower definition than that used by the UN.

1975 U.S. Embassies in Vietnam and Cambodia close in April when opposition takes over. Parolee status is granted to high-risk Vietnamese and Cambodians who have already fled Cambodia. Camps open in the U.S. prepared to handle 50,000 refugees. By May the Indochina Migration and Refugee Assistance Act appropriates $405 million for refugee programs. By the end of the year, the U.S. invokes parole to admit 130,000 refugees, mostly Vietnamese but including some Cambodians and Laotians as well.

1976 Attorney General expands parole program to admit additional refugees. Legislation is extended to include Laotians in larger numbers.

1977 Legislation ensures that refugees admitted under parolee status can change status to permanent resident (immigrant) after two years. Parolee status is granted to boat people.

1978 Attorney General authorizes parole for more boat people from the area of the South China Sea. Monetary appropriations provide special grants in language and vocational training. The number of refugees increases dramatically due to political events in Kampuchea (Cambodia), Vietnam, and Laos. U.S. steps up aid.

1979 In June President Jimmy Carter increases the monthly intake of refugees from 7,000 to 14,000. The U.S. contributes $9 million in food and medicine to starving people in Kampuchea.

1980 Refugee Act reduces waiting period for change of status from parolee to immigrant from two years to one year. It allows for 50,000 refugees to the U.S. per year through 1983. The act also redefines refugees to conform to the UN definition, eliminating specific references to communism, and establishes that Congress must be consulted about refugee admissions before the President allows additional "emergency" flows into the U.S. Full federal reimbursement to states for cash and medical assistance was approved for a period of three years following a refugee's arrival.

1981 Secretary of Education rules that school districts are not required to provide classes in foreign languages to students who do not speak English despite a 1972 Supreme Court decision. Congress reconsiders cash and medical assistance guidelines, to reduce aid guarantees to 18 months. Congressional committees consider reducing the number of refugee admissions. Over 300,000 Southeast Asian refugees remain in camps in first asylum nations. Worldwide refugee numbers exceed 12.5 million.

1981 120,000 refugees from Southeast Asia enter the U.S.

1982 Reagan administration establishes 1982 ceiling of 100,000 Southeast Asian refugee admissions. Reduction from the 1981 ceiling of 168,000 probably reflects congressional and administration concern about U.S. economic conditions, decreased refugee flows out of Southeast Asia, the desire to restrict immigration generally, and the impact of refugee resettlement on assistance programs and sponsorship organizations.

SIX

(Brendon-Jon Boyce)

Decades of Strife

Vietnamese Americans

"Before the war in Vietnam, the forest, the jungle, and the rice paddies were always beautiful. At night when we slept, we could hear the waterfall rolling down the jungle streams. Every morning we could hear the birds singing. That was the kind of life we had when the village was in peace. I knew almost everyone in the village. The area was small, the people were close together. We ate rice, fish, potatoes, and vegetables. Our houses were built of bamboo; for the roof we used long tall grasses. Every evening in the summer after dinner, the people got together and chatted while the kids were out playing games in the moonlight. They usually talked about harvest. Sometimes there was too much rain; sometimes there was too much sun. A big storm might flood the rice away. But whatever happened, the people always helped each other during the growing season and hoped for a better harvest next time." [1]

These memories of a boy from Vietnam now living in California suggest neither the long history of Vietnamese conflict with outside forces nor the grim record of war in Vietnam. His early childhood was peaceful.

Body counts quantify but do not personalize the depth of human misery spawned by conflict. Of the some 2,800,000 Americans who fought in Vietnam, 51,000 were reported killed, 270,000 wounded, and 1,400 missing in action. From 1965 to 1973, an estimated 1,435,000 Vietnamese out of a population near 50 million died. They were not just soldiers but included people from the bustling cities and quiet villages of both north and south. In addition, over 10 million Vietnamese were displaced by the turmoil. Over 180,000 were disabled. Of these, 83,000 lost limbs, 30,000 were blinded, and 10,000 lost their hearing. When the United States and her allies (Australia, New Zealand, South Korea, the Philippines, and Thailand) withdrew military support from the south, refugees from the northern part of South Vietnam crammed Saigon. Food supplies dwindled.

In terms of large populations, the figures speak for themselves. As an individual, the boy describing his village later experienced the horror surrounding him. His village was bombed; his school destroyed. His peasant father urged work in the fields. He hoped communism would unite Vietnam and end the inequality of the rich and the poor. Encouraged by North Vietnamese successes during the Tet offensive of 1968, the father attended a demonstration against American policies. Many Vietnamese felt Americans offered no long-term solution and only prolonged a war for economic reasons serving the United States.

The boy's father was shot at that demonstration. The son remained in the fields. Daily, American troops scouted his village. When there were no troops, bombs shelled the village. Then American tanks leveled it. During the last skirmish, the boy hid underground. A grenade killed his mother, grandmother, and a neighbor. When thirst drove him from shelter, U.S. gunfire wounded him. He continues: *"I was taken to Saigon. One morning I woke up and I was put on a stretcher on a plane bound for America. I landed at one of the air bases here and was transported to the U.C. Hospital in San Francisco. I saw all the strange people, talking differently. I couldn't understand a thing they said. That whole week I was scared to death, something I was close to anyway because of my condition. Every morning a lady came and took blood out of my arm. I thought I wouldn't have any blood left soon. When I saw the X-ray, I have never been so scared in my life. I thought they were going to use me for experiments. But I learned that there are some good Americans."* [2]

This boy's perspective is troubling. No doubt Americans died in the same conflict that wounded him. Some Americans would say the United States owes nothing to this son of a village rice farmer.

REFUGEE CAMPS

⬡ Vietnamese

Pulau Bidong, Songkhla, and twelve other Vietnamese refugee camps are in Malaysia and Indonesia.

CHINA

NANNING

Lao Cai

Dien Bien Phu

HANOI   HAIPHONG

Red River

Tonkin

Annam

Gulf of Tonkin

BURMA

Mekong River

Luang Prabang
(Royal Capital)

Xieng Khouang

Hainan

Vinh

L A O S

Sayaboury

VIENTIANE
(Administrative Capital)

RANGOON

17th Parallel

Moulmein

Nam Yom River

Mae River

THAILAND
(SIAM)

⬡ Si Khiu

Hue

Da Nang

V I E T N A M

Mekong River

Tavoy

BANGKOK

Angkor

Andaman Sea

KAMPUCHEA
(CAMBODIA)

Tonle Sap

Annam
Cochin China

PHNOM PENH

Kampot

HO CHI MINH CITY
(Saigon)

Gulf of Thailand

Mekong Delta

South China Sea

0   150mi
0   240km

Yet, his words show that his father's sympathies for the communist promise of equality and national unity were based on life in the village: hard work and the observation that American military maneuvers interrupted peaceful village life—just as the French had done earlier. Further, his misunderstanding of common Western medical practices suggests how little of European or American culture reached remote villages.

In a sense his story is not common. Most Vietnamese presently in America supported American war efforts even if they doubted certain policies. His story does reveal the extent of the turmoil caused at all levels by foreign intervention in Vietnamese affairs.

Conqueror and conquered

Quite early in their history, Vietnamese established a pattern of resisting outside political pressure. In 939 A.D., Vietnamese rebelled successfully against the Chinese who had controlled the northern region of what is now Vietnam since 111 B.C. by quelling sporadic revolts. As in other conquered regions, the Chinese had attempted to change the indigenous culture. Vietnamese, while retaining the Chinese style of law and government as well as Confucian customs of ancestor reverence and hierarchical social structures, formed their own nation.

Though the Vietnamese had ousted the Chinese and formed an independent country, fighting with Chinese troops continued until a conclusive battle in 1788 ended China's attempts to invade. Likewise, Vietnam also fought the Khmer and Champa empires of southwestern Vietnam and Cambodia in a series of push-and-pull border and land grabs that extended Vietnamese territory from the fifteenth through the seventeenth centuries. Both traditional border conflicts instilled a caution in Vietnamese policymakers to avoid two-front border wars, one reason for the recent occupation of Kampuchea (former Cambodia).

Besides warfare with neighbors, Vietnam has a tradition of political division, north against south, with the dividing line at or about the 17th parallel. At the end of the eighteenth century a family of lords known as the Trinh ruled in the north. Nguyen lords dominated the south. In 1778 three Son Tay brothers in central Vietnam rebelled, defeating the Nguyens. Within eight

(Ng Beh Leow; UNHCR)

A child in Asia
Unafraid of the sound of bombs and guns
Unaware of how much longer he has to live
Hoping that one day there will be peace

A child in America
Pretending to be in a war
Shooting his friends with his toy gun
Not knowing that somewhere a little boy like him
Wants it all to stop

Isa Cocallas *(Sojourner IV)*

years they also brought the Trinhs to their knees. One of the three brothers declared himself emperor of a unified Vietnam in 1788, another of the many attempts to unify the 1,400 mile span of mountains and lowlands comprising Vietnam.

The one surviving descendant of the Nguyen family did not submit to this defeat. In 1802 he reclaimed his heritage in battle to proclaim himself emperor. Aided by a French Catholic missionary who privately recruited French professionals to help, Nguyen Anh retained many French advisors in his court.

Nguyen Anh's descendants ruled Vietnam, at least in name, until the Japanese occupation in World War II. Neither Minh Mang nor Thieu Tri, who followed, were sympathetic to French or Christians. French advisors were dismissed; missionaries and their followers persecuted. In 1848 Christian villages were leveled. Christians were branded on the cheek with Chinese characters meaning corrupt religion. While Christian missionaries taught that God is supreme, Confucianism placed the emperor as the foremost ruler mandated from heaven. Christians also taught that everyone was spiritually equal, a new idea to Vietnamese accustomed to the Confucian hierarchy.

The persecution of Christians, French missionaries' promise of local support, and the desire to create overseas markets contributed to Napoleon III's decision to invade Vietnam. In 1858 French troops occupied Tourane (Da Nang).

French domination

The French conquest of all of Vietnam was slowed until 1886 by heavy French involvement in the Anglo-French war against China. In 1886 France abolished the name Vietnam in favor of the Indochinese Union, a name supposedly recognizing the combined cultural influences of India and China in Southeast Asia. Indian influence probably was strongest in Cambodia, which France took, along with Laos, in the next decade. Today most refugees prefer to be called Southeast Asians rather than Indochinese because the term describes their place of origin and carries no odious overtones of French colonialism.

French presence in Vietnam had profound effects. By 1945 Vietnamese schools were modeled on the French lycée system as

Vietnamese refugees often remained on their overcrowded boats until the Hong Kong refugee officials could find room for them. (Hong Kong Christian Service)

an overlay to the earlier Chinese reverence for scholastic achievement. The use of Romanized Vietnamese script, developed by missionaries and early Catholic Vietnamese clergy for prayer books, became widespread. Though slightly less than 10 percent of the Vietnamese converted to Catholicism under French colonization, Catholic schools became important as well-organized private institutions which also served non-Catholics.

The average Vietnamese did not learn to speak French, but some of the elite did. Older refugees in America who can speak French are generally those who held high social and leadership positions in Vietnam before 1954. French influence did filter down to the average citizen. Men adopted western dress. Girls cut and styled their hair.

The real impact was felt in government and economics. Vietnamese courts and imperial government officials became puppets of French administrators. Though French rule united the three political zones of Cochin China (south), Annam (central), and Tonkin (north), few Vietnamese had any influence. French colonialists controlled most rice fields and virtually all the rubber and tea plantations. When trade with the West, primarily France, poured wealth into Vietnam, few Vietnamese gained. Profits went to the French, who did not reinvest them. The majority of native Vietnamese were poor peasants who grew poorer. Few Vietnamese people gained positions of power, wealth, or leadership in the French colonial system.

Struggle for independence

Many Vietnamese rebelled. Nationalist societies attracted scholars, intellectuals, politicians, and journalists. Various emperors plotted to oust the French, who continually put down revolts.

In 1911 a thirteen-year-old boy named Nguyen Ai Quoc, better known later as Ho Chi Minh, left Vietnam as a mess boy on a French ship. In 1917 he settled in Paris where by 1920 he was involved in communist politics. During the years 1930 to 1945, Ho Chi Minh worked from outside Vietnam to unite his homeland against all outsiders, finally forming the Vietminh upon his return to Vietnam in the 1940s.

Vietminh tactics were to control rural areas and from there make guerrilla strikes against urban strongholds. As it turned out, preoccupation with World War II worked to the Vietminh's advantage. In 1945, while French and Japanese were primarily concerned with the larger war, Ho Chi Minh announced from Hanoi an independent Vietnam.

At the end of World War II, however, the Allies affirmed France's claim to Vietnam. Clashes continued between Vietminh and the French. By late 1946 various attempts at peaceful agreements among the nations involved had broken down completely and the First Indochina War began.

Nationalist and communist Vietnamese together defeated the French at Dien Bien Phu in 1954. At the Geneva Conference that year, the same one that partitioned Korea, talks on Indochina

Far from their country's battle front in 1964, Vietnamese women mend nets in the thriving fishing center at Rach Gia in southern Vietnam. (Ronald Rogers)

were attended by the United States, the USSR, Britain, France, the People's Republic of China, the three Indochinese states (Laos, Cambodia, and Vietnam), and Vietminh representatives. The Geneva Accords, signed only by the French and Vietminh military commanders, included a cease-fire line that would also be a temporary partition at the 17th parallel and provision for all-Vietnamese elections in mid-1956. The United States was there as an observer only. The South Vietnamese delegation was not a signatory. The other nations represented at Geneva pledged to uphold the agreements.

The partition at the 17th parallel resulted in the first mass movement of people within Vietnam. The Geneva Accords gave each side 300 days to withdraw troops to its side of the 17th parallel: the Vietminh to the north; the French and State of Vietnam to the south. Civilians could move from one zone to the other within a given time period. How many civilians chose to move north is not reported; some 850,000 moved south.

Before the signing of the accords, Emperor Bao Dai, nominal head of Vietnam under the Japanese during World War II, asked Ngo Dinh Diem to form a new government in Saigon. Diem succeeded, with U.S. aid, in stabilizing his government and making himself president of the newly formed Republic of Vietnam in 1955. Meanwhile, North Vietnam, with aid from communist countries, began reconstruction and industrialization. The all-Vietnamese elections to unify the country never happened. South Vietnamese leaders did not consider themselves bound to the accords they had not signed. They refused to consult with the North Vietnam government and hold nationwide elections.

Diem's leadership and military build-up did not halt internal dissent. By mid-1965, when Marshall Nguyen Cao Ky and his supporters gained power, Saigon had seen nine changes of government. The new government, reportedly as repressive as Diem's had been, imprisoned political opponents and restricted civil liberties, most notably freedom of the press.

Under the circumstances, growing opposition in the south was not surprising. Opposition came particularly from the National Liberation Front (NLF), composed of nationalists and communists. Weapons and military experts from North Vietnam also infiltrated and recruited people in the south.

United States involvement

Actions of the United States in Southeast Asia had their beginnings in post-World War II attitudes about communism and the need to develop a foreign policy given the new view of the United States as a world power. The question of Russian and Chinese intent was crucial to the resulting foreign policy.

While Russia and Soviet leadership were little studied topics in America, at the end of the war Russian military forces occupied much of eastern Europe, all of Poland, and what became East Germany. George F. Kennan, with the U.S. Embassy in Moscow, described the Soviet leadership as willing to use force if necessary in expanding Russian territory to ensure the country's security against what they saw as hostile forces. In 1947 Kennan outlined the need to contain such expansion. His words provided the U.S. State Department with a clear purpose. The so-called policy of

These refugees wait at Cheras transit camp near Kuala Lumpur, Malaysia. Resettlement nations often give preference to the young and healthy. The elderly and handicapped are often the last to find new homes. (John Isaac; United Nations)

containment became a major element in foreign relations. And a U.S. journalist, Walter Lippmann, introduced the term Cold War. Also affecting U.S. policy was the new Republic of China. In 1949, under the leadership of Mao Tse-tung, a revolution had replaced the dynastic regime with a form of communism.

The temporary division of Vietnam in 1954 disturbed those United States leaders, such as Secretary of State John Foster Dulles, who saw communism as the greatest threat to world peace and viewed the struggle in Vietnam in terms of communism versus non-communism. Dulles helped create the South-East Asia Treaty Organization (SEATO), formed in 1954, committed to the mutual security of its members in Southeast Asia and the western Pacific: the United States, Britain, France, Australia, New Zealand, the Philippines, Pakistan, and Thailand. Laos, Cambodia, and Vietnam by the terms of the Geneva agreement could not participate even if they wished. Although some Western leaders believed nationalism was a major issue in these countries dominated by the West or their neighbors for centuries, others believed with Dulles that communism was the issue.

Until 1960 the United States supported South Vietnam with military equipment, financial aid, and 700 army training advisors. When John Kennedy became president in 1961 the use of counterinsurgency to bolster governments against perceived communist insurgents was gaining support. U.S. Special Forces began training mountain peoples both for military combat and intelligence gathering. Political advisors together with United States Agency for International Development (USAID) personnel appeared in Southeast Asia. During Kennedy's presidency the number of Americans in Southeast Asian countries increased to an estimated 15,000.

In August 1964 President Lyndon Johnson put before Congress the Gulf of Tonkin Resolution, a response to unprovoked attacks by North Vietnamese torpedo boats on U.S. destroyers patrolling the gulf. The stated purpose was to approve and support actions the president might take to repel an armed attack against U.S. forces and to prevent further aggression. The resolution also declared Southeast Asian peace and security to be vital to U.S. interests and world peace. Both houses of Congress passed the

Refugees in all camps suffer from overcrowding. These Vietnamese refugees wait in a camp in Malaysia. (Marco Flaks; UNHCR)

resolution by resounding majorities. Only later did many in Congress see the wording of the resolution as possibly giving the president blanket power to wage war.

War

In 1965 President Johnson ordered bombing raids on North Vietnam, hoping to influence North Vietnamese to stop the movement of arms and men into the south. When the bombing failed, U.S. ground troops went into South Vietnam. The United States continued to support the struggle of South Vietnam economically and with air power and ground forces until the so-called Tet (lunar new year) offensive of February 1968 by the opposition. At the time Johnson began to de-escalate the war, there were over 500,000 U.S. combat troops in Vietnam.

U.S. negotiations with North Vietnam began in Paris in May 1968 and continued, off and on, for almost five years. President Richard Nixon began a gradual withdrawal of U.S. troops from

Vietnam. At the same time, fighting spread into Laos and Cambodia. Finally, in January 1973 the United States and the three Vietnamese groups involved signed a cease-fire agreement providing for rapid U.S. troop withdrawal and giving the NLF equal recognition with the Saigon government. An international commission was established to oversee the agreement.

For many reasons, Americans heaved a sigh of relief when the Paris Agreement was signed in 1973, ending American military involvement in Southeast Asia. Vietnamese, however, continued to fight each other until Saigon fell to the NLF in 1975.

Exodus begins

In 1975 Vietnamese began fleeing their homeland. Thousands of civilians who had helped the American military or diplomatic services or who had roles in the South Vietnamese government feared they would be considered traitors and executed. Others whose social or middle-class economic status made them enemies of communist philosophy suspected the new rulers would offer either death or "re-education." Some feared persecution for their religious beliefs.

A Vietnamese refugee describes her family's two flights from North Vietnam to South Vietnam in 1954 and to America in 1975: *"Our family was forced to move for three reasons. First of all, my parents are northerners. They moved to the south in 1954. If they had been caught (in 1975), they would have been doomed to die because the Communists would have accused them of being traitors. Second, we're Catholics. We had to move because the Communists wouldn't let us worship and condemned us. Third, my father was a judge. They would have arrested him because he was one of the highest judges in the Saigon court. They would have accused him of being unfair to the people he sentenced and for working with the old government. A friend just left Vietnam and he wrote to us. He said judges were put in one special camp and most couldn't endure it. Two of the judges dad knew died. It would have been the same for my dad if we hadn't left Vietnam. They wouldn't have let us go to school because they considered us to be traitors."* [3]

Few urban dwellers welcomed the new regime. In 1954 Saigon's population was about half a million. By 1974, 3 million people jammed the city. American and French influences had

Currently, boat people wait in camps in Hong Kong, Macau, Indonesia, Malaysia, the Philippines, Singapore, and Thailand. Since 1975 the United States, Canada, France, Australia, and West Germany, have led the list of nations accepting Southeast Asian refugees. (Tim Jewett)

turned Saigon into a cosmopolitan metropolis. Urban lifestyles and education made the prospect of forced labor in agricultural camps unacceptable to those who did not yet fear for their lives.

Unlike earlier immigrants from Asia, Vietnamese refugees had no time to make plans. They grabbed hasty moments to say farewell to family they were leaving behind. In April 1975 terrified civilians watched the U.S. government airlift employees and dependents to Guam and the Philippines. Bullets strafed helicopters lifting off the U.S. Embassy grounds. Those who could not expect to be airlifted by Americans jammed the public airports. Others pushed off from shore in rickety boats buffeted by monsoon seas. Some started the long overland trek to Thailand.

In May 1975 the United States began accepting its former allies as refugees. Processing camps opened in Pendleton, California;

Indiantown Gap, Pennsylvania; Fort Chaffee, Arkansas; and Fort Elgin, Florida. Federal and voluntary agencies helped the many thousands who arrived penniless and without extra clothing.

In 1975 American refugee policies called for sprinkling large family groups throughout the United States so a sudden influx of refugees would not overwhelm one local or state government. This policy changed when it was seen that the absence of community aggravated isolation and depression from loss of family members. Seeking communities, refugees migrated to places where other Asians had gone: Texas, Orange County in California, and other areas in the West. Some Vietnamese went to New Orleans because of the climate and the French influence.

By the end of 1975, over 130,000 Southeast Asian refugees had found new homes in America. Most were Vietnamese from urban settings. These early refugees were well-educated, young, and at least half were Christian, although in Vietnam only 10 percent of the population was Christian rather than Buddhist.[4]

These factors suggested that the early refugees would succeed here, but the refugees were not always welcomed warmly. A 1975 Gallup poll indicated 54 percent of the American public did not favor resettlement of Vietnamese in the United States. Some said the poll showed how fed up Americans had become with the war in Vietnam. Others pinned the response on the tendency to see all Vietnamese as "enemies" even though most refugees had been allied with the American cause. Whatever the explanation, this predisposition often made resettlement difficult.

Vietnamese found as their numbers grew in an area so did individual acts of violence aimed at them. Isolated calls of "chink" escalated to smashing windows in Vietnamese-owned stores. Clashes erupted in schools. Mai Khanh Tran describes teasing that prompted her to change her behavior: *"I hated when Americans teased me about my language. Maybe that's why I don't talk in Vietnamese in front of an American anymore. When I first came here, I used to talk in Vietnamese but ever since they teased me I don't feel comfortable doing it anymore. At home I do because my parents always talk Vietnamese and I'm trying to preserve what I have for as long as possible. But I can feel it's slipping away. I think, dream, and pray in English. I can still read Vietnamese, but very slowly. I can only spell easy words now."[5]*

Unlike the earliest immigrants to the United States, who were usually young men seeking their fortunes, refugees are often women, children, and the aged. Here Vietnamese refugees use the space allotted to each family—the equivalent of a double bed. (Hong Kong Christian Service)

Family and home

Vietnamese had trouble finding housing. When lodging could be found, frequently it did not suit large, extended families including cousins and grandparents. Zoning regulations prohibit "overcrowding." Families torn by war and resettlement wanted to reestablish themselves as close units but often could not find adjacent housing to accommodate up to thirty members. Grandparents missed regular contact with children. All missed the easy fellowship where neighbors looked after neighbors.

Vuong G. Thuy stresses the importance of the Vietnamese home: *"In a way, it is a mini-commune where its members live and share together, a maternity center where children are born . . . a funeral home where funeral rituals are performed, a religious place where the family altar is set up to revere ancestors or observe religious rituals, . . . a courtroom where conflicts or disputes between members are settled, a welfare center where assistance and social security services are rendered, a nursing home where the elderly are taken good care of, an educational institution where family and formal education is provided, a bank where money is available, a council where all important decisions affecting one or more than one family member are made and carried out, and a place where all members share the joys, the sadness, the enjoyments, the suffering of life.''* [6]

Pastor Tran Xuan Quang explains the Vietnamese reaction to the mobile American nuclear family structure, in contrast to the Southeast Asian concept of an extended family structure which might include five generations rooted to one ancestral location: *"Back in Vietnam the family is something precious for us—father, mother, children, But in coming here, we saw that the family here is too loose. The father works in one place, the mother works in another and they don't see each other at all. Sometimes the father works in the morning and the mother works in the afternoon and the children go to school. When they get home, they hardly see each other at all. We try to keep our family together as long as possible."* [7]

In addition, most Vietnamese believe in ancestor reverence, which ties in directly to the extended family social structure. Elderly Vietnamese, Buddhist or Catholic, worry about how to venerate ancestors buried in Vietnam and wonder what will happen to their own remains. One aging woman remarked that if she were buried next to Americans she would have no one to talk to; perhaps her family would not know where to find her at the New Year when families share memories of ancestors. In many parts of the United States, Vietnamese associations buy large cemetery plots in response to these concerns. The Los Gatos Memorial Park in California now features a section of 1,500 cemetery plots to serve Vietnamese who live in Santa Clara County.

Pastor Tran Xuan Quang further explains ancestor veneration among his fellow Vietnamese: *"When people worship their ancestors, they want to respect their ancestors. Sometimes I ask people, 'Why do you worship your ancestors?' Some say, 'Because our father did it, so I want to follow his steps.' Others say, 'I want to respect our ancestors.' So we must*

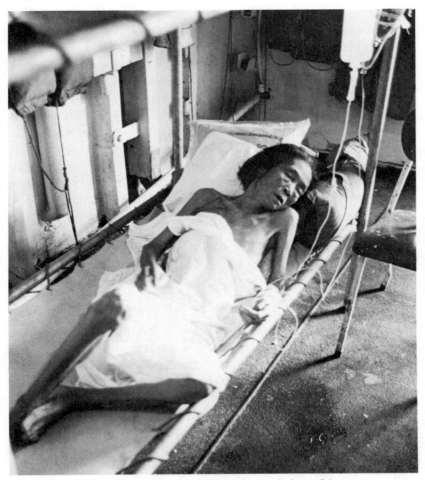

Many nations responded to the refugees' plight. This woman was treated in the French hospital ship Île de Lumière anchored off Tanjung Pinang camp on Binton Island, Indonesia. (John Isaac; United Nations)

have something to show that they respect their ancestors, usually once a year. It's in the New Year, and people prepare a meal. In every house they have an altar where they put the picture of the dead person, and they have candles, incense, and they put the meal on the altar, and they bow down in front of the altar and they ask their ancestors to help them, to give peace, to bless the family. So I think it's not a religion, but a way of life. Confucius taught people to venerate first of all the king, the teacher, and the father. So when you ask refugees, they usually say they are Buddhist, but actually they are not Buddhists at all. They worship their ancestors. 'To prevent the evil thing, doing good.' I think that's the concept of most Vietnamese.''[8]

Early arriving Vietnamese strived for self-respect and independence.[9] Some received assistance, but willingly accepted jobs with less social status and/or less pay than those they had left in Asia. By 1977, 95 percent had jobs whether or not they spoke English. As the months passed, they saved money. Family members pooled savings for a car or a home. By adding small loans, some opened markets where refugees could purchase familiar foods such as rice in bulk, hot red peppers, fish sauce, and rice paper as well as items regularly stocked in American supermarkets. Then came restaurants and churches, both Buddhist and Christian. Their presence added a new look to West Coast cities and towns.

Schooling

One scene of culture shock has been in American schools. Vietnamese culture values education—so much that a Vietnamese parent may apply more pressure on his child to study than his American counterpart (though the emphasis will not include athletic performance). Students are expected not to hold jobs while attending school. Teachers are regarded with the same Confucian respect as elders. Doing well in Vietnamese schools, however, often involved memorizing material, not analyzing it. American schools have different expectations: individual research, class debates, and choice of topics. Multiple-choice questions, learning by doing or experimentation, and group projects were unheard of in Vietnam. Group showering and clothes changing in American physical education classes offends the Vietnamese sense of privacy. So does sex education. A lack of school records complicated grade placement.

Later refugees from Vietnam have had to make the transition from schools fostering unquestioning loyalty to communist policy. Khan Nguyen, who arrived in 1980, describes his education in Vietnam from 1975 to 1979: *"In my district, there was only one*

English as a Second Language and cultural orientation training helps refugees find jobs, the first step to self-sufficiency. Early arriving Vietnamese, with good educational backgrounds, have found jobs more easily than later arriving, less educated hill people and fishermen. (H. Gloaguen, VIVA; UNHCR)

high school; that was 30 miles away from my house. At the beginning of the school year, the Principal, who was a member of the Communist Party sent to the South from the North, told the student that labor and morality was the basic requirement of attending school and passing. In the harvest season the students were sent to farms to harvest the crops free of charge for the government. I received food that was for animals. I didn't like farm labor in school. I thought labor is labor, and studying is studying. I always got a D or an F for labor because I had never done such labor under the burning sun before 1975. To have a better future, I should have been the son of a member of the Communist Party.'' [10]

American school routines also expose profound cultural differences. Vietnamese culture teaches individuals to hide fear, confusion, and disappointment behind an agreeing smile. Rarely would a Vietnamese student say he did not understand a topic even when asked directly. Instead, he would nod pleasantly to avoid upsetting the teacher. Too often this cultural habit has led American teachers to assume students understand when they do not.

Mai Khanh Tran tells of historical and cultural differences affecting understanding between Vietnamese and Americans: *"Generally speaking Vietnamese can more easily understand Americans than Americans can understand Vietnamese because we live in your country, we speak your language, and we've known a lot of Americans. But you don't really know us at all. What we say can sometimes be the opposite of what we mean. It's really hard for you to understand us, and we don't expect you to, but we do expect you to treat us as human beings and not be prejudiced."*[11]

Some Vietnamese, particularly the elderly, claim Vietnamese teenagers have understood too much American culture. Elders hear that students can get away with cutting classes. They regret children choose clothing that reveals more of the body than it should. They do not approve of American-style dating. Holding hands in public, much less kissing, is unacceptable to most Southeast Asians. One family drove their pregnant, unwed daughter out of the house. When her Vietnamese boyfriend's parents heard of it, they told their son to ignore her because she was a fallen woman. Only medical intervention saved her from the suicide she attempted.

Refugee numbers grow

In 1978 the Socialist Republic of Vietnam began a program to restructure society. Hanoi nationalized private businesses and announced city dwellers would be resettled in rural areas to work on agricultural communes. In response, a wave of 12,000 refugees a month, including Chinese living in Vietnam, poured out of Vietnam. Some trekked overland through the jungle to Thailand. More commonly they schemed to find places on boats leaving for Malaysia, the Philippines, Hong Kong, Singapore, or Thailand.

One Vietnamese official describes his escape as a boat person: *"I was an officer in the National Police under the Saigon government. After the fall of Saigon, like other Vietnamese, I thought the Viet Communists were not monsters and were not a threat to the people. At the time,*

Having lived under French domination for so many generations, many Vietnamese families are Christian. Here they celebrate the opening of a Southeast Asian community center in a Catholic Vicariate in Portland, Oregon. (Nguyen Ngoc Qui)

we did not feel it was necessary to leave the country. However, after living under the new regime for 4 years, I realized they were oppressors and we are their victims. They have applied an economic policy that impoverished the people and leaves nothing to us but an economic producing machine. My family attempted to flee but failed. . . . In 1979 we organized a group of 31 adults and 20 children, almost all were relatives. We bought a boat and disguised ourselves as fishermen. We left January 4, 1979, from an area between Long Xuyen and Chau Doc (2 provinces in the Mekong Delta). None of us were familiar with the sea. We chose to die rather than live under a perpetual threat of death."[12]

How many of the Vietnamese and Vietnamese Chinese who left Vietnam by boat died at sea can only be estimated. Some sources report 60 percent did not survive. Here is the story of a close escape: *"After we left Vietnamese waters we realized a compass and map would have been very useful but we dared not return for fear of being caught. Then we headed toward Thailand, a free democratic country that would welcome us. We drifted for two days, with no water, on the brink of death. On the third day we spotted a Thai fishing boat and they gave us water, food, and towed us to a Navy base. We rested two days and started again. A day later we found a fishing port but were told we could not stay. The local authorities would not let us stay because our fishing boat was still seaworthy. They forced us back to the boat and rowed us out to sea. Our fishing boat was very small compared to the big Thai ships. They had promised to give us enough fuel to reach Malaysia but instead gave us approximately 80 litres of diesel oil which could not be used in our engine. At first many wanted to return to Vietnam and die. However, one person said the Communists would not let us die so easily. Finally we decided to return to Thailand, to die in a free country rather than live in the hell of Vietnam. Returning to Thailand, we were robbed more than 10 times by Thai fishing ships. They had weapons when they boarded our little boat. One of them took away our water. When we arrived in Thailand, pirates claimed we hid gold in the boat. They broke open the engine in search for gold. They also stole our engine and our boat was broken in pieces after being struck by large waves. We had to swim ashore."*[13]

Starvation, murder, robbery, running aground on small atolls, rape, sinkings by pirates, treacherous seas—these were the dangers refugees who fled by sea confronted. Vile choices: to stay and be persecuted; to flee and risk death! Hundreds of thousands are reported to have died in the South China Sea. Most who survived say their ordeal was worth it. They relish freedom of speech, travel, press, and religion.

Struggle to succeed

For those who survived their flight to freedom and now live in the United States, success is possible. Vietnamese, some now Vietnamese Americans after five years residency and passing citizenship requirements, are finding jobs and are moving up the ranks. Some families have started to pay back loans they took to open small shops or buy homes and cars.

Counselors and principals see a high percentage of Vietnamese

Like all immigrants, Vietnamese refugees often accept low-paying, entry level jobs with the hope of saving money for education or supporting other family members. (H. Gloaguen, VIVA; UNHCR)

students on honor rolls. In 1981 one of the finalists in the Westinghouse Science Search for outstanding achievers was a Vietnamese refugee who had been here only one year. Adult refugees may begin as short order cooks, then switch to jobs in social service agencies, electronics production, manufacturing, accounting, or engineering.

Contact between cultures is sometimes awkward. Misunderstandings occur. No interaction between Vietnamese and Americans has been more inflamed than that in Seabrook, Texas, on Galveston Bay, and the surrounding Gulf Coast. The charge of unfair competition is part of the history of all Asian immigration.

The problem on the Gulf revolves around fish. Vietnamese fishermen admit that initially they misunderstood American fishing regulations and were overcatching. Recent checks by government agencies show this is no longer true.

When Texas fishermen complain about how successful the Vietnamese have been, the Vietnamese counter with their own charges. They say Texas fishermen sold them old boats at ridiculously high prices, but they now are succeeding for a number of reasons. They eat fish they catch and fix boats themselves. They live on the small boats rather than driving to homes in the suburbs. Some claim they work longer hours than Americans.

Americans accuse Vietnamese of having unfair access to federal money. They often do not understand the Southeast Asian custom of pooling family monies to make large purchases, a custom allowing some to make large cash deposits on a boat.

Of the 1,500 Vietnamese living on the Texas Gulf Coast north of Galveston Bay, 500 fish for a living. They own 200 of the 550 shrimp boats and say competition is basic to capitalism. Meanwhile, they endure Ku Klux Klan rallies which threaten mob action if the government does not intervene to stop competition from the Vietnamese.

These clashes are reminiscent of early anti-Asian mob actions. In 1979 a crabber in Seadrift, Texas, was killed in a quarrel with two Vietnamese brothers. Both brothers were acquitted in court on grounds of self-defense, but the incident is not forgotten. Two Vietnamese boats have been burned. Klansmen burn crosses on other boats and ride patrol on the bay dressed in hooded robes as they wave guns and rifles.

One Texas fisherman said on network television: "There's too many of them and there's not enough room for them and there's going to be lots of hard feelings if they don't get some of them out of here and teach the ones that they leave how to act and how to get along. I think they ought to be put on a reservation somewhere or some of them put in a compound to teach our laws and our ways, the way we live, our courtesy as a people."[14]

Reservations! Compounds! Chilling words to Native Americans, Americans of Japanese ancestry, and others who have experienced such places. Or to any American who believes everyone,

In many cases church organizations, as sponsors, have helped Vietnamese and other Southeast Asian refugees. (Brendon-Jon Boyce)

including immigrant and refugee, has the right to decide where to live, what work to do, and how to act as long as it is within the framework of American law.

That American law protects refugees is one of the most eloquent examples of the differing circumstances between early

Asian arrivals and today's refugees. Chinese and Japanese were often victims of local law, not the beneficiaries. In the Gulf Coast conflict, however, American law safeguards the rights of Vietnamese while insisting they comply with all laws too. The Texas state government has moved to reduce tension by creating councils and forums for communication between the two groups. Coast Guard and Texas Parks and Wildlife officials explain fishing regulations to Vietnamese and supervise catches. Vietnamese fishermen trust the courts for protection against the Ku Klux Klan. They won a suit in 1981 that accused the Klan of antitrust and civil rights violations as well as racketeering in their actions against the Vietnamese.

Population changes

As more refugees arrive from Vietnam, the profile of age, educational background, and religious affiliations is changing. They seem to have no more difficulty adapting to American culture than the early Vietnamese refugees. However, recent arrivals include hill, rural, or tribal people and fishermen who have resisted the current government's drives to resettle them. They lack the educational or urban background of those who came earlier. Fortunately, well-established, active Vietnamese communities with functioning mutual assistance associations greet and help them.

Early or late, however, the Vietnamese refugees share intense pressures to adjust to American society. A former vice-president of Saigon University, Le Xuan Khoa, argues that Vietnamese in America do not have to merge in the melting pot, losing their culture and traditions. There is another choice: offering America the strength and beauty of Vietnamese culture. Khoa says: "... I have no hesitation in stating that this melting pot concept is no longer valid in terms of cultural significance. Beauty and creativity consist in diversity, not uniformity. We can demand to be equal but we cannot and should not want to be alike. Insofar as we can fulfill our aspirations for freedom and equality, our cultural differences can only contribute to the beauty and diversity of the American nation."[15]

These are the words of a scholar who surveys the full spectrum of Vietnamese experience in America. Compare them with the thoughts of Khan Nguyen, now enrolled in an American high

Groceries and restaurants are often the first commercial ventures of new immigrant arrivals. They change the complexion of American cities just as Chinese businesses did a century earlier. Ninh Tran is the first cook at the Saigon Kitchen. (Brendon-Jon Boyce)

school: *"On October 27, 1980, I found my name on the list of people leaving for the U.S.A. I came to this country a day later. I was so happy the first day I arrived in this country. I could not understand everything the customs officer said to me at Seattle International Airport, but he was the first American I talked to. 'Americans are very kind,' were my first English words on the first day I came to this country."*[16]

The scholar yearns to preserve diversity in American culture. The student expresses gratitude for American freedoms. Now, more than ever before in the history of Asian immigration to America, basic laws guarantee a new arrival's right to live and worship freely, receive a fair wage for work, and participate in politics. Here is where the student and the scholar, the Southeast Asian and the American, stand on common ground.

Chronology

1858 French troops enter Vietnam in area which is now Da Nang.

1886 Vietnam incorporated into French protectorate known as French Indochina which eventually includes Cambodia and Laos.

1920 Nguyen Ai Quoc (who came to be known as Ho Chi Minh) joins the French Communist Party. He opposes French intervention in Vietnam.

1945 In March the Japanese take control of French Indochina. Later in the summer the Japanese surrender to the Allied forces. In September, with Ho Chi Minh as leader, the Vietminh proclaim Vietnamese independence and proclaim the Democratic Republic of Vietnam. Later in the same month, when Allied forces occupy Vietnam, nationalists in the south break away from Vietminh of the north.

1946 Negotiations between the Vietminh and the French break down. First Indochina War begins: eight years of battles and skirmishes, and developing guerrilla expertise of the Vietminh.

1954 A cease-fire in July ends the First Indochina War. The Geneva Conference places the northern half of Vietnam under the temporary rule of Ho Chi Minh. Southern Vietnam placed under the leadership of Emperor Bao Dai who appoints Ngo Dinh Diem as his prime minister. Citizens of north and south are given 300 days to relocate north or south of the 17th parallel.

1955-1960 Ho Chi Minh's government believes the Geneva Accords robbed him of his Dien Bien Phu victory. Communist forces in the south, organized as the Viet Cong, train guerrillas, hide caches of arms, and terrorize village officials who oppose them.

Refugees—Vietnamese, Laotians, Kampucheans—accepted by a resettlement country wait in transit centers to complete processing and receive transport. (J. Becket; UNHCR)

Diem becomes president of the State of Vietnam, but his leadership suffers as he is criticized for accepting American aid and for trying to usurp the role of village chiefs. Buddhist priests burn themselves to death in opposition to Diem government's denial of human rights.

1961 Diem government receives U.S. assistance in the conflict with the Viet Cong. Under President John Kennedy, the U.S. agrees to send military advisors.

1963 President Lyndon Johnson assumes office. U.S. withdraws support of Diem government in face of opposition to Diem.

1964 North Vietnamese torpedo two U.S. intelligence ships in Gulf of Tonkin. President Johnson pushes Gulf of Tonkin Resolution through Congress. This marks the beginning of increased U.S. forces in Vietnam and stepped-up bombing missions.

1965 U.S. sends Marines into Da Nang, Vietnam, the beginning of 549,000 U.S. troops going into Vietnam.

1966 President Johnson orders bombing of Hanoi. Vietnam becomes an important political issue in the U.S. Student demonstrations become common on college campuses.

1967 U.S. makes raids over Cambodian and Lao borders.

1968 North Vietnamese launch extremely successful Tet (New Year's) offensive. Richard Nixon is elected president on the promise of ending the war in Vietnam.

1969 President Nixon and Secretary of State Henry Kissinger agree to begin secret bombing raids to disrupt communist supply trails in Cambodia. U.S. and North Vietnam discuss bombing halts. U.S. troop withdrawals begin mid-year. Ho Chi Minh dies.

1970 President Nixon announces more troop withdrawals. Conflict continues. Protest in the U.S. centers on Vietnam War; the use of napalm and chemical defoliants.

1971 U.S. withdraws from ground combat in Vietnam but continues air and sea support.

1972 President Nixon orders bombing of Hanoi and Haiphong. Criticism erupts in U.S. over resulting civilian losses.

1973 Peace agreement reached in January. Despite agreement, North Vietnam sends soldiers and weaponry into South. Paris Agreement includes withdrawal of foreign troops from Cambodia. Direct U.S. military intervention in Indochina ends.

1975 North Vietnam breaks the Paris Agreement, moving into the South. As North Vietnamese forces approach Saigon, confusion mounts. During April thousands flee by boat or by overland routes into Thailand. The U.S. Attorney General authorizes parolee, or refugee, status for relatives of American citizens and other Cambodians and Vietnamese. The U.S. opens refugee centers. Southeast Asian refugees move into camps in Thailand, Malaysia, Hong Kong, and the Philippines.

1976-1980 Refugees from Vietnam move north by land to China. Others flee and receive international attention as "boat people," suffering enormous losses of life on the South China Sea. Others continue to move overland.

1980 U.S. Census lists 262,000 persons of Vietnamese ancestry in America, the fifth largest Asian group in residence here. (See also chronology of overseas Chinese, page 276.)

SEVEN

(T. Brian Collins)

Heritage of Diversity

Laotian Americans

Kingdom of a million elephants and white parasols, fields nodding with golden poppies, the tall spires of Buddhist pagodas—Laos mixes rich images. Geographical diversity underlies many of them, nurturing deep cultural, economic, and ethnic differences.

Landlocked, Laos' centers of commerce and agriculture cluster along the Mekong River. Tributaries drain rugged mountains and plateaus sheltering villages of tribes and clans which fled southern China 150 years ago. Lack of a developed internal transportation system and natural divisions of lowlands, dense jungle, and mountain peaks provide a backdrop for the coexistence of cultural groups varying in countless ways: language, clothing, methods of agriculture, religion, ethnic origin, and political affiliations.

The Lao people descended from Thai who migrated south from China in the thirteenth century. Of a national population never much over 3 million, only half are ethnic Lao. They control the lowland valleys of the Mekong River where rice is grown in wetlands. Ease of river transportation and abundant harvests helped the lowland Lao maintain political and cultural dominance in this country not much bigger than the state of Kansas.

To the north, in the mountains, dwell seven Thai tribes, including Thai Dam. These groups distinguish themselves from each other by dialects and color of dress. Near them live descendants of the Khmer people who inhabited this region and Cambodia before the Thai came. Khmer tribes number nearly sixty.

Hmong and Mien dwell near each other in the mountain passes, but their languages differ too much to allow them to communicate. Although their residence in Laos has been brief, about 150 years, both became deeply involved in the politics of Southeast Asia and the Western presence there. As a result, by 1975 large numbers of both tribes had fled Laos as refugees.

Given this complex mix of cultures, it is unfortunate that the U.S. Immigration and Naturalization Service lumps all Lao refugees together under one broad national category—saying 22 percent of the Southeast Asian refugees in the United States come from Laos. Estimates suggest half are Hmong and nearly all the remaining 50 percent are lowland Lao.

A divided land

The history of Laos, like that of other small countries in Asia, reflects foreign interests and internal factionalism. The first Laotian state, dating from the fourteenth century, was called Lan Xang: Kingdom of the Million Elephants. Lan Xang survived in relative tranquillity until the sixteenth century, when struggles broke out with Burma and Siam (Thailand). When the Burmese seized Vientiane in 1574, the Lao government collapsed. Under Souligna-Vongsa, Laotians regained control in 1637. During his reign, called the Golden Age by Laotians, the country made treaties with Vietnam and Siam establishing territorial borders. Vientiane became an art and intellectual center.

After Souligna-Vongsa's death, Laos split into three rival kingdoms. The kingdom that fell to Burmese invaders in 1752 soon came under Siamese rule, as did the other two kingdoms. The Siamese continued to expand toward Vietnamese territory, then a French protectorate. France, by agreement with Siam, annexed Laos in 1893. The French retained power until 1954 except for a brief interval during World War II when the Japanese pressured the Vichy government to relinquish all of Indochina.

The period of French domination of Laos as part of French Indochina from 1907 to 1954 had elements of solidarity, but it was a French imposed union, not a true Lao one. The French agreed to a

limited self-government in 1949, with a constitution and general elections. However, Prince Souphanonvong, the newly elected president, and his followers were unwilling to accept the French presence. A new political movement, the Pathet Lao, literally meaning Lao Country, began in 1950. Concentrated in remote mountain hideouts, they joined with the Vietminh of Vietnam to purge the French from their lands.

When the First Indochina War ended, the Geneva Accords established Laos as a unified, independent buffer state between Thailand, allied to the West, and North Vietnam, allied to the communist bloc. While internationally the agreement was acceptable, within Laos the new coalition government was unstable. Internal developments also became increasingly linked with events in Vietnam. Part of the North Vietnamese supply line, the Ho Chi Minh Trail, ran through Laos. The North Vietnamese gave aid to the Pathet Lao in the mountainsides.

In U.S. foreign policy terms, the Royal Lao needed aid to fight the Pathet Lao. The North Vietnamese posed a threat to both Laos and South Vietnam. In keeping with SEATO aims, U.S. technical and military advisors as well as United States Agency for International Development (USAID) personnel went into Laos.

Americans in Laos in the early 1960s provided various forms of aid. Some inoculated against disease, pieced together pumps to irrigate rice fields, or built roads. Under USAID programs they also spread throughout the countryside as recreation leaders, teachers, foresters, and specialists in animal husbandry. Talented pilots in cowboy hats flew rice deep into the mountains. They landed on scrubby airfields hewn out of mountainsides to deliver grain and guns to enemies of the Pathet Lao.

Meanwhile guerrilla activity heated up throughout Laos. The Pathet Lao dominated the mountain jungles full of places to hide from Royal Lao forces. Because Laos' population was divided into small villages, the heads of hamlets, clans, and tribal groups could swing loyalties one way or the other. The Royal Lao government held the Mekong River region. North Vietnamese controlled the Ho Chi Minh Trail in the north. The mountains split between the Pathet Lao allied with the North Vietnamese and Hmong tribesmen allied with the Royal Lao government.

An idyllic postcard shot of fishermen on the Mekong River between Thailand and Laos contrasts with many refugees' memories of the river—a border teeming with Thai guards and Pathet Lao soldiers intent on blocking refugee escape. (Anonymous)

American intelligence watched this build-up and the shifting political currents in Vietnam. Eventually the CIA moved into the mountains to recruit support for the Royal Lao government. Members of mountain tribes fought valiantly. They fired modern weapons, carried out surveillance against troop and supply movements, gathered intelligence for the U.S. forces opposing the North Vietnamese, and rescued American pilots. By the late 1960s, Hmong and Mien guerrillas fought both to disrupt communist supply lines and defend their homes.

Although the Vietnamese peace agreement was signed in 1973, rivalries erupted in Laos. Royal Lao supporters (primarily ethnic Lao of the lowlands and some mountain tribal people), neutralists, and the Pathet Lao unsuccessfully negotiated attempts at unified government. When the South Vietnamese and Cambodian capitals—Saigon and Phnom Penh—fell in 1975 and communist regimes took over, demoralized Laotian rightist leaders and soldiers, as well as merchants, fled to Thailand. The Pathet Lao moved rapidly, establishing control and founding the Lao People's Democratic Republic.

Flights from chaos

What followed resembled what happened in Vietnam. People fled the threat of forced work on communes. Food supplies dwindled. Rather than starve, lowland people pushed toward Thailand where huge camps formed to receive them until other nations would accept them for resettlement. Drought intensified poor harvests. Guerrilla fighting tore apart village life. Refugees told of the repression of civil liberties and religious freedoms. They also spoke of executions.

In the mountains, Pathet Lao took vengeance on those who had opposed them. Agonizing journeys began of the elderly, children, wounded soldiers, and women who trudged over mountain passes toward the Mekong River. Casualty figures ran high.

Nearly a tenth of Laos' population has sought refugee status since 1975. Reports trickle out of Laos of continuing subversive operations aimed against the communists. Refugees in the United States whisper among themselves about going back to fight again. Mutual Assistance Associations organize to send money to help anti-government forces or relatives in camps. One lowland Lao man describes their faith: *"We donate money—so much per member per month. We save it up to send home to refugees in Thailand. We take a chance. There may be corruption, but we just do it. We don't expect 100% results. We hope some of the money will go to Laos to resistance forces. Maybe it will go for Anacin and beer . . . Maybe it will help."* [1]

Meanwhile, the United Nations sends medical supplies and agricultural equipment in a relief program designed to support the fragile Lao economy. Hope grows that fewer people will leave and

The village of Vang Vieng, pictured in the 1960s, seems distant from worldly cares. Refugees from such villages recall cycles of dysentery from polluted water, storing rice in huts on stilts to foil rats, and the overpowering odors from unpenned animals and birds. They appreciate American luxuries like refrigeration and electric lights. (Galen Beery)

that some refugees in Thai camps will return to Laos.

The people of Laos, now people of America, for all their support of anti-communist forces back home, shyly confess they know they will never return. At the same time, they maintain the ethnic identifications that defined them in Asia. Only the lowland Lao call themselves Lao as a first label. To the Hmong and Mien, their tribal identities are most important, defining their religions, clan structures, and sense of history.

Lao, Hmong, Mien, and even small Thai groups understand that U.S. agencies classify them all as Lao. Statistics that report Lao refugees have the lowest average earned income or highest dependency on cash assistance of all the Southeast Asian refugees do not distinguish ethnic groups. When sponsors and government agencies speculate that Lao refugees face more difficult social and vocational adjustments in resettlement than either Kampuchean or Vietnamese refugees, again the tendency is to blend what in Laos was understood and appreciated: rich diversity.

Lowland Lao

"One night a young boy set a bamboo fish trap in a small river. When he examined the trap the next morning, he was surprised to find it empty. Looking more carefully, at the bottom he discovered some fish scales and bones. He straightened up and muttered to himself, 'Who stole my fish?' Eager the next day to return home with fish in hand, he approached the trap . . . he found only scales and bones. Turning away from the trap he noticed a line of footprints in the mud and guessed that children had interfered with his trap. Angrily he followed the footprints to where the river broadened out into a lake. Keeping his eyes on the footprints, he followed them forward until an evil forest spirit standing at the end of the chain of footprints startled him. Without hesitation, the boy said to the forest spirit, 'My fish trap is empty. Where are my fish? You stole them.' The evil forest spirit shook his head in reply. 'I did not rob your trap.' The boy clenched his fists. 'I followed these footprints all the way from my trap. They lead directly to you.' The evil spirit glanced at the boy. 'You talk too much. If you say anything more against me, I will eat you. Right here. Right now.' 'That means you are guilty. You ate all my fish,' the boy complained more quietly. He knew now where his fish had gone, but he knew by the tone in the evil forest spirit's voice he was helpless. Without another word, the boy turned to retrace his steps home. He never returned to where his trap had been to try to catch any more fish."

If the ending of this lowland Lao folk tale seems surprising, it may be because American culture praises heroes who vanquish villains: from the Biblical David to Superman and Wonderwoman. The boy's acceptance of the evil forest spirit's power is puzzling, as if this cannot possibly be the end of the story. Americans want underdogs to fight back and, eventually, to win.

This simple tale suggests that cultural assumptions of many Southeast Asians differ from the American norm. Just as the Vietnamese habit of ancestor reverence may not fit America's adoration of youthfulness, neither does the Lao awareness of the *pei* —spirits of the dead and nature who must be appeased to protect

In this photograph, taken in 1965 near Xieng Lom, older children care for younger siblings while their parents harvest rice. Physical contact builds strong, lifelong family ties. (Galen Beery)

mental and physical health—jibe with the American sense of rugged independence and self-determination. Even Buddhist temples, or wats, recognize these spirits: the pointed towers drive away bad spirits from the Buddha.

A refugee who fought fifteen years as a soldier in the Royal Lao Army says he has attended a Presbyterian church here and is now going to a Methodist one. When asked if he's a Methodist, he responds, *"I am right now. But I'm also a Buddhist. And I'm also an animist [believer in the power of spirits]."* To him one belief need not exclude the other. A Western attempt to categorize does not faze him. He is at ease with his mixed religious beliefs.

An American rural development worker in Laos, with a good grasp of spoken Lao, offers his view of the easy mix of religions in Laos: "Laos' official religion is Buddhism, but this is only an overlay on a deeper primitive animism. The practice is to give the

[Buddhist] monks food every morning at sunup. Long silent lines of monks parade past rows of women squatting beside the road, each monk extending his rice bowl for a ball of sticky rice from each donor, a handout which bestows merit on both the recipient and the giver. Yet, these women hang little amulets on their children to protect them from harm. These are curious little sacks of animal fibre with undisclosed things inside, little images and sacred items. The IVS nurses are amazed at supposedly-scientific Lao nurses, who as mothers, calmly continue the traditional use of magic charms for themselves and their children. The soldiers of Laos create their own lucky charms, shooting at little images of Buddha, purposely missing them, and wearing these on chains around their necks so bullets will not hit them. Some people are famed at being immune to injury or death."[2]

This is part of the mix of Laos. Buddhist monks and village elders tie strings around a sick person's wrist to keep the souls of the thirty-two parts of the body from escaping. Mountain people wail in high pitched voices to keep evil spirits away as they traverse dangerous paths. Families attend to the spirits of their relatives after death so they will not cause trouble for the living.

Lao villages

Theravada Buddhism, the form of Buddhism practiced in Ceylon, lowland Laos, Burma, Thailand, and Kampuchea, was the center of Lao village life. It is flexible enough to serve the variety of its followers' beliefs: the Buddhist concept of earning merit through performing good deeds for the monks, ancestor reverence, and spirit worship. A Buddhist monk consults astrology when helping name a child. In temples, visitors tell fortunes by tossing sticks. Monks meticulously celebrate elaborate funeral rites to mediate between spirits of the living and dead. Village exorcists and elders try to reduce the influence of spirits afflicting a person with bad luck, turmoil, or disease by using Buddhist rituals to overlay the animist ceremonies designed to restore the spirit to balance.

For centuries the monks played crucial roles in Lao villages by harmonizing with the older animist beliefs. How many monks and temples exist today in Laos is unknown. Once the village temple featured a chapel, dwellings for the monks, preaching

Monks near Vientiane accept portions of rice brought by villagers. Young women earned merit for their families by making these gifts to the monks. (Galen Beery)

halls, and the village school and meeting hall. Even before the French instituted national education, monks taught men reading, writing, and the precepts of Buddhism. Though the temple was usually at one end of the village, symbolic of the ascetic and spiritual retreat from the lay world, it was undeniably the center of Lao village life, illustrating how Theravada Buddhism mediates between the everyday world and the spiritual life—living humans and their ancestors.

In each village, days began at the temple with scriptural readings. Villagers offered ricecakes and fruit to the monks, who are not allowed to cook for themselves, own possessions, or earn a livelihood. A monk has always depended upon his community to support him: to provide his saffron robes and sandals, deliver his rice, and handle his money.

To many Americans the monks' dependency seems to be self-serving, perhaps selfish. In fact, the relationship between the temple and the village was a perfectly functioning exchange seen by villagers to benefit both. By offering veneration, food, clothing, and shelter to the monks, Buddhists earned "merit" only the monks could confer. Accumulated merit aided the Buddhist on the path to spiritual enlightenment, a rebirth blessed with happiness, and produced a virtuous state of mind in this life, a context for unselfish giving.

Merit-making took many forms in Laos. Financing the building of a temple was an important way, one restricted primarily to the rich. A poor person who donated time or labor to the temple was the spiritual equal of the rich donor. A man earned merit when he or his son became a monk, another tie between the temple and the village. A family could give money to repair the temple. At the simplest level, a family sent rice portions saved from their meals to the temple, earning merit for the whole family.

In return, the monk tended to the village. He performed rituals based upon the harvest and planting seasons to ensure well-being and started holiday festivities that provided immense entertainment. On certain days monks performed ceremonies in the cemeteries where the ashes of ancestors were buried. In this way they blessed family homes and ancestors. Monks also handled the funeral rituals which saw to the spirit needs of the dead and the living. They taught the guidelines of Buddhism.

Villagers never forgot that monks did not share the same kinds of lives they led. Five Buddhist precepts, taught by monks, define the proper life of the lay person: taking only what is freely given, preserving life, and avoiding adultery, lies, and alcohol.

The monk's life was much more demanding. He entered the monastery at fifteen and began learning the 227 precepts that govern a monk's life—compared to the layman's five. By twenty

Equipped with buckets to carry rice allotments, women line up at the Nong Khai refugee camp in Thailand. (Mohammed Benamar; UNHCR)

he might be ordained as a monk, but continue his celibate life of chanting, practicing recitations, and other spiritual practices. By living according to the precepts, he accepted a code of nonviolence that did not allow him to dig in the ground to produce crops, kill animals, consort with armies, or approach battlefields. He shaved his head. He wore only the saffron robe tinted by jungle barks to symbolize his desire to be free of material possessions.

Lao Buddhism in America

Lowland Lao, mostly Buddhists, are grateful when this way of life can continue. Though by the end of 1981 no more than twenty monks had arrived in the United States to serve a lowland Lao population of over 70,000, Lao communities freely support them. Lao refugees plan temples in San Diego, California; Washington, DC; Portland, Oregon; Rockford, Illinois; and St. Paul, Minnesota. Temples receive financial support from large areas. Supporters hope each temple may one day have a facility for cremation to ensure proper funeral rituals.

On a day-to-day level, though no refugee can yet make the merit-making gesture of funding the building of a temple, the community supports the monks as it did in Laos with smaller acts of merit-making. Families pledge monthly donations. Young children slip off their shoes before entering the temples with hot rice for the meals monks take twice a day. A monk sits quietly as a Buddhist kneels in front of the altar with the image of Buddha near the ceiling, closest to the spirit realm, and places a bag of fresh fruit on the floor as a gift to the monk. A father hopes his sons will spend several weeks at the temple, as most young men of his generation did in Laos.

Theravada Buddhist monks adhere to the old traditions. They keep their saffron robes, turning the heat up or adding extra layers underneath during chill weather. A monk walks slowly. He never stares out of the corner of his eye. He remains celibate. Precepts teach him correct posture, proper etiquette, and the spiritual way.

Monks maintain the way of life that people of Laos and Cambodia knew for centuries, providing a stability in the shifting atmosphere of culture shock and readjustment. Where there are monks to confide in, refugees say they do not need counseling services or tranquilizers to ease the ache of loneliness, loss, and displacement. When Lao families move, they turn to the monk to bless their new homes. He cleanses the home of whatever spirits reside there by sprinkling holy water and flower petals, and he never objects when someone attends another church, possibly Christian. Monks are there when needed. Temples are always open for personal devotion.

The presence of a temple and Buddhist monks in Portland, Oregon, helps unite the lowland Lao refugee community. The temple is a modest, older home supported by pledges from Buddhist believers. Flowers and gifts adorn the altar, complete with a Buddha figure brought by one of the monks in his flight from Laos. (Kathleen Ryan)

Temples radiate a compelling calm. The delicate, handmade offerings to the Buddha—flickering candles, paper spires, fresh flowers, ricecakes, and tapestries—testify to the community's commitment to show cohesion in the way it maintains the temple. Serene wood and stone figures of Buddha brought by monks and refugees from Laos or Thailand grace altars redolent with the scent of chrysanthemums.

Certainly, this serenity will be challenged. Boys who go to the temple for two weeks during summer vacation later quarrel with their parents over how much television they may watch. No novices presently study to become monks, the only way the culture can be preserved over the long run. Though plans are in the preliminary stages for bringing the curious and interested into monasteries yet to be built, one wonders if eventually the young will find the daily tasks of merit-making too arduous, preferring to pay by check. In addition, Americans who do not understand the reciprocal services of the monks and their communities criticize the monks' dependency.

Though presently Lao people and monks work to preserve their traditional patterns of leadership and worship, both recognize how far it is from Vientiane to San Diego or Seattle. Lao Buddhists point out that a majority of the Pathet Lao were Buddhists, that they dare not destroy That Luang, the famous monument of Laos which survived wars with Thailand, Burma, Japan, and the Pathet Lao. Yet, when the Pathet Lao took over in Laos, they expelled the monks from the temples to work in the fields. The temple, the traditional focal point of Lao villages, became living quarters and office space for communist workers. Lao in America wish to avoid any secularization of their temples here, yet they also realize how hard it will be to collect money to build temples, monasteries, and crematoriums of their own.

Lao concerns

Like all Southeast Asian refugee groups, Lao who arrived earliest were most familiar with Western culture and most educated. Vongthongthip Kiat, who came to the United States in 1975 and is now a citizen, recalls his first impression: *"One thing I tell you, I think Americans are crazy: they get up in the morning, they rush, rush, rush, rush. They eat breakfast, they rush, rush, rush to work. In the evening they rush, rush off to play somewhere; then they rush back. They do this five days a week, fifty-two weeks every year, then they have heart attack. I think you are all crazy—but I will learn your ways."*[3]

Beyond adjusting to the pace of life, other conflicts arise. A father dislikes the way his teenage sons ignore discipline and behavior he demands. They refuse to become monks. He feels his children outstep him in becoming American in action, language, and dress. Yet, when they cut a lawn, they share their earnings with the family. They accompany him to a friend's small farm where they help butcher a pig so the family can have fresh meat as

In America this Laotian continues the practice of older children caring for younger, while his parents work in berry fields. (T. Brian Collins)

it once did in Laos.

A 1980 California study of refugee assimilation describes Southeast Asians as frequent victims of fraud. One was sold a mobile home, but not told the land the home stood on cost extra.

Another paid a large fee to a Los Angeles attorney to help him reunite his family. Nothing was ever done. Others have been visited by door-to-door "tax collectors," wearing business suits, who insist upon payment in cash.

These events prompted a leader of the Lao Family Community in Santa Ana, California to say: *"We have been living in a jungle for a long time in Laos. This is another kind of jungle—a technological and bureaucratic jungle."*[4]

Bureaucratic concerns are very much on the minds of Lao now in America. Many note that when bilingual education programs exist, they are most extensive in Vietnamese, not Lao. They understand there are more Vietnamese, but they also want education for their children. In addition, recent fact-finding trips to Southeast Asia by Congressmen have yielded suggestions that ethnic Lao in Thai camps no longer be considered "refugees." The argument runs that ethnic Lao are not presently persecuted for reasons of ethnicity like the Hmong in Laos are: Lao farmers who protest the New Economic Zones and communal agriculture are really "economic migrants." As such, they may not be eligible for resettlement here. Lao in the United States believe returning economic migrants are just as likely to be persecuted as those classified as refugees.

Those who live here, refugees with poetic, long first and last names—like Phoxay Vansirivong and Phengsy Douangpayvong—begin to take oaths of citizenship. Their Theravada Buddhist temples, humble buildings, join the ranks of Buddhist temples of other types—Japanese (Mahayana) and Vietnamese (Mahayana or Hirayana)—that dot our cities. They practice the creed of *king-chai*: respecting others, maintaining modesty, and avoiding confrontation. They teach their children to respect the authority of the father and the monk.

Mien

Mien travelled from southern China to Laos less than 200 years ago. Their origins are traced in myth. One myth tells of a Chinese emperor who in 2435 B.C. offered his daughter to whoever destroyed his enemy. A multi-colored dog, P'an, accepted the challenge and vanquished the foe. Then P'an married the princess and

Clothing that may be reserved for festive events since resettlement often was everyday wear in Laos. Red yarn pompons around the women's necks and brightly embroidered pants make a brilliant contrast to the black cotton of the blouses. The style of turban tells other Mien where these women live. (Lois Calloway)

retreated into China's mountains with his bride. Their twelve children became the originators of the twelve Mien tribes scattered throughout the mountains.

Later history, confirmed by Chinese accounts, tells that in the later fourteenth century Mien were driven from Nanking in China toward the sea. As confirmation, some Mien still reside on the Chinese island of Hainan. Drought and poor crops pushed most Mien into the mountains of southern China. Chinese persecution in the nineteenth century pushed them south again. Most settled in Laos, though some entered Thailand and Vietnam.

Mien culture retains vestiges of Chinese influence. Leaders still use Chinese characters to record traditions and social customs. Complex ancestor scrolls and ceremonies, which form the basis of

Mien ancestor reverence and spirit worship, may show Chinese Taoist influences. On the other hand, Mien reject the name Yao, a derogatory term used by Chinese and used by most historians. Yao meant thieves.

The Mien are a people with a strong oral tradition. Young men generally received only rudimentary instruction in the Chinese characters forming Mien texts. Men of religion learned the subtleties of the Mien use of Chinese characters. Missionaries developed a Romanized alphabet for Mien, but it is not widely used.

Only the older men are able to read the few texts that exist in Mien-adapted Chinese characters. These rare books narrate accounts of Mien origins strikingly similar to the Biblical Genesis, with an exile from a Garden of Eden Mien-style, a flood, and people living to be several hundred years old.

In Laos, the Mien became a minority among minorities, a status they had faced in China. Numbering over 3 million in China, fewer than 50,000 lived in Laos. One of dozens of ethnic minorities in Laos, they moved into the mountains between the altitudes of 3,000 and 4,000 feet. Mien lived just below the Hmong, but spoke a different language and virtually never intermarried. In small villages ranging from a low of ten to a high of a hundred families, but averaging around fifteen, they clustered into strong clan and family groups.

Mien moved constantly. Like the Hmong, they practiced slash and burn agriculture. First they burned stands of tropical forest. Using the ash for fertilizer, they planted rice, corn, vegetables, and beans for as long as the soil stayed fertile. When it gave out, they moved their villages of bamboo and split logs to begin again. Chickens, pigs, buffalos, horses, and donkeys went along.

Eventually the Mien produced opium. Encouraged to grow the colorful poppies by Chinese traders and later by the French, they traded opium for silver bars. Silversmiths forged elegant jewelry for the Mien costume. Bracelets, rather than rings, became the symbolic gift at weddings. In Lao cities silver bought medicines and other necessities. Neither the Hmong nor the Mien developed the technology to render opium into heroin. Few became addicts: opium was too valuable as a trade good to consume. The terminally ill or aged received it to soothe pain.

A rare look inside a Mien home shows family life in a highland village. (Lois Calloway)

Dependence on a written history of complex Chinese characters few can read combined with the severe social dislocations of war dating back to the 1940s—no wonder a Mien man describes Mien in America by saying, *"The Mien people don't even know where they are from and who they are."* For those under thirty-five, war has disrupted most of their lives. North Vietnamese passed through the mountains of Laos to build supply trails and move equipment. South Vietnamese and their allies fought to disrupt the supply lines. Hmong and Mien villages were trapped in the crossfire. To the Mien, residence in Southeast Asia became another segment in a history dotted by war and flight. The turmoil of war forced them to move, join the Hmong in fighting, or flee to camps in Thailand.

Mien in America

In America, the Mien are once again a minority among minorities. Estimates place 3,000 to 4,000 in the United States: 1,500 in Portland, Oregon, and smaller groups in Richmond, Oakland, San Jose, and Long Beach, California. Others scatter in isolated pockets. Mien sense their history must be preserved—recorded in English—or it will soon be lost. One Mien says. *"I am very positive the Mien will lose their traditional religion within the next ten years. There will be no more shamans. There will be no more scroll."*[5] He works to preserve this old culture, photographing traditional needlecraft patterns and the religious scrolls each clan should possess. The scrolls represent a sacred pantheon of gods, heroes, ancestors, lords of the forces of nature, and the lord of hell.

Traditional Mien know how hard the fight will be to preserve this culture. Girls say they are too busy to learn needlecraft, the basis for the colorful beauty of Mien clothing. Sponsors and missionaries join to counter the old ways. What the Mien call spirit worship or ancestor reverence, many missionaries privately label devil or demon worship. Church people condemn the techniques of the shaman, or spirit doctor, who is paid to exorcise bad, or "outside," spirits by calling up the aid of benevolent, guardian ones. They challenge the shaman's role as healer of the sick and depressed and as leader of the Mien marriage and funeral rituals.

Some Mien have mixed reactions toward missionaries. Those who do convert say they feel free from the threat of outside spirits (spirits who died without parents or relatives to revere them and who consequently have a malignant influence on the living). They say that in America it is time for the old ways to pass, so accept Christian marriage and funeral rites.

In the largest Mien enclave in the nation, Halsey Square in Portland, Oregon, two missionary groups maintain apartments. They teach English, advise Mien women on how to make money selling handicrafts, and offer tapes in the Mien language on everything from urban survival skills to Bible stories. In Seattle similar groups undertake a "pea patch" program to help Mien start their own vegetable gardens. One missionary group maintains a Mien directory to help family and clan groups locate each other and

A Mien scroll shows Tu Ta and lesser deities of Mien legend and bears Chinese inscriptions. In spite of long and dangerous overland treks, many families and clans brought scrolls with them. Painted in striking patterns of red and neutral colors, the scrolls are only used on ceremonial occasions. (Mike Sweeney)

seeks to publish a Mien dictionary. Mien agree with missionaries who claim their work finally persuaded the Mien in refugee camps that no man-eating giants lurked in America to gobble them up as Mien legends of eastern lands claimed.

Some Mien, however, wish new arrivals had more time to think through their religious commitments. Mien were not alone among Southeast Asians in assuming that because missionaries were so visible in refugee camps, conversion to Christianity brought faster resettlement. Sponsoring agencies have always argued religious preference has nothing to do with the resettlement decision—that interviews by U.S. immigration officials decide a refugee's fate long before sponsoring agencies become involved.

Some of the 65 percent of the Mien who have not converted insist there has been pressure to do so. They think of themselves as a kind, grateful people. Some Mien think that many who become Christians simply want to repay kindness from their sponsors. Most remain committed to animistic spirit worship, the way of the Mien for countless generations. They hope this tradition survives as an option.

The early stages of resettlement challenge Mien in other ways. Like hill people from Vietnam and Laos, Mien were exposed to many of the miracles of Western technology in the homes of U.S. officials, but never had to deal on a day-to-day basis with such things as Western stoves, crosswalk stoplights, and refrigeration units. When a sponsor explains American tap water is safe to drink, a newly arrived refugee may find this just as puzzling as that in America raw pork is not considered safe to eat. In Laos the water was bad; the pork was good.

Medical practices are another problem. Because villages in Laos were remote from city centers, Mien cared for each other or went to their shaman minister. Infant and fetal mortality rates in Laos were high. Dr. Tom Dooley's work in Laos documented the causes: malaria, dysentery, small pox, cholera, parasites, childhood diseases for which no immunizations were given, TB, and pneumonia. Mien often blamed the high death rates—over 50 percent—on evil spirits. To keep threatening spirits from finding out about an imminent birth, custom decreed a pregnant woman not discuss her condition with either close friends or husband.

Missionaries from the United States urged Mien to convert to Christianity. Over several years, nearly half have converted. (Anonymous)

Conflicts arise when Western ways challenge custom. In the refugee camps, women learned to accept prenatal care along with classes on preventive medicine and family planning. Despite knowledge of Western practices, many Mien women are shy about being examined. Many do not wish to confide the date of their last menstrual cycle so the doctor can pinpoint a due date for delivery. They blush at undressing in front of a male doctor. They remember that in Laos, women with years of experience in childbirth assisted at births. The husband's only role was to fetch water, though he lovingly cared for the children after birth.

Though most Mien do not fear hospitals, many rely on traditional remedies. They practice "coining," applying pressure to bruise painful areas as a counterirritant to disease. Women eat pumpkin to facilitate conception. Most seek help from a shaman at the same time they accept prescriptions for medication.

Mien women receiving maternity care mix the traditional and the Western. They expect their baby to wear a cap festooned with red pompons, delicate embroidery, beads, and silver ornaments. Sometimes a mother adds good wishes with folded bits of paper and bead work. She believes the hat protects her child from evil spirits. In addition, Mien women subscribe to the custom of not eating fruits or vegetables containing seeds or ice for a one-month period after delivery. If her doctor does not specifically order rice, small cubes of chopped chicken, and broth for the recovering mother in the hospital, she may go hungry rather than violate Mien folk health beliefs.

Mien mothers do modify other aspects of child rearing as they observe American ways. In 1979 one government-sponsored program found that 100 percent of the Hmong and Mien women it aided breastfed their children. One year later, only 47 percent did. Mothers cite convenience as the reason, and say they seldom see American women baring their breasts in public. Unfortunately, infant hospital admissions for diarrhea among refugee children has increased. Not all refugee mothers understand how to prepare formula or sterilize bottles.

Mien family traditions

As with other refugee and immigrant groups, Mien find much that is different here from what they have known. They blend old traditions and new necessities.

Members of the same Mien clan may marry (unlike the Hmong) but several rules dictate what marriages may be successful. An astrologer determines the most propitious time for the wedding ceremony even if it is 3 a.m. This custom remains unchallenged. Other traditions determine whom an individual may marry. A father's brother's daughter (first cousin) is never suitable, but a mother's sister's daughter (also a first cousin) might be.

Will the young honor tradition? For the moment they do. Older Mien worry that the youth will not always base their marriages on family considerations coupled with astrological predictions. The American concept of love is too strong, they say.

Historically, in Laos the groom's father had to pay the bride's

Mien mothers embroider pomponned baby caps to ward off evil spirits that might afflict the child. From the design of the cap, Mien can tell at a glance whether the baby is a boy or a girl. (John Maher)

family as compensation for the time they had spent rearing her. Rituals attended the engagement and marriage process. First, a son informed his father that he favored a certain woman. The father inquired about her birthdate and consulted a fortune book to see if the marriage could harm the family. Then, after a series of bracelet trades, the parents of both parties arranged costs. As many as 300 to 400 guests would need to be fed for many days. Specific quantities of food would be negotiated: perhaps 50 pounds of small dried birds, 22 pigs, 100 chickens, and 100 pounds of fresh fish. The bride's family decided whether the food would be fried, steamed, or baked. Then the groom's family took up to a year to gather the supplies needed for the wedding. For a poorer family the party might only last a day.

These negotiations took time. Marriages waited while families raised money. No one thought it amiss for the betrothed to start a family in the meantime. Pregnancy was considered a good indication that the eventual marriage would produce a large family. Consequently, the phenomenon of the unwed mother carried no social stigma. All children are wanted, loved, and assured of family to support them.

In the United States this custom raised problems between sponsors and Mien families. The suggestion of abortion shocks Mien. Most have mixed feelings about family planning. They also remember receiving contraceptive shots in refugee camps which are not legal for use in the United States but were being tested by drug companies in Southeast Asia.

Mien realized some modifications were needed in their marriage traditions. Americans claimed the bride fee was like a sale of livestock though Mien called it a social exchange that tied families together. Also, few Mien have amassed the kind of wealth that the opium trade brought in Laos. Thus, at a meeting in December of 1980, representatives from Mien communities set a ceiling of $1,000 for what the groom's family could pay for a wedding party. This figure fits the cost of many American weddings. A family can no longer demand live pigs in trade for a daughter. The father must accept goods available from grocery stores. Weddings now take place all in one day so people can return to jobs. Though these compromises changed traditions, the structure is still based on the father's active role in the selection of a marriage partner.

In America it is common to discuss divorce in the same context as marriage, one so often follows the other. This is not true in Southeast Asia. The Mien procedure for divorce was used infrequently; many Mien do not know anyone who has used it. Usually the couple with trouble went to the headman of the village for help. His counseling was usually enough.

Mien also settle disputes in the old way. Mien communities avoid establishing the kind of official associations the Hmong and Lao have formed, preferring the system that still works informally

Mien women display family wealth in the form of ten centime silver coins and silver jewelry. Turbans and shawls are all hand embroidered. (T. Brian Collins)

through well-respected leaders. Elders lead religious affairs and provide counseling on other matters, though younger men who speak English and are more bi-cultural often help interpret laws.

In the panoply of family traditions, one of the most important to Mien is the funeral. Here the family assures that a deceased member's spirit moves peacefully into the spirit world as a guardian for descendants. Friends and relatives gather to reaffirm social ties. Because Mien never embalmed their dead, they accept quick burials, waiting patiently for an astrologically propitious date for the separate funeral ceremony.

In the United States, Mien funerals hold to the traditions of Laos.[6] Substitutions are made only where necessary—such as dressing the son of the deceased with the remnants of a bed sheet tied around his forehead because the traditional apparatus was abandoned when Mien fled their homes. In other ways, the old patterns continue. Mien women don their embroidered pants and colorful tunics, moving quietly in the background to prepare food. Either the shaman or elder, dressed in a black tunic, gingerly unrolls the ancient ancestor scrolls and hangs them so the ritual displays of the lords of nature and the ancestors is complete. He leads chants while the other men, also in black tunics, take turns dancing and chanting. Rituals release the dead into the spirit world as men sound gongs and drums and blow ox horns.

Mien regret most mortuaries will not allow their noisy ceremonies inside. They resist overtures by funeral directors to cremate bodies because cremation is reserved for limited circumstances when the body is thought to be unclean. In Laos the shaman chose the best spot for burial. Here that option is not so available. Mien understand these constraints, yet they also know funeral traditions patch holes in the society that death has ripped open. Like early Chinese immigrants who wailed and moaned in long white robes as they carried their dead in parades through Chinatown and Vietnamese who dedicate their own cemeteries, Mien seek to fulfill the demands of their culture's funeral traditions.

New lives

The process of adaptation presses on, offering little time for thoughtful meditation on how things ought to be. Mien youngsters fall away from needlecraft, though once a woman's skill determined part of her value to the community. Some older women sell festive baby caps and backpacks to appreciative Americans. Others make untraditional ties, eyeglass cases, and potholders for fleamarkets and church socials. They are puzzled that other American women seem more interested in their art than their own children are. Mien Christians disappoint other Mien by not showing up for traditional Mien New Year's feasts in early spring.

The old and the new—these opposites sadden Mien when they separate the community. Perhaps their small numbers will determine what survives. Where families have clustered, they retain parts of their culture as Chinese and Japanese have. Their need for community explains what otherwise might seem like luxury phone calls to distant relatives resettled in France, the secondary migration of a Mien family from Vermont to Portland, Oregon, and the cassette tapes filled with gossip and news that shuttle back

In traditional garb of black cotton with bright embroidery, Mien musicians begin the New Year's festivities which they celebrate in February, as do the Chinese. In Laos New Year's day itself was followed by a series of fifteen superstition days. No one talked on Tiger Sleeping Day or used a knife on Knife Day. On Wind Day children who spoke too loudly risked provoking destructive winds. In the United States, refugees celebrate one day only, but they continue old traditions of cleaning their homes and exchanging eggs dyed bright red. Everyone wears yarn pompons in observance of the beginning of a new year. (T. Brian Collins)

and forth between refugee camps in Thailand and new homes on the West Coast.

What will the Mien be in ten years? Ay Choy Sae Lee, a young Mien man, sighs. To his right is a three-year-old girl playing with the red embroidery thread, needle, and black cloth her mother put in her hand. To his left is his television. As his phone rings, he hastens to say: *"In ten years Mien will be just Americans."*

Hmong

Throughout the mountains of Laos, clusters of eight to forty hand-hewn houses nestled in the highest reaches. One door of each home faced a saddle between two peaks to facilitate the flow of good fortune to the family within. Hmong chose these heights to escape centuries of Chinese persecution and the malaria that thrives in the tropical lowlands. Their remote location, however, did not protect them from the political intrigues and wars between colonialist, communist, and royalist forces centered far beyond village confines.

Hmong have never been able to attach to one homeland. Origins lie deep in Central Asia. Though they have had no written language historically, legends tell of black winters, fur clothing, and frigid snows. Slowly they migrated southward. Later oral histories relate how they were driven from southwestern China beginning in the eighteenth century. As they moved southward once more, they battled Chinese warriors intent on driving them into unproductive highlands or exterminating them.

Following a series of Hmong rebellions in China in 1698, 1732, and 1735, Chinese officers lured Hmong leaders to Peking where they were tied to stakes and hacked to pieces. Chinese displayed the heads of Hmong warriors in baskets to intimidate other Hmong rebels. Despite Chinese suppression, Hmong fought back and led major rebellions between 1855 and 1881.

The Chinese had a demeaning name for the Hmong: Miao or Meo, meaning "slaves." Like the Mien, the Hmong lived their own view of their history. They are Hmong, or "free men." Though 2.5 million Hmong remained in China, starting in the 1850s many resettled as a response to harassment and the threat of murder. A quarter million found homes in Vietnam, 50,000 in

Many Laotians measured their wealth in silver, and silversmithing was a highly respected craft. Artisans hope to find markets in America for their skills. (Lois Calloway)

Thailand, and at least 350,000 in Laos—forming 10 percent of Laos' population.

Throughout conflicts and migrations, Hmong retained a strong social organization. Their highly structured clan system based on twenty patriarchal groups—sixteen of which are the most commonly occurring last names for Hmong in the United States—held them together. Neither war nor the threat of genocide upset reciprocal clan marriage agreements, leadership based on seniority, and the religious authority of spirit doctors, or shamans, who ministered to spirit ills.

In Laos this cohesive tribal group was free. Remote from wet lowland ricelands, Hmong practiced slash and burn agriculture, like the Mien. At first they survived on dry mountain rice, corn, vegetables, and livestock. They maintained the Hmong language and seldom intermarried with Laos' other ethnic groups. Clothing made them easily recognizable. Women wore black turbans, appliquéd skirts, and silver necklaces and stitched, brightly colored baby packs. Subtle variations in design identified members of tribal subgroups: White Hmong, Blue Hmong, Striped Hmong, and others. Hmong claim the custom started at the order of Chinese officials who wanted variations by geographical location to fracture Hmong unity.

Hmong did make some adaptations to other cultures. Chinese first encouraged Hmong to grow opium as a cash crop. Though Hmong consumption of opium was restricted to the sick or aging, they accepted high Chinese payments for the sticky balls of poppy resin. Because the product was easily portable, its high mountain source was no disadvantage. Opium poppies require soil and weather conditions found only above 3,000 feet, the Hmong's homeland. When missionaries arrived, Hmong offered wrapped blobs of opium to collection baskets. They resisted trading opium for currency, recognizing silver had a permanent value beyond the shifting monies of governments. Hmong never underestimated the value of their cash crop, one kilo of which could be traded for one-half ton of rice or several bars of silver.

By the middle of the twentieth century, Hmong produced 90 percent of the opium grown in Laos. Of the world's opium 70 percent comes from the Golden Triangle: Burma, Thailand, and Laos. On an international market hungry for morphine and heroin, derivatives of opium, the Hmong were important producers. They did not manufacture heroin. Nor did they have the smugglers and street dealers to sell the final product. Not until 1971 did U.S. pressure prevail in Laos to make opium production illegal. By then the spreading conflict between the Pathet Lao, supported by the North Vietnamese, and the Royal Lao government endangered Hmong existence.

Hmong fighters

Crucial to understanding the role of the Hmong in this war is an overview of their past military commitments. Clan affiliations during World War II prompted Hmong to fight Japanese invaders. Most guerrilla leaders of the Hmong who emerged from World

In 1969 Hmong troops loaded U.S. supplied 105 mm cannon as part of an effort to stop North Vietnamese use of the Ho Chi Minh Trail through Laos. A high percentage of Hmong men living in the United States have combat experience. (Galen Beery)

War II sided with the Royal Lao when Laos gained independence from France in 1954. Fewer clans threw their support to the Pathet Lao. Following clan lines, then, Hmong allied themselves on one side or the other of the conflict that ripped Laos apart. Hmong who supported the emergent Royal Lao government (backed by U.S. aid and military advisors) form the bulk of Hmong refugees in the United States today.

The United States became involved with the Hmong in numerous ways. In the early 1960s the CIA taught English, methods of guerrilla warfare, and radio communications. Hmong boys often manipulated sophisticated weaponry. Many were pleased to have this education, whether or not they wanted to fight. CIA officials hoped the Hmong would become a potent guerrilla force acting as a buffer between U.S. bases in Thailand and North Vietnamese who threatened the mountain borders of Laos.

The United States Agency for International Development (USAID) supported the CIA's efforts. It sent personnel to train Hmong in noncombat skills. Providing tin roofs, chalk, blackboards, and teacher training, the USAID encouraged the Hmong to build schools. For the first time children had public education. Some learned to read and write in Lao. Very few had learned the Romanized script developed by missionaries for the Hmong language. Fifty years before, Hmong received only oral lessons in Hmong from village elders. When Lao national education programs reached the Hmong highlands in the 1960s, the mountains were already a war zone. Educational opportunities offered by USAID helped create strong loyalties to America.

Air transportation became the link between the mountain Hmong and the world outside. Some critics argue Air America guaranteed Hmong loyalty by assisting in the opium trade. Other officials respond that although an individual pilot may have made money on the side in this way, it was never government policy. Innuendo and rumor surround the relationship between the CIA and the Hmong.

American involvement with the Hmong encouraged the emergence of strong leaders who accepted broad roles in national Lao politics and later played important roles in Hmong resettlement here. General Vang Pao is best known. At thirteen, Vang Pao joined French colonialists in reporting movements of Japanese troops. Later he helped U.S. military efforts in Laos by organizing networks of Hmong soldiers with communicators to relay messages of Vietnamese communist and Pathet Lao supply movements through the mountains. Hmong soldiers harassed the communists and rescued downed American pilots. In the 1960s, as the Pathet Lao scoured the mountains, Vang Pao recruited soldiers and established order among villagers fleeing from bombed-out war zones. He also solidified his political strength among the Hmong according to custom: he chose six wives from the most powerful Hmong clans.

Today Vang Pao moves from one U.S. resettlement area to another counseling Hmong. Vang Pao is one important spokesperson for the Hmong refugee community. He opposes cash assistance, encouraging Hmong to find jobs, join resources, and fend

Vang Pao was a Hmong military leader and, according to some reports, CIA functionary in Laos. Pictured here with his son, Chu Leng, in Montana, he is now a United States citizen and a leader in the developing U.S. Hmong community. (Jo Rainbolt)

for themselves as they always did in Laos. His 400-acre farm in the Bitterroot Valley near Missoula, Montana, forms one principal resettlement center of Hmong in America.

Hmong flee

From 1955 to 1972 fighting between the Royal Lao and the Pathet Lao tore through villages and uprooted clans and families. During those twenty years, 30,000 Hmong died in action. War widows became common. Families fled their homes and left their livestock behind. Unable to stay in one place long enough to grow opium, Hmong lost their most important source of income. They depended increasingly on USAID planes to drop rice to dusty airfields where families crouched at the fringes, waiting.

From 1972 to 1975, Hmong experienced a sort of breathing space in the wartime pressures on their villages while the Pathet

Lao and the Royal Lao held to a ceasefire. Then, in 1975 the agreement collapsed. Royal Lao withdrew to Thailand; Pathet Lao rapidly came to power.

Hmong knew how vulnerable they were to the Pathet Lao. Vang Pao and other military aides evacuated quickly. Soldiers by the tens of thousands, accompanied by their families, started the long trek overland. At the Mekong River they made bamboo rafts to cross to the safety of Thailand.

Chen Vang describes flight, one typical of many: *"I remember the first evening that people in my village, Ban Nam Hia, Sayaboury, Laos, fled to Thailand. Before making a decision to flee on that evening in June, 1975, the entire village, young and old, men and women, over 1,000 people were outside filling the road that passed the village. They talked and discussed what to do. The goal was decided: Thailand and then America, but it was a dark and unseen goal. The decision was passed along from person to person. At 10:30 p.m. most of the villagers were gone. By midnight they had all fled. During the flight, children five years old and up carried as much as they could. The adults carried food, clothes, and young children or babies who couldn't walk. Each person carried a plastic cover for protection from the rain. Every night each family built its own tent for sleeping and fire for cooking. Every day it was as though a new village was built and left the next day. The walk was slow. You could see people moving along the trail from mountain to mountain like a mass of ants carrying things in many colors. When there was jungle, you could only hear their voices from the near side of another mountain. When it rained, the trail became muddy. As it became more slippery, you took careful steps down the hill so you wouldn't slip. After crossing the border in Thailand, Thai soldiers stopped us and took our weapons. We were held for two weeks until we were moved to another camp. There were 12,000 to 16,000 people there divided into eight groups. When food arrived, they divided it among the groups, then each group divided it into small groups and finally to families. The camp was built on the side of a hill and fenced so no one could get out until the gate opened. The rest of the world has opened its door and accepted those qualified to leave. The final unseen goal has been reached. However, thousands are still left in camps. Thousands were punished and killed before they reached Thailand. Many died from hunger. Those who died and suffered left us living in the worst terror of tears in the history of mankind. Thanks to God, the whole*

Hmong women in the Sobtuang camp, Thailand, dandle their children and practice needlecraft that is now an admired art form in America. (John Isaac; United Nations)

world has given us their humanitarian help."[7]

The Pathet Lao tried to halt these refugee flights by exterminating the Hmong. Their targets were not just soldiers. Entire villages were slaughtered. Pathet Lao hunted fleeing Hmong with napalm and tear gas. Refugees report strange nerve gases were used against them. Livestock were killed as well. If refugees hid, Pathet Lao burned the jungles looking for them.

Hmong estimate one-half the people who fled died en route to Thailand. Disease and persecution claimed many. Adults gave up food to feed their young and died from starvation. Communist soldiers shot women to make it easier to take off silver necklaces.

Hmong who could not swim the Mekong or find a raft did their best by tying empty water containers to their waists to help them float. Babies strapped to backs drowned as parents weakened. An American journalist reported what a Hmong man told her at the Thai border: *"I feel sad for my wife. Her clothes are shreds and she's sick with malaria yet she cares for my brother's five children . . . my brother and his wife are dead. I often think of my American friends. They gave me their addresses but I've lost them. It seems so long ago that the Americans left—maybe four years and now the fighting is even more difficult, with so few weapons and no one to help us. We Meo [Hmong] are all so tired. So many Meo are dead. We Meo people are so pitiful."*[8]

Pitiful was a new word in the Hmong self-concept. Wounds and diseases needed urgent treatment. Uneducated and poorly skilled compared to earlier Vietnamese refugees, they were given low priorities for resettlement. Most languished in the camps until 1979, when educational background was downgraded as a criterion for resettlement. Many were confined for three to four years. They could not search for jobs in Thailand. Parents worried about the physical and emotional health of children born within the camps' fences. Four out of five Hmong listed America as their first choice for resettlement when registering with U.S. interviewing teams. Most felt their lives were stagnating despite medical care and missionary attempts to teach them or encourage them to make traditional needlecraft for sale outside camps. All waited for word they had been chosen to go to France, Australia, Canada, or the United States.

Hmong resettle

Hmong who made it to the United States followed the pattern of building ethnic enclaves. Communities coalesced in Missoula, Montana; Santa Ana, California; Portland, Oregon; Seattle, Washington; and the St. Paul-Minneapolis area of Minnesota. Others sprouted in Denver, Honolulu, Des Moines, and in Providence, Rhode Island. Like other Asian groups, the Hmong were attracted to southern California.

Hmong in America face all the problems common to immigrants. In addition, lack of familiarity with Western customs and educational structures creates frustration. Where first arrivals had

Like millions of newcomers before them, Hmong in Montana find virtually every aspect of life different in the United States. While in Laos, few foresaw snowy winters, metal mobile homes, and car ownership as part of their way of life. (Jo Rainbolt)

been employed by the U.S. government, more recent arrivals tend to be independent guerrilla fighters, peasants, and farmers with no formal education or job experience beyond manual labor. The destruction of homes, livestock, and farms disrupted whatever opportunities they had for planning futures in a modernized world. Hmong men were too busy fighting to attend school regularly. Women and children scurried between the jungle, hideaways in caves, and neighboring villages avoiding the fury of war. The Thai camps offered little in the way of language, cultural orientation, or job skill training.

School is a new experience for many Hmong, not just a matter of adapting to a different structure as it is for most Vietnamese and lowland Lao refugees. Fifth graders might need to be taught how to hold a pencil. Others face trials riding buses or participating in group reading sessions. Waiting lists clog all language training programs. One frequently mentioned reason for the secondary migration of large numbers of Hmong from their initial resettlement area to some other American city—mostly in family or clan groups—is the availability of better job training or cash assistance. Wherever they go, teachers working with Hmong note high motivation to learn, good behavior, and dependable class attendance.

Old ways and new

Like the Mien, the Hmong balance ancient traditions with Western customs. Some wonder if the spirits of home, hearth, forest, water, and thunder exist here. Households decide whether to convert to the Christianity they were exposed to by missionaries. Traditional belief in a supreme creator and the promise that someday a Hmong leader will arise to lead the Hmong against all oppressors is easily seen as a spiritual metaphor for the arrival of Christ: a promise of peace, happiness, and prosperity.

More traditional Hmong, still forming the majority of the some 60,000 refugees here, believe in their complex world of spirit deities, the *tlan*. Their shaman, who is called to his position by the ancestor spirits, goes on long "shaman's rides," or spirit journeys, to find the spirit afflicting a sufferer and drive it out. As he starts on the journey, which may take hours, he beats a drum with his face covered. His patient waits.

One Hmong shaman, Joua Pao Vang, describes his spirit journey that helped him become a shaman: *"I was dead for seven days. My spirit was gone. My body still breathed. I was warm under the armpits. The journey took me to a King's palace, Shi Yi, the king of the shamans. It is not an easy journey, and few shamans make it all the way. Shi Yi sets tests for each person. First you must cross a great field of fire. Second you approach a gigantic creature, resembling most closely a caterpillar. It writhes menacingly in your path. You must jump over it. Third there is a door with slashing blades like scissors and no one may enter without the power bestowed by the ancestors. The scissors door is meant to cut the bad from the good. You must be a faithful and trustworthy person*

A teacher shows a group of Hmong refugees in Minnesota how to price foods and deal with the American supermarket system. (Kurt Foss)

who would use the shaman's power for good. You must never use it to kill people. If you are a bad person, this door will kill you and you will never come back a shaman. The Shi Yi writes on your chest and back, left and right. Books of knowledge are placed on your chest. Then Shi Yi sends you to another who gives you the shaman's bell, rattle, and drum. They are used to travel the world of the spirits and as weapons to protect from or frighten spirits.''[9]

Though Hmong here turn to both, neither shamans nor Western medical doctors have been able to halt the mysterious pattern of death that has struck down scores of Hmong. Apparently healthy Hmong, mostly men, have died suddenly. Coroners, psychiatrists, military doctors, and specialists cannot explain why. Theories range from stress or cardiac arrhythmia to the effects of unidentified gases North Vietnamese used against Hmong which may also be associated with internal bleeding, headaches, and high miscarriage rates suffered by Hmong. The Center for Disease Control and other agencies seek causes for these deaths, but none has emerged. The so-called sleeping deaths of the Hmong remain another mystery to shroud their history.

Some Hmong find it hard to understand why they have to stop growing opium. On suburban lawns they see poppies growing they are sure could produce opium at the right season. One Hmong who receives word that one of his wives, whom he thought was dead, has just arrived in another part of the country cannot understand his sponsor's reaction. He humors the sponsor who is upset about possible bigamy charges, but he wants his second wife back with him. His first wife is ready to accept her. The sponsor is not.

In a similar vein, a Hmong woman waits in the lobby of a doctor's office. She nods her head at a houseplant on a corner table. It makes sense to her that a doctor would cultivate the traditional Hmong cure for diarrhea in babies. She does not understand someone might grow a plant simply for decoration. Later, she and several friends may gather by freeway right-of-ways to collect wild herbs to treat burns or cure snakebites. This is part of what was once her job as a woman.

Like other refugees, she may be homesick. She does not leave the house as often as the men or her children, and is embarrassed that she does not learn English. She remembers that in Laos when the men chopped firewood or cleared the field, she cooked rice, fed the chickens, pigs, and horse, and then went into the fields. When she came back, she fed the animals again, fixed dinner, and milled the rice. Later she bathed the children, straightened the house, and made preparations for the morning. Here she feels confined because she has not learned to drive. When the children leave, there is little for her to do but watch television shows she may not understand. Too often her married children do not live close enough for her to visit daily.

Out of this experience as refugees, Hmong try to leave behind the pitiful and regain the proud. MAAs, usually known as Hmong Family Associations, capitalize on the strong system of clan leadership. Hmong pool investment monies, structure job training

Soda pop and Hmong needlecraft—this youngster grows up literally surrounded by two cultures. Her mismatched hand-me-downs are typical attire of a newly-arrived refugee. (Miriam Weinstein)

programs, and reach out to help the American community understand who they are.

Occasionally Hmong leadership experiences some shakeups. Young men play roles once reserved for the eldest heads of clans or shamans because they understand American culture or speak English better. Most Hmong still prefer to concentrate decision-making in the hands of the elder patriarchs or household heads, within the old tradition, but they also see that these men are sometimes overlooked by government or sponsorship agencies. Americans tend to turn to those who speak English.

Hmong Family Associations encourage members to use skills they already have. Older women exercise their needlecraft skills in either the Blue Hmong style of small squares appliquéd on top of each other or the White Hmong appliquéd designs made from intricate folds of fabric. The strong geometric patterns of dazzling primary colors in the form of wall hangings, baby packs, burial pieces, and purses are finding a place in America's art and commercial textile markets. Hmong silversmiths seek markets for their handcrafted necklaces, bracelets, and earrings. Other Hmong set up contracting services employing crews of Hmong in cleaning, landscaping, and security services.

Given their history, it seems likely the Hmong will succeed here in the long run just as they did in Asia. Their clan and leadership structure still provide cohesive group decision-making. Strong communication networks develop as Hmong form larger settlements to help others find jobs and take advantage of services. Short-run prospects, however, are not so bright. Cutbacks in cash assistance and high unemployment mean Hmong have little chance for financial security while they seek education and build communities. Though distinctions between sub-tribal groups based upon geographic origin tend to blur, most Hmong believe in the old rules governing clan leadership and marriage. Even today no Hmong marries a person with the same last name.

What is not so clear is what will happen to tradition. The desire to be simply American—not Hmong American—is already being heard from some teenagers, though most have not taken the next step of rejecting the old or being embarrassed by it.

A Hmong high school student wrote an essay describing his life in Xieng Khouang, a Lao province. Chia Moua concluded with a promise, suggesting he appreciates how the Hmong struggle to be free in a world threatening genocide, which began centuries ago and is still endured in Southeast Asia: *"If someday I have children . . . I will describe to them all I know about a long time ago. I will tell my story to them."*

Chronology

1700s Laos is caught in the middle of border pushes by both Siam (Thailand) and Vietnam.

1800s Siam dominates most of what is now Laos.

Hmong musician in traditional dress—silver jewelry, silver coins, and appliquéd belt—plays a small instrument useful in courtship. He can play it so softly outside a woman's window that only she hears. The Hmong language is based on voice tones, so musical instruments can be made to "speak." Music and poems are part of the oral history of this people with no established written language. (T. Brian Collins)

1907 Treaty between Siam and France sets the present borders of Laos. Annexation as part of French Indochina protects Laos from Vietnamese and Thai invasions but ties Laos to France.

1945 Japanese troops occupy Laos and urge Lao king to proclaim independence from France. Japanese surrender to Allied forces. By late fall the Free Lao (anti-French) forces dethrone the king and install him as head of state. Lao prince Souphanouvong meets with North Vietnamese communist leader Ho Chi Minh who promises to support the independent Lao movement. North Vietnamese backed forces establish liberation committees primarily in northeastern Lao mountains.

1946 French forces return to Laos. Souphanouvong's forces, no match for the French, flee to remote regions. Until 1949 Laos is ruled by Lao leaders in exile in Thailand under the direction of the French. Anti-French forces (communist and nationalist) look for aid from North Vietnam, strongly communist and anti-French.

1954 Geneva Conference refuses to seat the Pathet Lao (communist Lao) as a government but agrees that in 1955 Laos will hold elections to determine government leadership. Laos also gains independence from France. Pro-Western forces rule in Laos though many factions vie for power. Prince Souphanouvong leads the Pathet Lao. His older brother, Prince Souvanna Phouma, leads a neutral faction allied with rightists. Rival factions quarrel over power and influence.

1955-1958 Pathet Lao and neutralist forces under Prime Minister Souvanna Phouma work to unite Laos. Pathet Lao gain ministerial positions. The effort at unity fails when rightist forces arrest and jail Pathet Lao ministers.

1959 Military clashes break out between Royal Lao and Pathet Lao forces in northeastern Laos. UN commission finds North Vietnam was providing military aid but finds little evidence of troop presence. Royal Lao government charges North Vietnamese do have troops in mountain hideaways to protect North Vietnamese supply trails through Laos into South Vietnam.

1960 Neutralist Souvanna Phouma is returned as prime minister.

Hmong and Mien fine needlework is finding a receptive audience in the United States because of the intricate patterns and careful attention to technique. Embroidery is used as well as cutting and folding back to expose a contrasting fabric color underneath. This example is Hmong. (Kathleen Ryan)

1961 Pathet Lao make military gains in Laos. U.S. sends military advisors to help the Royal Lao Army. Non-military advisors also arrive, including USAID (United States Agency for International Development) and CIA personnel.

1962 U.S. agrees to encourage a cease-fire agreement in Laos at a 14 nation conference in Geneva. Before settlement, Pathet Lao secure all access points into North Vietnam. The new agreement calls for all foreign military forces to withdraw. U.S. complies; North Vietnam does not. Non-military USAID workers remain in Laos building roads, hospitals, and airstrips; teaching plumbing and carpentry; advising on agricultural techniques; and providing medical assistance. Final agreement creates tripartite coalition of neutralists, rightists, and communists.

1963 Coalition falls apart. Fighting between neutralist and communist forces resumes.

Late 1960s North Vietnamese step up movements of supplies and troops along Ho Chi Minh Trail in Laos. U.S. bombs trail and North Vietnamese outposts; enlists Hmong and Mien men to work as guerrilla fighters.

1969 In March the Hmong guerrilla base in northeastern Laos falls to communists. Hmong people continue to flee their mountain homes. In May U.S. jets heavily bomb communist towns on Laos' Plain of Jars. In December the U.S. Senate prohibits using Defense Department money to support U.S. ground troops in Laos or Thailand.

1970 President Richard Nixon admits 400 U.S. aircraft have been lost over Laos. U.S. bombing intensifies against Cambodia.

1973 Pathet Lao forces control two-thirds of Laos' territory but not the Mekong River Valley where most of the population lives. Royal Lao government and Pathet Lao sign a cease-fire.

1974 No Royal Lao forces are allowed inside Pathet Lao zones. A provisional government seeks to reunify Laos.

1975 South Vietnam and Cambodia fall to Communist forces. Royal Lao government falls to the Pathet Lao who direct the new Democratic Socialist Republic of Laos. Royal Lao officials and U.S. agency employees flee Laos. U.S. halts aid to Laos. Pathet Lao arrest and execute thousands of Lao as traitors, including Hmong.

Most Hmong leave for the lowlands or Thailand. New Lao government allies itself with the Soviet Union and Vietnam.

1976-1977 Border skirmishes occur between Laos and Thailand. Drought compounds problems of economic and agricultural comebacks in Laos.

1978 Pathet Lao support Vietnamese movement into Kampuchea. U.S. sends aid to Laos, mostly rice to aid shortages caused by mismanagement and drought. Communists order farmers into agricultural collectives. Many farmers choose to become refugees.

1979 In the first half of the year 5,000 refugees a month flood into camps just inside the Thai border. By late summer the number decreases to 2,000 a month. Many are mountain tribespeople.

1981 100,000 Lao await resettlement from refugee camps in Thailand. 300,000 Lao have fled Laos since 1975. UN aid in the form of irrigation and farming supplies and medical dispensaries pours into Laos to bolster the economy and halt refugee flight.

EIGHT

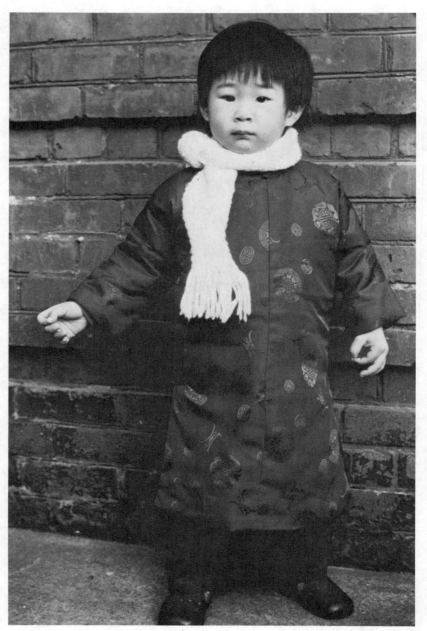

(T. Brian Collins)

The Boat People

Overseas Chinese Become Americans

As early as 200 B.C. Chinese merchants sought foreign markets for silk, paper, brass, and tea. In Southeast Asia they traded with Vietnamese for rhinoceros horn, ebony, fish, gold, pepper, rice, cinnamon, and sugar.

By the 1850s the forces of flood, famine, and overpopulation causing Chinese laborers to sail for California prompted Chinese merchants to expand their role in Southeast Asia. They established themselves as middlemen between Western traders drawn to rich markets and local producers in Siam (later Thailand), the kingdoms of Cambodia and Laos, and the empire of Vietnam. Akin to the early merchants who sold goods in the gold rush settlements in California, these Chinese left their homes to make fortunes not in labor but in commerce, making deals in silk, lacquerware, and porcelain.

Supported by strong family ties to trade headquarters in Hong Kong, Singapore, Taiwan, and mainland China, ethnic Chinese who lived outside China, called overseas Chinese, prospered. No exclusion acts restrained them from bringing families. Chinese enclaves sprouted all over Southeast Asia. No laws prohibited intermarriage, and some married into local families. In 1889, 23,000 Chinese, or Hoa as they were called in Vietnam, lived near Saigon alone. By 1921, 200,000 Chinese called Vietnam home and by

1975, almost 2 million.

The success of these merchants varied. For some, "trade" meant a stall that resold vegetables raised by Vietnamese or Cambodian farmers. Others established small market gardens or orchards on the outskirts of towns and delivered fresh fruits and vegetables to their family-owned shops.

The role of overseas Chinese as middlemen between local producers and European traders broadened as more European ships sailed into Southeast Asian harbors. Chinese had practiced the customs of trade for centuries. Because of longer acquaintance with each, they understood both Southeast Asian and European cultures better than those two did each other. Later they helped the French, operating as bankers to finance deals with Vietnamese and Cambodian traders.

Relations between overseas Chinese and local communities were sometimes uneasy. The Chinese paid special taxes as foreigners to own land and businesses. As their economic influence grew, Vietnamese farmers in debt to them became resentful. Chinese tended to keep to their own communities, another irritant to local populations. They held Taoist and Confucian ideas, while most Southeast Asians practiced Buddhism. Few Chinese declared themselves citizens of a Southeast Asian country even if their families had lived in Southeast Asia for many generations. Like the laborers in the United States, they described themselves as sojourners. They were Chinese, taught their children the Chinese language, and celebrated the Chinese lunar rather than the Buddhist New Year.

Citizenship disputes

China also called them Chinese. In 1909 the Chinese government ruled that any children born of parents of Chinese ancestry were Chinese. When a Chinese citizen married a Southeast Asian, Chinese law said the spouse became Chinese. These decrees conflicted with local laws. Vietnam accepted anyone born in Vietnam as a Vietnamese citizen.

World events at times obscured such citizenship issues. When worldwide depression in the 1930s dampened trade opportunities in Southeast Asia, large numbers of Chinese returned to China.

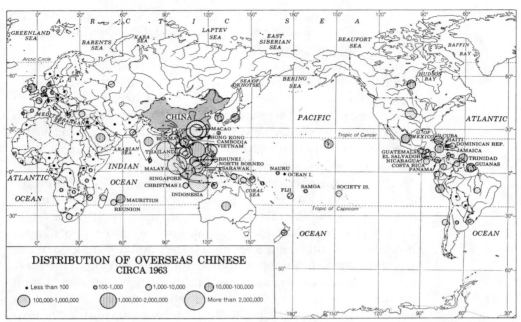

DISTRIBUTION OF OVERSEAS CHINESE
CIRCA 1963

• Less than 100   ⊙ 100-1,000   ⊘ 1,000-10,000   ◍ 10,000-100,000
◍ 100,000-1,000,000   ◍ 1,000,000-2,000,000   ◍ More than 2,000,000

During the early fifteenth century thousands of Chinese emigrated to the countries of Southeast Asia. Mass immigration did not begin until commercial contacts with Western nations began in the 1840s. During the next fifty years approximately 2 million men left China to seek gold in the United States, Canada, New Zealand, and Australia; build railroads in the United States, Panama, India, and Russia; or work plantations in Cuba, Brazil, Hawaii, and Tahiti. During these years emigration to Southeast Asia continued. As many overseas Chinese live in Thailand, Indonesia, and Malaysia as inhabit the rest of the world combined. (Sen-Dou Chang, "The Distribution and Occupations of Overseas Chinese." *Geographical Review* 58 (1968): 89-107. Reprinted with permission of the American Geographical Society)

When Japan established bases in Indochina during World War II, Chinese trade dropped off because China and Japan were at war. From 1946 to 1954, while Vietnam fought France for independence, most Chinese remained neutral, selling goods to either side.

With full independence of Vietnam, Laos, and Cambodia affirmed at Geneva in 1954, concern grew over the status of overseas Chinese. These three small nations—with a total land area less than that of California, Oregon, and Washington combined

—remembered past struggles against stronger foreign nations. Suspicion of overseas Chinese' politics and dislike of their continued economic influence was natural.

Vietnam demanded Chinese born there recognize Vietnamese citizenship. Law compelled Chinese to change their names to sound Vietnamese. Some complied: Wongs became Nguyens to remove the danger of arrest and beatings. Tension mounted when the Chinese government promised easy immigration to any Chinese who found these demands unacceptable. With China's backing, most Chinese ignored the Vietnamese orders.

Various Southeast Asian laws focused specifically on the Chinese minority. In 1956 non-citizens of Cambodia were banned from jobs classified as relating to national security. Chinese could not become longshoremen, private police, river pilots, auto chauffeurs, or intelligence agents. At that time Chinese were the largest minority in Cambodia and included 95 percent of the merchants in Cambodia's rural areas. In urban areas, Chinese formed the majority of shopkeepers. As in the United States, when Chinese came under attack, district and clan associations tried to protect their interests.

Vietnam went further than Cambodia in restricting what Chinese could do professionally. Anyone refusing Vietnamese citizenship was forbidden to own a grocery store, process rice, or act as middleman in the sales of goods—roles traditionally filled by Chinese who retained Chinese citizenship.

Chinese made up 7 percent of Vietnam's population but controlled 80 percent of retail trade. Like Japanese farmers in America who bought land in the names of their young children when they could not own it in their own names, Chinese reacted to legal restrictions with subterfuges. To hide their business interests they formed partnerships with Vietnamese citizens or created elaborate corporate structures that concealed Chinese investments.

Chinese survived through the 1960s and early 1970s because free market conditions prevailed in Vietnam and Cambodia. Americans dealt through the Chinese as the French had before them. Though citizenship laws seemed rigid, the pressure of war and the immediate postwar atmosphere allowed Chinese to continue in business.

At the turn of the century, many Chinese left behind China and the Boxer Rebellion to live in other countries. (Library of Congress)

Conditions deteriorate

Beginning in 1975 the new regime in unified Vietnam moved to socialize southern Vietnam and strengthen the nation's economy. At first, small businesses such as food markets and retail shops stayed in private hands; the government nationalized other businesses such as banks and shipping.

One refugee remembers the day in 1976 when his family's department store in Saigon was closed. Months later they were allowed to reopen it as a vegetable stand. Eggs and produce lined shelves that had once held fabric and clothing. Within months the national currency changed, reducing the value of other currency held. Though the family store remained open, trade fell drastically. The family grabbed its savings and fled.

Two problems facing Vietnam were increasing unemployment in a fast-growing labor force and urban congestion sapping tight resources. "New Economic Zones" begun in 1977 moved people, regardless of background, into the countryside to develop agricultural communities. The government encouraged migration by providing free transport, guaranteeing provision of essentials on arrival, and giving credit on basic supplies until the first harvest.

"Re-education" also began in 1975. Defeated armed forces' members were the first to be registered. Courses talked about people changing their old ways to fit into the new society, previous foreign interference, and the duties of Vietnamese citizens in reconstruction and socialization.

The second wave of people to leave Vietnam, those leaving after 1975 and before 1978, were mostly those who saw no benefit in staying, who had suffered economic loss, or who had unsuccessfully relocated under the new government. Three years in which flooding following droughts destroyed crops and livestock aggravated already poor conditions. Those who saw little or no hope of change determined to leave, not knowing whether their escape would be successful or what awaited them.

As socialization of agriculture in southern Vietnam speeded up in 1978, farmers (mainly Vietnamese) and middlemen (mostly Chinese) lost their independent economic positions. Ethnic minorities, especially Chinese, and Vietnamese who disapproved of the new programs were blamed for the food shortages. Closure of more shops also heavily affected Chinese. It was not long before merchants and traders who had never spent an hour in a rice field or vegetable patch were ordered at gunpoint to desert businesses their families had run for generations. They stood by as stores were looted, then were marched off to agricultural communes. Young Chinese men feared they might be forced to enter the military. In the countryside, harsh weather wrecked crops and housing. Hardship threatened lives as much as guns. Larger numbers began leaving southern Vietnam.

By the 1890s the simple black dress and long queues of Chinese appeared in cities all over the world. Children were rarely seen; adult men made up most of the immigrant population. (California State Library)

Conditions in Cambodia also worsened after 1975. Urban populations, Cambodian and Chinese alike, were hard hit by the sudden flood of peasants fleeing the countryside. American bombing and war had swelled Cambodia's capital, Phnom Penh, from

500,000 in 1963 to 3 million in 1975. Destroyed crops had not been replanted. People went hungry.

In 1975 Pol Pot's regime shoved people out of cities into the ravaged countryside. From 1975 to 1978 Chinese in Kampuchea (Cambodia's new name) joined Kampucheans in fleeing from the Khmer Rouge. Many fled to Thailand and Vietnam. Starvation and persecution reduced the differences between Chinese and Kampucheans; they suffered equally.

In northern Vietnam Chinese wanting to leave often crossed over into China. How many did so before 1978, when Beijing (formerly Peking) accused Vietnamese leaders of forcing overseas Chinese out, is not certain. When Vietnam responded with accusations that China was deliberately fomenting trouble, Chinese in Vietnam worried about possible war between the two countries.

Deteriorating relations with China may well have led to a Vietnamese policy change in 1978 toward Chinese. Hanoi began to encourage emigration. Middlemen began negotiating flights by boat between refugees and shipowners under the supervision of government employees. The middlemen also paid a secret fee to the government for each refugee they helped.

One Vietnamese describes the process of meeting the middleman. All the boat people, ethnic Chinese or Vietnamese, who had to buy their way on boats rather than leave in their own fishing boats, submitted to this process of secrecy and extortion: *"We [sixty-three people] came to the secret house. It was a house in a community by a Communist factory which made fish sauce. The owner of that house took us into a somber living room. We stayed there and waited until it got dark. In the meantime, I remembered what the people said about him—that he was a wily man. He had much money but he always wanted to have more. He organized a separate group and found many ways to go out to the sea. He looked for the folks who wanted to leave Vietnam and he talked with them. He knew many ways to get out of Vietnam that the Vixi [Viet Cong] didn't know. If people wanted to go, they had to give gold, diamonds, money to him. Of course they agreed and for that reason he made many trips for people and became a millionaire. This time we needed his help and he was ready to help us."* [1]

Costs of the boat trips were enormous. Fishing boats with rotten planks sold for $20,000. Bribes to officials could swallow up

More than 80 percent of the refugee boats have been boarded by pirates, sometimes several times. Many boats were blown off course by the monsoon winds. (Hong Kong Christian Service)

$1,000 to $3,000 for each refugee. One refugee paid a middleman $1,000 to help him get a place on a boat. Shortly after embarking, all hundred people on the boat were captured—possibly due to a report turned in by the middleman. Vietnamese sailors arrested them. Family members paid $1,000 for bail; then the bribes began all over again. This refugee figures his family spent $10,000 to get him out of Vietnam. He now lives in the United States in a small house with his aunt, uncle, and four cousins. He is unsure where the rest of his family is.

A Chinese invasion of North Vietnam in February 1979 heated up the campaign against Chinese in Vietnam. The Vietnamese government ceased to single out only Chinese merchants for the heaviest attack. They launched propaganda campaigns against all Chinese in Vietnam: fishermen, farmers, and merchants alike. Vietnamese feared to associate with their Hoa friends.

Refugee flood

What had been a trickle of overseas Chinese and Vietnamese leaving by boat became a flood. Shoving off to an unknown fate they became known internationally as "the boat people." Of the people clinging in desperation to those overcrowded ships about 70 percent were Chinese, most under the age of thirty-five. How many survived can only be estimated. The media reported fewer than 60 percent: nearly 200,000 died at sea. Monsoon rains swamped their small vessels. Hostile navies in Malaysia and Thailand threatened to turn them away.

Hundreds of thousands of people left Vietnam between March and July of 1979. Receiving nations protested they could not handle the sudden influx. International response to the castaways mushroomed. In July 1979 a sixty-five nation conference met in Geneva to consider the problem. Under pressure, Hanoi agreed to halt the flight of boat people. Australia, France, Canada, and China accepted refugees. The United States agreed to take 14,000 refugees each month for the indefinite future.

International compassion did not end the horrors boat people endured. Some still sit in refugee camps waiting for resettlement. Others are still bobbing on crafts in the South China Sea. Some who are resettled dwell on what happened to them. A young bilingual Chinese who graduated from a Seattle high school tells his story: *"I am a foreigner who has grown up in a mass of fire and war called Vietnam. My family was not rich but we were happy. In 1975 the Communists took away South Vietnam and with it went my future hopes and happiness. I could not endure living under Communist control so I was determined to escape in search of freedom. I remember the night we left. A dull moon filled the lake and little stars twinkled brilliantly in the sky. The night wind swept the leaves to and fro. It seemed like nature was playing a farewell song for us. The fishing boat which we were to use for our escape lay waiting on the water. We left quickly and while we were leaving I waved goodbye to my adopted homeland, Vietnam. 'Goodbye my relatives and goodbye my . . .' Before I went away I didn't want to say a word to her because I was afraid the tears would never leave her eyes. I could not bear seeing those tears on her face. The ocean was freezing and pitch black. I could hear its mighty sounds coming from the bottom of the*

In Laos, as in other Southeast Asian countries, overseas Chinese sold *ga lat pao*, sweet rolls, from streetside carts. Because of their commercial success (and middle-class values) ethnic Chinese were unacceptable to the socialist government. (Galen Beery)

ship. There were more than 100 people on the boat though it was only twenty-two meters long and six meters wide. I had to sit by the side of the boat on top of an oil drum. If I wasn't careful, I would have fallen overboard. Early the next morning the sun was burning brightly. Each movement of the boat took me further and further away from all that I had known and loved. The whitecaps in the water reminded me of fare-well tears. Ming . . . forget me! Hate me! I am sorry! The boat traveled a day before we reached international waters. During the night I woke up with a strange feeling. The boat was shaking. It started to rain and continued throughout the day. The waves were getting higher and stronger. The ocean turned from blue to gray. The waves attacked our vessel like wild dogs. The ship was silent and everybody was praying. The water came over the rail and hit me in the face. It felt like someone was slapping me. Suddenly, the owner of the ship came out of the control room. He wore a very pale expression. His body was shaking. He had terrible news! The captain was sick and he needed someone who knew how to pilot the ship. The rain was getting harder. It seemed like the sun was gone since the ship looked so gray. We felt very close to death and we prayed for God to help us. The captain recovered and everyone took a long breath. All of a sudden we saw a black shape coming toward us. 'At last!' we thought, 'Someone is coming to rescue us.' Everyone began to cheer up. As the black shape became bigger and closer, we also heard gunfire. Someone was shooting at us! People were afraid. The captain shouted. 'We must escape. Throw everything overboard!' Everyone threw their things into the water. The little packages flowed alongside the ship until the waves claimed them and swept everything away. The black ship came closer and closer, still shooting at us. Toward the end of one's life, some people curl up their body, others just cover themselves . . . I couldn't even think toward the end of my life. I sat still on the oil drum. I just wanted to laugh . . . laugh at this sour and bitter life. We waited for the robbers to come but the storm was too great even for them. We were saved. The sky turned from gray to black. It was extremely cold. During the attack the drinking water was thrown overboard. The angry sound of the waves mixed with the crying of a little child. Two days later we were still without water and everyone began to lose hope. It was a slow and painful torture. All aboard the boat were waiting to die. With dawn came a beautiful morning mist. I beckoned the ocean to take a message to my relatives and to Ming: Freedom, no matter how much we have to sacrifice, is worth-

Some Southeast Asian shipowners, once involved in drug running or smuggling, collected exorbitant fares from desperate Vietnamese and ethnic Chinese to help them escape. Ships were often unseaworthy, overcrowded, and vulnerable to attack by pirates. These boat people made it to Indonesia. (V. Leduc; UNHCR)

while! Suddenly a dark shape came toward us again. Should we go ahead and signal for help? The captain sighed, 'Let us gamble for our life. We have nothing to lose.' Everyone felt so weak but their restless eyes and dry lips reflected the bitterness of having their lives decided by chance, as if in a game. Perhaps that is what life is: a series of gambles. The dark ship became bigger. There was no gunfire and everyone felt relieved. Gradually, as the ship came closer we could see its colors clearly. It was a big military ship from Malaysia. Everyone rejoiced as it stopped next to us. Even the elderly smiled like little children. I felt I was smiling too. I remember talking but now I can't recall who I was talking to or what we were saying. Life is very precious. Once you are close to death and still are able to live, life has a greater value. Even though we have much pain and hardship, life is worthwhile if we are free.''[2]

The cumulative weight of the stories these refugees tell is overpowering. One girl tried to catch seagulls for her brother to eat. He slid into a coma and died from starvation and dehydration. A mother watched Thai pirates rape her teenage daughters. The pirates took the girls, probably to sell into prostitution. Boatloads of refugees were stripped and left naked on the decks of rotten ships as pirates searched, mostly in vain, for treasure. One man lost a finger when a Thai pirate hacked it off because the refugee did not remove his wedding ring. Other refugees watched pirates steal the pump and motor from their boat before leaving them adrift. Pirates killed wantonly and stole anything from hoarded gold to half-filled oil drums. One refugee said bands of pirates boarded his boat ten different times, taking what they could find, if only a map or a rudder.

Rescue did not necessarily mean security. At Pulau Bidong in Malaysia, one of the most crowded UNHCR camps receiving boat people in 1979, 42,000 people crammed into a quarter-square-mile rock island. Refugees waited in line for twenty-four hours for a drink of water. Babies and children wept from hunger. Garbage and waste rotted on the shore. Old people whimpered in the night. Ingenious refugees dug holes in the sandy cliffs and used scraps of wood stripped from the hillside to throw together huts. Other camps—Laemsing and Songkhla in Thailand—were no better. Neither the Thai nor the Malaysian government could handle the flood of refugees in 1978 and 1979.

Resettlement

Meanwhile, relief and resettlement officials predicted Vietnamese Chinese would have an easier time adjusting to American society

After an arduous voyage in open boats, many refugees were too weak to wade ashore. Some deliberately sabotaged their boats so they would not be forced back to sea. (Kaspar Gaugler; United Nations)

than any other Southeast Asian group. Prior Chinese communities existed here. By changing their names back to their original Chinese versions, they might find a place in family associations. They could buy Chinese-English dictionaries, translated novels, Chinese newspapers and magazines. Chinese benevolent and family associations might provide jobs.

Like early Vietnamese arrivals, ethnic Chinese from Vietnam

are predominantly urban. They understand diplomacy, economics, Western thought and dress. As a group they have the most experience with rigorous educational institutions. While the average Southeast Asian refugee arriving in the United States after 1979 had less formal education and less experience with Western culture than those who arrived in 1975 and 1976, this is not true of the ethnic Chinese.

Chinese refugees from Vietnam and Kampuchea understand status as an ethnic minority. They are grateful for the support of Chinese Americans when it is offered. Occasionally a new arrival finds that people of Chinese ancestry here resent the federal help available to Southeast Asians that was not available to their parents and grandparents. Or, he finds long residency in Southeast Asia mingled Chinese customs with Southeast Asian ones, setting him apart from Chinese Americans whose ancestors came from Canton. Established U.S. Chinatowns, however, do wait for these new arrivals—along with the problems accompanying ethnic ghettos: housing shortages and low wages for long work days.

Ethnic Chinese refugees try not to lean too heavily on existing Chinese American communities. In Seattle, overseas Chinese formed their own Indochina Chinese Association. Like the MAAs and benevolent associations, these groups strive to pull together the interests of ethnic Chinese from Southeast Asia. They recognize that the established Chinese American community does not necessarily owe them anything. They are products of a different history, a later struggle.

Overseas Chinese, despite their urban backgrounds, do have to make adjustments here. A young man whose family lived well on the top floor above a Saigon department store now works as a bellhop in a hotel. He saves money to pay for college classes in business and economics. In this way he accepts the tradition of starting at the bottom. Though he regrets what he has lost, turning fondly through old photo albums of leisurely afternoon strolls in Saigon parks or large family gatherings, he wants to work.

Some Americans worry that Chinese youth from Southeast Asia will follow those Hong Kong refugee and immigrant youth who formed gangs in Chinatowns, harassing people on the street and vandalizing businesses. Some of these youth recognized how

Goods imported from China were in great demand, and the overseas Chinese made use of trade opportunities across the globe. Chin Gee Hee's office, near Seattle, was typical of the turn-of-the-century merchant. (Asahel Curtis; Washington State Historical Society)

they differed from more established Chinese Americans—in dialect, attitude toward family, and the necessity of accepting menial jobs. Their response contrasted with that of their parents, who accepted those jobs and toiled hard to keep them.

A teenager whose family came to the United States from Hong Kong in 1972 describes her mother's first employment in San Francisco: *"After a few months, one of our relatives walked by a fortune cookie factory in Chinatown. They were looking for a Chinese worker for a full-time job. She told my mom right away and the next day, she was accepted. So from then on, my mom became a factory worker. In the beginning, she didn't have any thick gloves and her fingers were always burned by the hot cookies. The temperature in the factory is terribly hot, especially in the summer. It's stuffy and noisy inside. It takes a long time to practice the skill of folding and bending the cookies. During these times, the beginning workers don't get full pay. They have to wait 'til they can handle a machine all by themselves. Eight and a half hours was too much for my mom. Besides she didn't get used to conditions there. So later, I began to go help her and became a fortune cookie worker myself. In my opinion, I hate this job absolutely. It did nothing good to us except harm for my health and time. My mom gets sick very often. But she can't ask for a day off unless she is very, very sick. So sometimes she has to work even though she has a toothache. Few years ago, they all had day off on Sundays. Now, they have to work seven days a week. After work, my mom has to sweep the floor without pay. We have to make our own gloves and mend them after we go home.''*[3]

She may not have liked the job, but she kept it. This gutsy determination to survive earns the admiration of schoolteachers, sponsors, and neighbors. After well-educated overseas Chinese and other students from Vietnam attend English as Second Language classes, long chains of Nguyens, Lees, Wongs, and Chens appear on scholastic honor roles.

There are challenges mixed in with success, not the least of which are the temptations of a different educational system. A recently arrived Chinese high school student from Hong Kong describes what happened to her younger brother: *"I can't stand any person who changes their personality. For example, my little brother. Before he came here, in Hong Kong, he was a hardworking schoolboy, scared or polite to anyone who taught him. But after he came here, although he is so small, he knows how to change too. He began to be a naughty boy because school here never gives any work for students to do. When they are in the first grade, they just teach a little bit and let them do nothing when they get home, just fool around on the street every day after school. It happens to most of the Asians or Chinese and that's why my little brother changed into some kind of naughty gang of boys. Whenever I scold him or teach him, he will scold me back. When I slap him, he gives me a slap back, but I never said anything because he is already too spoiled by my parents. The only one he is scared of now is Ken, our older brother. He is not even scared of my parents. I don't know what he will do when he grows up.''*[4]

Bruce Lee's parents were itinerant musicians from Canton. Lee spent his early years in California and graduated from high school in Seattle. His prowess in the martial arts, captured in four action films in the 1960s, has become legendary. Chinese recently arrived in the United States will sometimes travel days to visit his grave in Seattle. (Anonymous)

If history is any indicator, despite his sister's fears he may well become once again the person she remembers. Unlike the Chinese sojourners who arrived one hundred years before him, he has a good grasp of Western values and culture that will help him in school, business, or a profession.

Chinese refugees of today can dream beyond stoop labor, menial domestic positions, or pick-and-shovel railroad building. This example was set for the overseas Chinese refugees by those lonely Chinese who came to America so many years ago. Newly arrived Chinese struggle to earn the opportunities they visualize on the horizon. A prediction of their success does not discount the disillusionment, painful memories, culture shock, and dejection they may feel along the way. Statistics on educational background and cultural tradition do not ease pain in that way. They do hold out hope to those who only a year or two ago had none.

Chronology

1850s Chinese immigration to Southeast Asia increases as Chinese merchants perceive business opportunities. Generally the Chinese remain in Chinese settlements rather than assimilating into Southeast Asian cultures.

1890s After France incorporates Vietnam in 1884 into French Indochina, French increasingly turn to Chinese to establish banking services and handle import business with the Vietnamese.

1909 Chinese government rules that children of Chinese nationals remain Chinese citizens. This sparks decades of controversy about whether Chinese in Southeast Asia are Chinese or French Indochinese citizens.

1930s Many Chinese in Southeast Asia return to China as Southeast Asia is hit by worldwide depression.

1940s-1950s Chinese merchants act as middlemen in trade to both nationalist and French forces.

1954 Vietnam split in two by Geneva Convention. Many Chinese leave North Vietnam, moving to south.

Late 1950s Vietnam harasses Chinese in Vietnam. Similar events take place in Cambodia as Southeast Asian governments insist that Chinese who have been living in their countries for many decades or were born there are no longer Chinese citizens.

1975 Saigon falls. Several hundred people leave Vietnam by boat.

1976 More than 5,000 Chinese leave Vietnam by boat in fear of persecution.

1977 Border disputes between North Vietnam and Kampuchea intensify. Some 21,000 Chinese leave Vietnam by boat.

1978 Vietnamese nationalization of private enterprise angers Chinese merchants. Rumors of war between Chinese-backed Kampuchea and Vietnam prompt many Chinese to flee Vietnam. China cuts off all aid to Vietnam. Vietnam invades Kampuchea. U.S. establishes diplomatic relations with China. Of some 106,000 people fleeing Vietnam by boat, 70 percent are Chinese.

1979 Vietnamese- and Soviet-backed Heng Samrin becomes the puppet ruler of Kampuchea. He replaces Chinese-backed Pol Pot. In July Vietnam agrees at Geneva Conference to stop encouraging the flow of refugees. 300,000 people leave Vietnam by boat.

1980 Number of people fleeing Vietnam by boat slacks off slightly.

1981 In May alone 15,000 Southeast Asians become boat people. High monthly figures give resettlement workers and asylum nations reason to fear that the plight of the boat people has not ended. Persecution of Chinese in Vietnam is reported.

NINE

(P. Jambor; UNHCR)

Survivors of an Asian Holocaust

Kampuchean Americans

Like pieces of a jigsaw puzzle, Vietnam, Kampuchea, and Laos snuggle along the Mekong River. Before independence in 1954, they formed the composite of French Indochina. Despite this proximity, Kampucheans retain their sense of a separate history. For Khmer, the predominant ethnic group of what was once Cambodia, this history goes back at least two thousand years.

Memories include the magnificence of Khmer civilization from the eighth to the twelfth century. Homes contain pictures of Angkor Wat and other massive temples built in the old capital city of Angkor. These temples, combining Hindu and Buddhist influence, cover some seventy-five square miles of plain. Though in need of restoration, they retain their grandeur.

At its largest, the Khmer Empire ranged from the border of China into present-day Thailand, Laos, and southern Vietnam. Expansion and contraction of territory continued until the fall of Angkor to Thai attackers in 1444. The Khmer court then moved southward to Phnom Penh. Rivalry in the royal family and continued struggles with other countries weakened the Cambodian state. The tug-of-war between Britain and Thailand, on one side, and France, on the other, led to the signing of a protectorate treaty with France in 1863.

Pressed by the French to change their government structure,

Cambodians rebelled in 1885. After a two-year battle they gained some concessions to the monarchy, but the French gradually took greater political control. France, remaining in nominal control when Japan occupied Cambodia during World War II, placed Prince Norodom Sihanouk on the throne in 1945. The monarchy, too, was more nominal than real. After the war, the French regained control throughout Indochina by Allied agreement. Cambodia became autonomous—at least in name. From 1945 to 1953 two main groups continued to work for true independence: supporters of the crown and those who supported parliament.

Early in 1953, while the French were fighting the Vietminh, Sihanouk dissolved parliament, imposed martial law, and sought world support for true Cambodian independence. France did grant full autonomy. At the 1954 Geneva Conference, Sihanouk's government was recognized as the only legitimate authority. Although internal political division continued, Sihanouk viewed nearby countries as a larger threat. Thailand to the west and South Vietnam to the east, historical rivals of Cambodia, were U.S. allies; he distrusted the United States' intentions. He also viewed a unified Vietnam under the Vietminh as a potential threat. Finally, in 1965 he decided to align Cambodia with China, North Vietnam, and the National Liberation Front in South Vietnam. He also allowed the North Vietnamese military to use Cambodian territory to move and store supplies.

Sihanouk's decisions and his internal policies dissatisfied both the political left and right. The left resented intolerance of their dissent; the urban right feared for their economic interests. In 1970 General Lon Nol and other leaders deposed Sihanouk, who then established a government in exile in China. This change did not bring stability. Cambodia became a battleground. The United States supported and gave aid in goods and money to Lon Nol. North Vietnam supported the leftists, dubbed Khmer Rouge (Red Khmer) by Sihanouk, who had taken to the countryside. When the U.S. bombing of Cambodia ended in 1973, the Khmer Rouge continued to fight Lon Nol's regime.

While military forces clashed and bombs fell, the economy of Cambodia disintegrated. Rubber production ceased; few crops were planted. The urban upper and middle classes began to feel

the pinch; the poor struggled along as best they could. Then, in April 1975, Phnom Penh fell to the Khmer Rouge. Sihanouk returned as titular head of the new government. When a new constitution took effect in January 1976, in the country newly named Kampuchea, he resigned.

Kampuchea's nightmare

With Sihanouk's leave-taking, the Khmer Rouge moved to consolidate their power. Weakened by the overflow of the Vietnam War into Cambodia from 1970 to 1975, royalist and neutralist forces were unable to resist a takeover. Under the leadership of Pol Pot, the Khmer Rouge military evacuated Phnom Penh.

In 1975 urban populations were much larger than they had been five years before. Cambodians had fled the barrage of bombs —more than were dropped on the whole Pacific theater during World War II—that blasted rural Cambodia. Pol Pot set out to return the urban population to what had once been 90 percent agricultural workers. His decrees closed schools and hospitals. Crowds were forced at gunpoint to leave the cities.

Those who fled Phnom Penh recall soldiers tossing patients out hospital windows to die in the streets. Fleeing pregnant women delivered babies at roadsides. Businessmen who dared to look back saw troops looting and burning stores. People who wore glasses learned corrected vision was "elitist, too intellectual."

Anti-communists, intellectuals, middle-class merchants, and everyone connected with the American-supported government of Lon Nol ran for their lives. Refugees reported mass executions and death from disease. People even suspected of resisting were killed—brutally. There were no trials. No second chances. No reasons for hope.

In the countryside, soldiers bludgeoned farmers who refused to relocate to forced labor camps, using farm implements to conserve bullets. To instill discipline, troops used terror. They dismembered and burned children in front of parents. As farmers fled to Thailand, troops swept rural villages, killing thousands at a time. In some places, remains were plowed into mass graves. Carrion fouled the jungle, wells, and fields.

Few observers ventured inside Kampuchea's closed borders

Bone fields scarring the Kampuchean countryside bear silent testimony to mass killings under Pol Pot's regime. (American Friends Service Committee)

during Khmer Rouge rule. Recent reports confirm refugee stories. Bone fields scar the gently rolling greenery of tropical Kampuchea. How many died is not known. Estimates range from 2 to 4 million of a population of some 7 million. By the hundreds of thousands, civilians fled to Thailand through steamy jungles. At the beginning some took trucks and possessions. Soldiers stalked and harassed them. At the Thai border they met suspicious guards who often turned them back. After months on the move, Kampuchea's refugees appeared to relief workers as shocking images of woe. In 1977 their pictures flooded the world's newspapers.

Refugee camps played a desperate catch-up game with the enormous numbers arriving daily. Well into 1980 camp conditions were deplorable. Children and adults, mere skeletons, lay wrapped in black rags on bamboo cots. Weeks of starvation swelled bellies. A teaspoon of rice after endless days of chewing on banana leaves, papaya bark, and grass caused violent illness.

Most suffered multiple medical problems. They shivered from malaria and dysentery. Hollow-eyed, they stared at cameras out of an abyss of hopelessness. Flies swarmed near eyes; bone-thin arms were too weak to brush them away. At Camp Khao I Dang, ten miles from the Kampuchean border, hacking coughs from pneumonia punctuated the soft nights. People died faster than relief crews could remove corpses.

Those remaining in Kampuchea from 1975 to 1979 fared little better. Agricultural production came to a standstill as farmers fled. Mass starvation threatened the entire population. By 1978 wire services referred to Kampuchea as the "Auschwitz of Asia," an Asian holocaust of starvation and mass extermination. Refugees reported as many as eleven of every fourteen family members had starved, been tortured, or been executed.

From the camps, Kampuchean refugees wrote to sponsorship agencies around the world. One West Coast agency has received 100 resettlement requests every day for several years. Officials file the names and addresses, send form letter responses, and search for church congregations or individuals to act as sponsors.

The tone of these letters has not changed. Though the English in the following letters from 1981 has been slightly regularized, their messages recall the urgent desperateness of the past. *"I am a Khmer refugee, age twenty-five. In the four years gone by I have lived in Pol Pot's regime. My uncle, my aunt, and my two brothers were killed and buried in the same hole because Pol Pot's elements knew that my relatives were soldiers. Pol Pot's men killed my older sister's husband because they accused him as a political man who betrayed their Communist Party. I live with wretchedness. I work hard day and night without anything to eat. My parents, my older brother and sister died because the Thai sent them back into the mountains. Nowadays because of steadfastness I stay at Kampot New Camp."*

Or, *"Would you please save my life by contacting the government of United States and ask a favor for me so that I and my family could be accepted for resettlement in your country? Because I have not any relatives abroad not even in the States, they were all killed in a harsh manner by the jungle law of Pol Pot's regime. My belongings and property were completely destroyed. Nothing is left to me except my true heart with faithfulness for my Saviour. I have no one else to turn to."*

Refugees stream into Camp Khao I Dang in Thailand, ten miles from the Kampuchean border. At one point in 1978, Khao I Dang contained more Khmer people than any city in Kampuchea. (M. Munz; UNHCR)

Similarly, *"Excuse me, Sir. I want you to help me soon because I'm very poor. I feel it's difficult for you to believe the despotic and barbarian regime of the Communist because the murderers killed without consideration. People get killed with hoe handles, by starving to death, by throwing people alive into wells. Sometimes they took a few months to die, forcing them to work from 5 a.m. to 12 p.m., stopping fifteen minutes for lunchtime. One milk tin rice cooks for fifteen to thirty persons. They will kill people for fertilizer. I can't tell you much because I can't speak or write well. When I enter your country, I make up my mind to learn English, to speak and write well, and learn all politics against the Communist regime. Kindly be confirmed that I haven't money in my pocket. Forgive my mistakes without purpose. With deep respect."*[1]

In December 1978 Vietnam invaded Kampuchea, occupying Phnom Penh. The Heng Samrin government, with Vietnamese support, replaced Pol Pot's regime in January 1979. Vietnam sought to reduce the danger of a two-front war by eliminating Chinese influence in Kampuchea. China had supported Pol Pot. China did invade northern Vietnam in February, then began a withdrawal one month later.

By the end of 1979, 200,000 Vietnamese troops occupied Kampuchea. The change offered some hope that the Kampuchean nightmare would end. Mass exterminations did come to an end. Other charges of abuse surfaced. International agencies reported that though Vietnamese soldiers helped dispense medical and food supplies to villagers during the day, they stole them back at night. Relief supplies ended up in Vietnam or sold on black markets for high profits.

The occupying army also fleeced relief agencies. Soldiers taxed entering relief vehicles and refugees fleeing for camps. OXFAM, an independent development and relief organization, reported in late 1979 that a barge carrying 1,500 tons of food was held for forty-eight hours and charged $9,000 before it could finish the journey up the Mekong River. A French relief ship had to pay $5,750 for handling charges and piloting fees on the Mekong. The pre-1975 cost would have been no more than $800.

Relief efforts

UN Secretary General Kurt Waldheim in 1979 called the plight of Kampucheans "a national tragedy with no parallel in history." For the survivors, aid began. Though guerrilla fighting disrupted food production as Khmer Rouge, Vietnamese, and Khmer Serei (Free Khmer) skirmished, worldwide relief sped to Kampuchea. Rosalyn Carter, visiting Thailand on a fact-finding trip for President Jimmy Carter in 1979, called the problem "inconceivable." Pope John Paul II appealed for the rights of Cambodians.

Media stars volunteered to lead efforts to save Kampuchea. In early 1980, Joan Baez and Liv Ullman led a march to the Kampuchean border of 160 celebrities including Coretta Scott King and Winston Churchill III. They begged Vietnamese soldiers to deliver the twenty truckloads of medical and food supplies that followed. Ullman explained her presence: "I want to go that road tomorrow because it is the same road that went to the gas chambers."

This young boy waited in line for food at Sa Kaeo camp in Thailand in 1979. Parents worried about how the abnormal environment of the camps might affect family life later. (P. Jambor; UNHCR)

Large international agencies such as UNICEF, Red Cross, American Friends Service Committee, World Vision, the United Nations, OXFAM, Church World Service, CARE, Lutheran World Relief, and Catholic Relief Services mobilized volunteers worldwide to collect money for Kampuchean relief. Individuals in small groups did what they could. A fifth-grade class organized a bake sale. In Oregon, a "Run for Cambodia" organized participants to collect per-mile pledges of money for donations. A California group sold tickets to a classical piano concert as a benefit. The former press secretary to California's Governor Jerry Brown and a Los Angeles attorney collected supplies in a movement known as "Operation California." An American nurse working in a Thai camp ended up offering her own breast milk to a starving child whose mother suffered from acute malnutrition.

Though refugees suffered from the knowledge that close to one-half their nation's people had died in a five-year period, by the end of 1980 new pictures appeared of camps with adequate sanitation and children with hesitantly trusting smiles. No one predicted a speedy return to prewar well-being, but careful words of optimism appeared in the news. The millions of dollars of international relief flooding Kampuchea had slowed the vicious cycle of malnutrition. By the end of 1980, most relief goods were getting into the hands of the people who needed them.

Through 1981 observers watched nervously as crops came to harvest in Kampuchean soil. Where Pol Pot had ruled by controlling the food supply, collecting and doling it out to those who supported Pol Pot-style communists, a solid market economy slowly regrew. Vegetable and fruit stands popped up in a once-again bustling Phnom Penh. International assistance propped up the delicate food supply by sending rice seed, agricultural pumps, and hand tools to aid rebuilding what the war and Pol Pot's regime had destroyed. Schools and hospitals reopened. A strong symbol of the psychological recovery of Kampuchea was the reestablishment of the well-loved National Ballet. A more tangible sign is the reduced number of Kampucheans in Thai camps; by the beginning of 1981 camps that had held 500,000, held 230,000.

Most observers, however, temper their optimism. They point to the likelihood of continued guerrilla fighting between anti-communists and the Vietnamese occupiers that could disrupt agriculture not fully recovered. And bad weather, epidemics, or reduced international aid could reverse the trend. Although traffic now clogs Phnom Penh and shops open regularly, a 1981 UNICEF survey reported that 80 percent of the Kampuchean population had just enough food to survive.

Pol Pot's regime attempted to create an agrarian utopia in Kampuchea, forcing all people out of cities into agricultural communes. In fact, the destruction of the economy combined with poor weather and the chaos produced by warfare created widespread starvation. Swollen bellies show typical signs of malnutrition. Many died before they could be helped by medical staff in refugee camps. (OXFAM America)

Legacy of loss

The Pol Pot legacy of horrors torments resettled Kampuchean refugees. One man has sent handfuls of letters to Thai camps in a vain search for his family. Despite the full support of his state's senator, he knows only the frustration that caused one of his sons in France to commit suicide: *"I did not know if my other sons and daughter or mother had been killed by the Pol Pot regime or tortured by them or starved. It was that way for five years and all the bad stories came out of Cambodia. Then the Vietnamese invaded, and there were more bad stories. I swam in my tears of misery until they were dry, and when I pleaded for help, people would tell me to be patient. I say to the United States, help me or shoot me. I am so miserable. Don't just tell me to be patient again. I was patient for five years."*[2]

In contrast, newspapers headline family reunions, even when only one or two members of an extended family of thirty find each other again. These meetings are only the beginning, as one refugee who attended school in Paris when Phnomh Penh fell explains: *"One of the biggest problems Cambodians in America face is adjustment. They've never experienced a touch-on oven, television. I see tremendous change. It makes me a little sad because I come from where principles are conservative. Fathers have really big authority. They are not always right but act for the children's own good. Here there is so much freedom."*[3]

So far this young man's perceptions sound like any immigrant's, any refugee's. He moves on to discuss how resettlement challenges his sense of identity. A past president of a Cambodian student association at a West Coast university, he remembers with gratitude those students who joined him in a hunger strike for a day as a fundraiser for Kampuchean relief. He hesitates and recalls how different, how remote he felt when he celebrated with Americans the next day. He says: *"Something strikes me quite often in the past two years when I'm brushing my teeth. I look at myself in the mirror and the first words I say are, 'Good morning.' It sounds really strange. It seems like there is another person right beside me. I say, hey who are you really? Where does that come from? Why do I speak English? It's very hard for me to feel at ease."*

Those feelings eventually intensified. After graduation with honors, he moved into his uncle's house in a middle-class suburb of a large West Coast city. The yard is well-groomed, the house tidy. Inside, three family groups live. In the living room is a Buddhist altar covered with offerings.

He appreciates his life. Proudly he displays his record collection and tells of the job he will start in one month at an aircraft company. Then he opens his eyes wide, glances over his shoulders at a nearby bedroom, and describes how he spends most of his days curled up in bed, facing the wall. Old memories, deep-rooted fears surface in this in-between time when he is neither in school nor working. He feels guilty for surviving. The experiences of Vietnam veterans have led mental health experts to call such symptoms "post-traumatic stress disorder." He says: *"Two years ago when I found out my mother was killed in Cambodia, I almost went crazy. It's ok*

Relief in the form of supplies and equipment from all over the world poured into Thai camps holding Kampucheans. Refugees eat at the Ban Mai Rut camp in Thailand. (John Isaac; United Nations)

now, but I have to see a counselor and take several pills to go to sleep. I lost all motivation to be myself. I wanted to tell her I hadn't been goofing around. I almost wanted to quit school.''

Though he is willing to try Western-style counseling and medication to ease his pain, he confesses that neither is doing much good. In his heart lies a conviction that a Cambodian Buddhist monk could help his spirit's conflict, but he knows of only one on the East Coast and two others who live 800 miles south.

Memories do not show to outsiders and Kampucheans do not share them lightly. One teenager, an unaccompanied minor by immigration terms, sat on the floor at a 1981 New Year's celebration tapping his foot in time to the beat of a Kampuchean rock band. His apparel—running shoes, designer jeans, and a fashionable t-shirt—testified to the adaptations he has made. When his foster mother and sponsor volunteered his story, he stared into space. Less than a year ago he and his sister ran through the jungle after hostile soldiers entered their village. She grabbed his sleeve, whispering to him to keep running and never look back. When he stopped, she was no longer with him. Days later his parents died of starvation. He could barely scrape up enough dirt in his hands to cover their bodies. He does not know what happened to his last family member, another sister, except that when the communists found out she was an artist, they broke her hands with a hammer. Art is elitist. While the woman talked, the boy's foot never lost the beat of the music.

Overcoming memories

Kampucheans resettled in the United States face perplexing problems. Their small numbers, perhaps less than 50,000 compared to the Vietnamese population of over 250,000, make a sense of community difficult. Family structures barely exist. A 1980 survey of 100 Khmer in Thai camps reveals the extent of loss.[4] From eight camps, the people questioned represent a cross-section of farmers, urban workers, and professionals. Of the 100, 40 lost 88 close family members. A third reported executions of family members. Deaths of more distant relatives mounted to more than 200. Of the survivors, 42 had seen executions. Those deaths have left many survivors in a shock that time has not healed.

Like other Southeast Asian refugees, those Kampucheans who escaped in 1975 tended to be from cities, where they received formal education and gained some understanding of Western customs. They understand that Americans want to shake their hands, thus they save the formal Khmer gesture of pressing their palms together with their hands near their foreheads while bowing to use among themselves. Newspaper articles feature countless stories of Kampucheans who have risen from janitorial positions to jobs in accounting firms or electronic design companies after one year—during which time they mastered English.

Those who fled later generally had less education and exposure to Western customs. They must learn that Americans do not nap

In July 1979, these two refugees lived in Ban Mai Rut camp near Klong Yai, Thailand. (John Isaac; United Nations)

after lunch. American traffic regulations seem too complex. Sponsors need to show them what to do with sheets and blankets which were not needed in tropical Kampuchea. Refrigerators strike them as luxuries. Most continue shopping for fresh meat and vegetables daily.

Some refugees make substantial career changes. Hardest hit are those who held the highest social rank in pre-1975 Cambodia. One Cambodian film star, Huy Sann, who acted in seventy-seven films as a martial arts "bad guy," now has steady work as a machinist in an electronics factory. He appreciates his job, knowing that many Americans would like it, but he misses his old life: cameras, publicity, and fame. At celebrations, Kampuchean youth still flock around him, but there is a difference. Their numbers here are so small. He dreams of going to Hollywood even as a stunt man riding motorcycles.

Many Kampuchean refugees have job skills and educational backgrounds suiting them for work here. Working as "family" groups, they buy homes and sponsor other arrivals. They look forward to New Year and other celebrations. They satisfy longings for new beginnings at the New Year by attending dinners, watching Cambodian ballet, and greeting other Kampucheans who have driven long distances to participate. But they do not forget.

Beyond carrying the burden of memories, Kampucheans struggle to adjust to the different moral values they find here. Families in Kampuchea tend to be very strict with young girls, not allowing them to go out at night or to talk casually with young men. Co-ed public schools, community events for refugees, and school gatherings put parents in a difficult position. Teenagers who want the same privileges as their American counterparts are usually not granted them, particularly girls.

Family dislocations created large numbers of single parent families headed by women. One relief agency estimates 60 percent of the Khmer population in Kampuchea today is female. In America these single parents feel trapped. If they refuse to date, they limit their chances for remarriage. If they date, members of their community are quick to judge. The women fear becoming outcasts from their ethnic group. Increasingly, Kampuchean women search for careers to help support their family. As this happens they experience conflict with the traditional view that women should stay at home to tend the house and children.

Political issues remain important. Concern prompts Kampucheans to flock around speakers, newsmen, and relief agency workers just returned from Kampuchea. Most confess to being homesick. The lack of reliable news complicates their efforts to track down relatives.

Refugees look with dismay on the current United Nations policy toward Kampuchea. Though the Vietnamese-backed Heng Samrin government bids for international recognition, the Khmer Rouge representatives of Pol Pot's regime hold the United Nations seat. Despite Pol Pot's appalling human rights record, the United States supports his regime's place in the United Nations rather than support any form of Vietnamese aggression in Southeast

Angkor Wat is the crowning architectural symbol of ancient Khmer culture. The structure rivals Chartres, Westminster, and St. Peter's cathedrals in size, age, and complexity. Begun by King Suryavarman about the year 1755 (1113 A.D. on the Western calendar) the temple's perfect perspective, massive towers, and Hindu bas reliefs make it a world treasure. When Buddhism swept the Southeast Asian peninsula centuries later, Buddhist statuary was built onto the sandstone foundation. Angkor Wat and dozens of other temples from the same era stand forlorn in the jungles of central Kampuchea. Monkeys chatter the only rituals as art thieves and the dense foliage eliminate the classic grandeur. (Mark Beach)

Asia. Vietnamese troops continue to occupy Kampuchea. From exile, Sihanouk claims China has offered infantry weapons to aid anti-Vietnamese forces in taking Kampuchea back. Refugees watch for international diplomacy to sort out which government—Sihanouk's coalition, Pol Pot's regime under varying leadership, or the Vietnamese occupiers—will gain the legitimate place in world affairs.

Conflicts and readjustments are inherent in the decision to relocate in a country as remote from Southeast Asia as the United States. What stirred the world's compassion, however, was the mass extermination of Kampucheans. That experience is still close to most Southeast Asians. Some tremble when they hear the roar of planes and helicopters. Children fear to walk through forests, anticipating hidden communists. In addition, Khmer wonder how their once proud people are to survive now that half of them are dead, so many others dispersed.

Americans often ask Kampucheans if they harbor any bitterness toward the U.S. government for initiating the bombing that devastated former Cambodia. Some shrug their shoulders. Others smile to avoid a conflict. Most do not hesitate to express gratitude for resettlement opportunities. They speak of America in terms of salvation, a promise of hope.

Perhaps one Southeast Asian refugee expressed the overriding feeling of new arrivals best when he said: *"There are some people who don't understand the cause and consequences of the Indochinese War and they have a tendency to feel we are cheating and stealing from them by being here. But we are a proud people and while we fought to the last minute in the war because we love our land, we are proud to say this is our home now. We feel the least we can do here is contribute in terms of our labor, our brain power, and our cultural heritage. We want to become part of this country. It is a chance for a new life. But, inside, the memories are still there. We won't ever forget."*[5]

Chronology

1850s Cambodian people (the Khmer) are subjugated by the peoples of Thailand and Vietnam, the result of centuries of border disputes and conquest all over Southeast Asia.

1864 France establishes Cambodia as a French protectorate. Cambodia becomes the second part of French Indochina.

1941 Prince Norodom Sihanouk is crowned King of Cambodia.

1954 Prince Sihanouk gains Cambodian independence from France as part of reshuffling of French Indochina after North Vietnam's defeat of France at Dien Bien Phu. Geneva Convention on Indochina recognizes Cambodian neutrality.

1955 Sihanouk abdicates throne but remains chief of state.

Khmer New Year's festivities, celebrated in mid-April according to the Buddhist calendar, help knit immigrants into a community. The Buddhist year 2524 corresponds to Western year 1982. (T. Brian Collins)

1955-1965 Trying to maintain Cambodian neutrality, Sihanouk juggles Chinese, American, and Russian interests in Southeast Asia and specifically renounces U.S. economic and military aid.

1965 U.S. airstrikes begin in Vietnam. Vietnamese communists and U.S. forces cross into Cambodia, which breaks off diplomatic relations with U.S. and aligns with China, North Vietnam, and South Vietnamese National Liberation Front (Viet Cong).

1967 U.S. spies begin missions into Cambodia to determine extent of Viet Cong and North Vietnamese activity along the Ho Chi Minh Trail which runs through northeastern Cambodia.

1968 Richard Nixon elected president. U.S. troop involvement in Vietnam reaches peak. Publicly President Nixon promises to respect Cambodian borders, but U.S. spies continue activity.

1969 President Nixon authorizes B-52 air strikes against Vietnamese strongholds in Cambodia upon recommendation of Secretary of State Henry Kissinger. Army Joint Chiefs of Staff warn that civilian deaths could run high since Vietnamese supply depots are close to Cambodian villages. Over a 14-month period 3,360 bombing raids devastate large tracts of land and kill Cambodian civilians along with North Vietnamese soldiers.

1970 Sihanouk, deposed while out of the country, calls upon Khmer Rouge to fight with his forces against the American-backed Lon Nol regime.

1970 American news media uncovers bombings of Cambodia; protest in the U.S. mounts. By April Nixon admits U.S. troops entered Cambodia. Four students at Kent State University shot by National Guardsmen become a symbol of student opposition to Nixon's administration, the Vietnam War, and American presence in Cambodia. By June U.S. troops withdraw from Cambodia.

1970-1974 Lon Nol's government, weakened by corruption and incompetent leadership, faces civil war against the Royal National Union Government of Kampuchea, a Sihanouk-communist coalition. Hundreds of thousands of Cambodians die as Vietnamese communists, Sihanouk supporters, and Khmer Rouge fight throughout Cambodia. Massive rice shortages threaten lives. Food prices rise. U.S. bombing also continues until 1973 when House of Representatives halts funds.

1975 North Vietnamese take Saigon. Khmer Rouge under the leadership of Pol Pot seize Cambodia's capital, Phnom Penh.

1976-1977 Cambodia renamed Democratic Kampuchea. Kampucheans continue to flee. No precise figures exist on how many resettled in the U.S. during this period as refugees from Southeast Asia were not counted by country of origin.

1978 Pol Pot's regime tightly controls the food supply. Refugees flood out of the country. Relations between Vietnam and China sour. Vietnam faces spectre of a two-front war against China and the Chinese-supported Pol Pot regime in Kampuchea. Vietnamese forces step up incursions into Kampuchea. By late December, Vietnamese forces take cities. Pol Pot's forces flee into mountains to establish guerrilla bases.

1979 Heng Samrin, backed by Vietnam, becomes the puppet ruler of Kampuchea. Vietnamese are backed by the Soviet Union. Samrin's leadership stops some of the atrocities of the Pol Pot regime. Agriculture, however, has been so severely disrupted that hundreds of thousands of Kampucheans starve to death or die of disease and malnutrition. World relief organizations send rice and medical supplies. Poorly organized refugee camps in Thailand struggle to take care of as many as 400,000 refugees at a time. Vietnamese vow to remain in Kampuchea until there is no further threat from China.

1980 Kampuchea's population of more than 8 million in 1970 is reduced to 4 or 5 million. Protesting the Vietnamese invasion, UN recognizes Pol Pot regime as officially seated government.

1981 Observers report crops growing almost normally. Vietnamese occupation continues. The situation remains tenuous, but some refugees leave the camps to return home. Pro-Vietnamese leaders win the first national elections since the 1978 Vietnamese invasion. Opponents of pro-Vietnamese candidates are not allowed on the ballot. Sihanouk claims from exile in Peking that China agrees to arm the Khmer Rouge and anti-communist soldiers to fight the Vietnamese troops still in Kampuchea.

1982 No firm statistics exist on how many Kampucheans live in the U.S. since they were not counted separately in the last census. Government estimates suggest between 10 and 12 percent of the Southeast Asian refugees in America are Kampuchean. It is likely more than 52,000 Kampucheans lived in the U.S. by mid-1981.

(N.Y. Convention and Visitors Bureau)

Epilogue

Despite all the problems in our cities today, despite all the burdens that our communities are bearing with unemployment, inflation, housing and taxes, you should recall that the record of history is clear: Whenever we have helped others to come here and build a new life, whether it was the Irish in Boston long ago, or the Chinese in San Francisco, or the Cubans in Miami, there have always been those who would close the golden door, but afterwards we have always been able to say, "By helping these people, we have helped ourselves." Our role as the beacon of freedom in a darkening world is too precious a part of our tradition, too central to our strength as a free people, to allow it to weaken even in the hardest of times. If we ever determine that the Statue of Liberty has become obsolete, we may find that we have become obsolete also.

Victor Palmieri
U.S. Coordinator for Refugee Affairs
1980

Chronology of United States Law

Appendix One

1743 Population of American colonies passes 1 million mark. Until 1880 most immigrants came from Great Britain, Germany, Ireland, Scandinavian countries, France, Belgium, the Netherlands, and Switzerland.

1789 U.S. Constitution gives Congress the sole power to limit, encourage, or prohibit immigration to America.

1790 First Census records 4 million people. U.S. Congress limits citizenship by naturalization to free, white aliens.

1820 Population reaches 9.5 million. U.S. starts keeping records on immigrant arrivals.

1870 By congressional act, people born in Africa or of African descent become eligible for U.S. citizenship. Asians do not.

1882 Chinese Exclusion Act becomes the first American law specifically to deny citizenship by naturalization to one nationality.

1894 Saito, a Japanese man, applies for U.S. citizenship. In court he is refused because he is neither white (Caucasian) nor black (of African descent).

1900 Hawaiian Islands become a U.S. territory.

1906 An 1878 California statute prohibiting intermarriage between negroes and whites is extended to include "Mongols." The U.S. Supreme Court declared all antimiscegenation laws unconstitutional in 1967.

1907 President Theodore Roosevelt signs Gentlemen's Agreement with Japan to limit Japanese immigration.

1911 U.S. Immigration and Naturalization Service reaffirms only whites and persons of African descent may become naturalized U.S. citizens.

1913 California law holds that persons ineligible for citizenship may not own land or property. Over the next few years, Oregon, Idaho, Montana, New Mexico, Minnesota, Nebraska, Washington, and Kansas follow California to bar Japanese and Chinese immigrants from owning land.

1924 Immigration Act sets immigration quota of 2 percent for the nationals of a given country living in the U.S. in 1890. No one ineligible for citizenship can immigrate. Combined with 1790 congressional act, this act effectively halts immigration of non-whites, except nationals. Filipine nationals' immigration opens to fill jobs once held by Japanese.

1931-1940 The smallest number of immigrants were admitted to the U.S. during this decade of any decade since 1830. In the U.S., as in many countries, residents suffer financial hardship due to Great Depression.

1940 Nationality Act allows Eskimo aliens and Native Americans not born in the U.S. to become U.S. citizens by naturalization.

1941 December 7—Japan bombs Pearl Harbor. U.S. enters World War II.

1942 Executive Order 9066 signed by President Franklin Roosevelt authorizes U.S. Army to remove persons of Japanese ancestry from the Western Defense Command, a large portion of the West Coast states.

1943 Chinese Exclusion Act is repealed. China and the U.S. are allied against Japan.

1946 With Philippine independence, Filipinos in America become eligible for citizenship by naturalization.

1948 U.S. Supreme Court holds that alien land laws violate the equal protection clause of the Fourteenth Amendment.

1948 President Harry Truman signs the Evacuation Claims Act, which authorizes payments of settlements to people of Japanese ancestry who suffered economic losses during internment.

1952 McCarran-Walter Act revamps immigration policy. It gives the right of citizenship to all immigrants. It also establishes a rigid quota system based on ancestry not birth, restricting immigration from the Asia-Pacific Triangle (including Afghanistan, Indonesia, Burma, Cambodia, China, India, Pakistan, Korea, Laos, the Philippines, Samoa, Thailand, and Vietnam) to 100 per nation, total not to exceed 2,000 in one calendar year. Some non-Asian countries are also limited to a quota of 100 per year, including Egypt, Ethiopia, Iran, Iraq, Israel, Jordan, New Zealand, Australia, and Saudi Arabia. European countries, on the other hand, are given more liberal quotas: Italy, 5,645; Germany, 25,814; France, 3,069; Ireland, 17,756; Greece, 308.

1965 Public Law 89-236 eliminates the quota system established under the 1952 act and the Asia-Pacific Triangle provisions. Under this law 20,000 immigrants are allowed annually from each independent nation outside the western hemisphere—though this is revised in 1978 to create a hemispheric ceiling. It establishes a system of preferences for selecting immigrants. For example, first preference is given a son or daughter of an American citizen. The seventh preference is for refugees. Refugees do not enter the U.S. as immigrants. They are considered parolees, or conditional entrants, who must wait two years for change of status to immigrants, or permanent residents. Parolees are defined as people fleeing persecution because of race, religion, or political ideas who are afraid to return to their country of origin. From 1965 on, immigration legislation is directed at assisting the world's huge refugee populations. (See Chronology of legislation as it affects Southeast Asian refugees, page 166).

Graphs

Appendix Two

The graphs on the following pages are based upon information from three sources: U.S. Bureau of Census, U.S. Immigration and Naturalization Service, and U.S. Department of Health and Human Services, Office of Refugee Resettlement. These agencies gathered data under circumstances which often changed. The figures must, therefore, be understood in their historical context.

Who is of Asian background? Starting in 1970, census takers recorded ethnic and racial backgrounds according to self-reports. Each person could identify a heritage or omit the question. Before 1970, census takers themselves decided on a person's heritage based upon factors such as appearance and accent.

What is an Asian nation? Political history has often changed answers to this question. For forty years, Korea was considered part of Japan. For almost as long, the Philippines were considered part of the United States. Then, starting in 1936, people from those islands were counted as foreign nationals.

Decisions about efficient ways to categorize people also affect what nations get counted. Nations sending only small numbers typically have their people listed only as "other Asians." Thus Koreans did not appear as a census category until 1960 and Vietnamese until 1980. In the 1980 census, Laotians and Kampucheans were enumerated as "other Asians" along with people

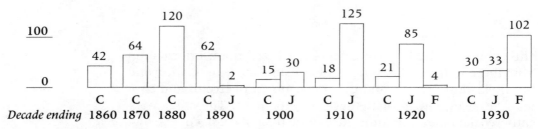

One: Arrivals in the United States and territories from Asian nations by decade from 1851-60 through 1971-80. 1981 arrivals have been included here in the decade 1971-80, their numbers given parenthetically and shown at the top of the bar. (Sources: 1851

from Thailand, Burma, India, Indonesia, Malaysia, and the islands of the Pacific.

What is the United States? During the 19th century, the Hawaiian Islands were a U.S. territory commercially, but not politically. Data from those years come from the records of the Royal Hawaiian government (which skipped its own census in 1880). During its six decades of territorial status, Hawaii was enumerated by the census but not by immigration authorities. Thus, for example, a person going from the Philippines to Hawaii in the 1920s was considered as going from one U.S. territory to another.

What is an immigrant? Figures from the immigration authorities include only people with official immigrant status. Thousands

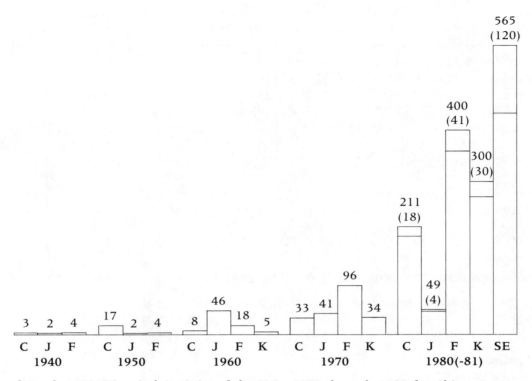

565
(120)

400
(41)

300
(30)

211
(18)

49
(4)

96

46

33 41   34

17
18
8   5
3 2 4   2 4

C J F   C J F   C J F K   C J F K   C J F K SE
  1940   1950   1960   1970   1980(-81)

through 1970, Historical Statistics of the U.S.; 1971 through 1981 for China, Japan, Philippines, and Korea, U.S. Immigration and Naturalization Service; 1971 through 1981 for Southeast Asian nations, U.S. Office of Refugee Resettlement)

of others came—and still come—unofficially, thus were not counted. Additional thousands have some other official status, such as student or parolee, so are counted by other agencies.

In addition to these factors, census data usually underrepresent minorities. Because minority peoples are often also poor, they frequently must move their households. Sometimes there are two or three families sharing one living space. Census takers have a hard time getting an accurate count. Some minority people also fear or resent government, thus avoid census takers. This is especially true for recent arrivals whose previous government took the census only for purposes of taxation and military conscription.

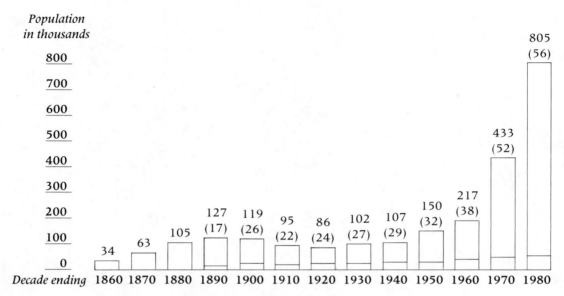

Two: Cumulative totals of Chinese heritage in the United States and territories by decade from 1851-60 through 1971-80. Residents of Hawaii are shown at the bottom of the bar, and their numbers given parenthetically. (Source: U.S. Bureau of Census)

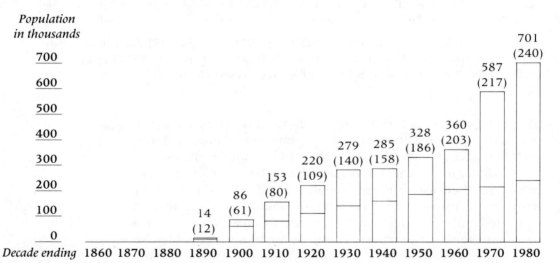

Three: Cumulative totals of Japanese heritage in the United States and territories by decade from 1851-60 through 1971-80. Residents of Hawaii are shown at the bottom of the bar, and their numbers given parenthetically. (Source: U.S. Bureau of Census)

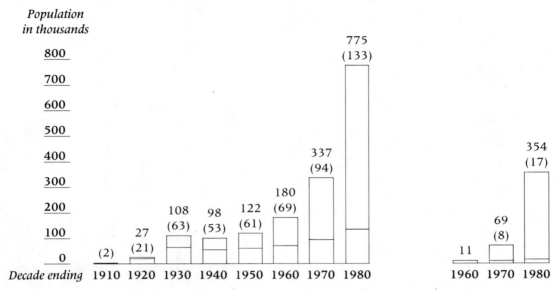

Four (left): Cumulative totals of Filipino heritage in the United States and territories by decade from 1901-10 through 1971-80. Five (right): Cumulative totals of Korean heritage in the United States and territories by decade from 1951-60 through 1971-80. Residents of Hawaii are shown at the bottom of the bar, and their numbers given parenthetically. (Source: U.S. Bureau of Census)

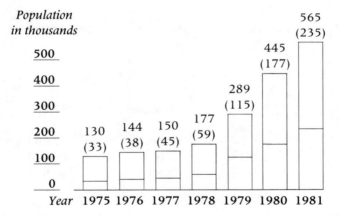

Six: Cumulative totals of Southeast Asian refugees in the United States by year from 1975 through 1981. Residents of California, Oregon, and Washington are shown at the bottom of the bar, and their numbers given parenthetically. (Source: U.S. Department of Health and Human Services, Office of Refugee Resettlement)

Ethnic heritage	Population	Percent of all Asian Americans
Chinese	433,000	28
Japanese	587,000	38
Filipino	337,000	22
Korean	69,000	5
Other	100,000	7
Total	1,526,000	100

Seven: United States populations of Asian heritage for the year 1970. (Sources: U.S. Bureau of Census; U.S. Office of Refugee Resettlement)

Ethnic heritage	Population	*Percent of all Asian Americans*
Chinese	805,000	23
Japanese	701,000	20
Filipino	775,000	22
Korean	354,000	10
Vietnamese	322,000	8
Laotian	141,000	5
Kampuchean	102,000	3
Other	300,000	9
Total	3,500,000	100

Eight: United States populations of Asian heritage for the year 1981. (Sources: U.S. Bureau of Census; U.S. Office of Refugee Resettlement)

All Names are American Names

Appendix Three

Kie Ho, who lives in Laguna Hills, California, wrote this article for the *Los Angeles Times* in the spring of 1982. It is reprinted here with permission.

At a recent seminar that my company sponsored, where many of the participants came from our overseas offices, a gentleman from the Netherlands looked at my name tag and said, "I see that you are from our division in California, but your name does not sound American." I told him that mine is indeed a Chinese name; however, I am an American citizen.

I should have told him that my name is as American as Lucille LeSueur or Margarita Carman Cansino before they became Joan Crawford and Rita Hayworth. My name does sound as foreign as the name of the Japanese slugger Sadaharu Oh, but does it not also sound as American as Joe DiMaggio?

I have already simplified my name for Yankee ears. I was born Kie Liang Ho, which means Ho the First-Class Bridge. I skip the name Liang because it is so difficult for many to pronounce correctly. Even so, the short name has caused much confusion. Some secretaries write it as Keyhole. Others, deciding that such a short last name is impossible, change it arbitrarily to something more common, like Holm or Holt.

When I was sworn as an American citizen, I could have become Keith Ho, or Kenneth Ho, or even Don Ho. I decided to keep my Chinese name;

this is one privilege that my new country gives me—the right to maintain my ethnic identity—and I cherish it.

Having a Chinese name does not necessarily mean that culturally I am a Chinese. I was born in Indonesia (which a lot of people misunderstand to be Indochina), and I do not write or speak Chinese. The only Chinese characters I can write are my name and my father's. Still, to everyone I am a Chinese. When somebody in my office has a birthday and we are all signing a card, people often say, "Come on, Kie, write something in Chinese." What I write is my dad's name, and I tell them that it means "Abundance of Fortune and Long Life." Actually, my father's name means Ho the Gold Fish.

Many people are confused by Asian names and nationalities. One day, my wife and I asked a patio contractor to give us a reference. He turned over page after page of his reference book and at last, with a friendly, victorious smile, he said: "Here you are, this one is a Chinese lady, Mrs. Nguyen." I hated to disappoint him by telling him that Nguyen is a Vietnamese name, and, since we do not speak Vietnamese at all, she might not be the best to call.

When our daughter was born, we did not give her a Chinese name. We thought that the name should be selected for the child, not for the parents' sake. We would have liked to name her May Hoa Ho, "Ho the Pretty Flower," but imagine the problems that she would face in school among children who like to make fun of "funny" names. So we gave her a "common" American name: Melanie. We hope that she will be as gentle as Melanie Wilkes in "Gone With the Wind." I wonder if Melanie Wilkes' mother ever knew that "Melanie" refers to something black: Would she still have named her so? Only Margaret Mitchell could tell.

So what's in a name? Benjamin Kubelsky changed his name (Jack Benny). Zbigniew Brzezinski did not. I will not, either.

Notes on the Text

Appendix Four

ONE: Chinese Americans; Pages 9 through 45

1. Stephen Williams, "The Chinese in the California Mines" (Ph.D. Dissertation, Stanford University, 1930).
2. Stan Steiner, *Fusang: The Chinese Who Built America* (New York: Harper and Row, 1979), p. 114. Copyright 1979, Stan Steiner. Reprinted with permission of Harper and Row.
3. Williams, p. 53.
4. *Ibid.*, p. 59.
5. Mary Lee Chan interview. Reprinted from *Opening Doors: Vancouver's East End* by Daphne Marlatt and Carole Itter (Sound Heritage Series, Volume 8, Nos. 1 and 2), Provincial Archives of British Columbia, 1979.
6. Steiner, p. 133. Copyright 1979, Stan Steiner. Reprinted with permission of Harper and Row.
7. Eng Yin Gong and Bruce Grant, *Tong War!* (New York: Nicholas L. Brown, 1930), p. 10.
8. David Newsom, *The Western Observer 1805-1882* (Portland: Oregon Historical Society, 1972), p. 205.
9. Ming-tai Chen, "What I Hope For the Chinese Community in Portland," *Chinese Language School Quarterly*, Vol. 1, No. 2. Trans. Chia-lin Chen, Oregon Historical Society, 1973.
10. Reprinted from Marlatt and Itter, *Opening Doors*, p. 41.

11. *Ibid.*

12. From a collection of interviews, Portland, Oregon, Oregon Historical Society, 1973. Reprinted with permission.

13. Tommy Woo, "12 Hours A Day," *Sojourner IV*, Asian Writers Project, Berkeley Unified School District, 1974. Reprinted with permission.

TWO: Japanese Americans; Pages 47 through 85

1. Ito Kazuo, *Issei: A History of Japanese Immigrants In North America* (New York: Japan Publishing, 1973), p. 291. Reprinted with permission.

2. K. K. Kawakami, *The Real Japanese Question* (New York: Macmillan, 1921), p. 252.

3. William Petersen, *Japanese Americans: Oppression and Success* (New York: Random House, 1971), p. 15. Reprinted with permission of Random House.

4. Paul Mayeda, "Sword in the Air," *Sojourner IV*, Asian Writers Project, Berkeley Unified School District, 1974. Reprinted with permission.

5. Esther Boyd, Testimony before Select Committee, House of Representatives, National Defense Migration Hearings held in Washington, March 1, 1942, Part 30, p. 11583.

6. Dan McDonald, Testimony before Select Committee, Part 30, p. 11583.

7. National Defense Migration Hearings, House of Representatives, Part 30, p. 11465, in *Final Report: Japanese Evacuation from the West Coast*, by General J. L. Dewitt (Washington, D.C.: Government Printing Office, 1943).

8. From *Issei and Nisei: The Internment Years*, by Daisuke Kitagawa. Copyright © 1967 by The Seabury Press, Inc. Reprinted with permission.

9. Joey Ouye, "Oka-San," *Sojourner IV*. Reprinted with permission.

10. Jeanne W. and James D. Houston, *Farewell to Manzanar* (Boston: Houghton Mifflin, 1973), pp. 27-29. Copyright 1973, James D. Houston. Reprinted with permission of publisher, Houghton Mifflin Company.

11. Gordon Hirabayashi, "A Case for Redress," Speech at Japanese

American Citizens League Conference, Portland, Oregon, March 14, 1981.

12. Amy Eto, "A New Happening With Mother," *Sojourner IV*. Reprinted with permission.
13. Houston and Houston, *Farewell to Manzanar*, pp. 146-147. Copyright 1973, James D. Houston. Reprinted with permission of publisher, Houghton Mifflin Company.
14. Darrel Montero and Gene N. Levine, "Third Generation Japanese Americans: Prospects and Portents," Revised (San Jose, California: Pacific Sociological Association, 1974).

THREE: Filipino Americans; Pages 87 through 113

1. Bruno Lasker, *Filipino Immigration to the Continental United States and Hawaii* (Chicago: University of Chicago Press, 1931), p. 233.
2. Willie Barientos quoted in *First Generation: In the Words of Twentieth Century Immigrants*, by June Namais (Boston: Beacon Press, 1978), p. 85.
3. Pete Silifan, *Why America?* (n.p.: Asian Americans for Community Involvement, 1978), p. 13.
4. H. Brent Melendy, "Filipinos in the U.S.," in *The Asian American: The Historical Experience*, ed. Norris Hundley (Santa Barbara, California: Clio Press, 1976), p. 108.
5. Alfonso Engalla, *Sojourner IV*, Asian Writers Project, Berkeley Unified School District, 1974. Reprinted with permission.
6. Interview with Silvestre Pulmano, Portland, Oregon, March 18, 1981.
7. Carlos Bulosan, "Selected Letters of Carlos Bulosan," *Amerasia Journal*, 6 (May 1979): 143.
8. Buaken, Manuel, "Where is the Heart of America," *New Republic*, September 25, 1940, p. 410.
9. Connie Noblejas, "Invasion: WWII," *Sojourner IV*. Reprinted with permission.
10. Interview with Silvestre Pulmano.
11. *Ibid.*
12. Interview with Greg Oliveros, Portland, Oregon, April 9, 1981.
13. Carlos Bulosan as quoted in "Introduction" by E. San Juan Jr., *Amerasia Journal*, 6 (May 1979): 26.

FOUR: Korean Americans; Pages 115 through 139

1. Warren Y. Kim, *Koreans in America* (Seoul, Korea: Po Chin Chai Printing, 1971), p. 82.
2. Wayne Patterson and Hyung-chan Kim, *The Koreans in America* (Minneapolis: Lerner Publications, 1977), p. 34.
3. Interview with Dr. David Kim, Director, Holt Foundation, Holt International Children's Services, July 21, 1981.
4. Studies of Koreans in America appear in *Korean Diaspora*, ed. Hyung-chan Kim (Santa Barbara, California: Clio Press, 1977).
5. All of Dr. Sammy Lee's comments are from an interview by the author in May 1981.

FIVE: U.S. Refugee Administration; Pages 141 through 169

1. U.S. Department of Health, Education and Welfare, *Report to Congress on Indochinese Refugee Assistance*, 1978.
2. Julian L. Simon, "What Immigrants Take From, and Give To, the Public Coffers," Paper by Professor at University of Illinois, Urbana, September 15, 1980.
3. Interview with Pastor Tran Xuan Quang of the Vietnamese Mennonite Church of Euphrata, Pennsylvania by Mel Lehman, *Indochina Refugee Update*, Church World Service, New York, June 1980.
4. Thomas Mortenson, "Factors Influencing Refugee Sponsorship in the U.S.," *Journal of Refugee Resettlement* 1 (March 1981): 8.
5. *Ibid.*, p. 15.
6. Ed Sponga, Office of Refugee Resettlement, U.S. Department of Health and Human Services, Washington, D.C. Correspondence with author, April 6, 1981.
7. Tran Cong Nghi, "Refugees Resettlement Policy on the Role and Responsibility of Indochinese Mutual Assistance Associations," Speech presented to General Assembly of Indochinese MAAs in Portland, Oregon, November 1980.
8. Graduate paper for Asian American Studies Program, "The Lao and Cambodian Refugee Communities in Seattle-King County" (Seattle: University of Washington, 1980), p. 17.
9. Le Xuan Khoa, "Cultural Adjustment of Indochinese Refugees," *DAT MOI*, March 20, 1980.

SIX: Vietnamese Americans; Pages 171 through 203

1. Pham Than, "Always Vietnam," *Sojourner IV*, Asian Writers Project, Berkeley Unified School District, 1974. Reprinted with permission.
2. *Ibid.*
3. Mai Khanh Tran, Class assignment, Madison High School, Portland, Oregon, 1980.
4. Darrell Montero, *Vietnamese Americans: Patterns of Resettlement and Socioeconomic Adaptation in the United States* (Boulder, Colorado: Westview Press, 1979), pp. 29ff.
5. Mai Khan Tran, Class assignment.
6. Vuong G. Thuy, *Getting to Know the Vietnamese and Their Culture* (New York: Frederick Ungar Publishing, 1976), pp. 21-22.
7. Interview with Pastor Xuan Quang of the Vietnamese Mennonite Church in Euphrata, Pennsylvania by Mel Lehman, *Refugee Update*, Church World Service, New York, 1980, p. 2.
8. *Ibid.* p. 3.
9. Darrell Montero, *Vietnamese Americans*, pp. 42ff.
10. Khan Nguyen, Class assignment, Roosevelt High School, Portland, Oregon, 1981.
11. Mai Khan Tran, Class assignment.
12. Asian Relations Center, "Voices of the Refugees," *Refugees—the Cry of the Indochinese* (Tokyo: Sophia University, n.d.), p. 74. Reprinted with permission.
13. Asian Relations Center, "Voices of the Refugees," p. 75.
14. Citizen from Seadrift, Texas on ABC's "20/20," September 21, 1979.
15. Le Xuan Khoa, "Vietnamese Immigrants and Their Adjustment to American Society," *DAT MOI*, April 27, 1980.
16. Khan Nguyen, Student assignment.

SEVEN: Laotian Americans; Pages 205 through 255

1. Interview with Vongthonthip Kiat, Portland, Oregon, April 29, 1981.
2. Report from Galen Beery to International Voluntary Services, January 20, 1964.
3. Vongthonthip Kiat in "Children of Laos: A Descriptive Report,"

by Terri Lee Kubow, Spring 1977. Reprinted with permission of Vongthonthip Kiat and Galen Beery.

4. Jeffrey Kaye, "Yearning to Breathe Free," *New West*, April 7, 1980, p. 57. Quoted in "The Assimilation and Acculturation of Indochinese Children into American Culture" (Sacramento, California: Department of Social Service).

5. Interview with Ay Choy Sae Lee, Portland, Oregon, March 10, 1981.

6. Mike Sweeney, "Southeast Asians," *Cityfolk*, ed. Steve Siporin (Portland: Oregon Arts Commission, 1981), pp. 16-17.

7. Chen Vang, Class assignment, Roosevelt High School, Portland, Oregon, 1981.

8. Jane Hamilton Merritt, "Flight from Laos," *New York Times*, September 4, 1979.

9. Mike Sweeney, "Southeast Asians," pp. 13-14.

EIGHT: Overseas Chinese; Pages 257 through 277

1. Nghiep Nguyen, Class assignment, Mills Junior High School, Sacramento, California, 1980.

2. Quan Ngo, Class assignment, Cleveland High School, Seattle, Washington, 1980.

3. Anne Lee, "Just A Trap," *Sojourner IV*, Asian Writers Project, Berkeley Unified School District, 1974. Reprinted with permission.

4. Millie Huey, "Gang of Boys," *Sojourner IV*. Reprinted with permission.

NINE: Kampuchean Americans; Pages 279 through 299

1. Letters edited and reprinted with permission of Sponsors Organized to Aid Refugees (SOAR), Portland, Oregon, 1981.

2. J. Crick, "Beaverton Cambodian Man Searches Camp on Thai Border," *Oregon Journal*, May 10, 1980.

3. The next three quotations are from an interview by the author with a Kampuchean refugee on April 17, 1981. His name has been withheld upon request.

4. *Far Eastern Economic Review*, survey, June 6, 1980, p. 21.

5. Diane Carman, "Refugees' Memories Still Hurt," *Oregon Journal*, November 19, 1979.

Resources

Appendix Five

Here is a list of books and articles most readers could find in a good public or university library. This is not a bibliography for research scholars, although it does include a few quite specialized titles. In addition to citations for books and articles, this list has information about resources such as bookstores, agencies, and Asian American organizations.

General background

Daniel, Cletus E. *Bitter Harvest: A History of California Farm Workers, 1870-1941.* Ithaca, New York: Cornell University Press, 1981.

Daniels, Roger. "American Historians and East Asian Immigrants." *Pacific Historical Review* 43(1974):449-72.

Endo, Russell, ed. *Asian Americans: Social and Psychological Perspectives.* Palo Alto, California: Science and Behavior Books, 1980.

Fairbanks, John K. Jr., and Reischauer, Edwin O. *East Asia: Tradition and Transformation.* New York: Houghton Mifflin, 1973.

Fall, Bernard B. *Two Vietnams: A Political and Military Analysis.* New York: Praeger, 1967.

Herring, George C. *America's Longest War: The United States and Vietnam, 1950-1975.* New York: Wiley, 1979.

Hundley, Norris, ed. *The Asian American: The Historical Experience.* Santa Barbara, California: Clio Press, 1976.

Kalb, Marvin, and Abel, Elie. *The Roots of Involvement: The U.S. in Asia, 1784-1971*. New York: Norton, 1971.

Latourette, Kenneth S. *Short History of the Far East*. 3rd ed. New York: Macmillan, 1957.

Lyman, Stanford M. *The Asian in North America*. Santa Barbara, California: Clio Press, 1970.

Perrin, Linda. *Coming to America: Immigrants from the Far East*. New York: Delacorte, 1981.

Price, Charles A. *The Great White Walls are Built: Restrictive Immigration to North America and Australasia*. Canberra: University of Australia, 1974.

Reischauer, Edwin O. *Beyond Vietnam: The United States and Asia*. New York: Alfred Knopf, 1968.

Sowell, Thomas. *Ethnic America: A History*. New York: Basic Books, 1981. (Specific chapters about Chinese and Japanese along with good comparisons with European immigrant groups.)

Takaki, Ronald. *Iron Cages: Race and Culture in Nineteenth Century America*. New York: Alfred Knopf, 1979. (One of the first general accounts of white exploitation of all peoples of color.)

Thernstrom, Stephen, ed. *Harvard Encyclopedia of American Ethnic Groups*. Cambridge: Harvard University Press, Belknap Press, 1980. (This single volume reference work is the starting place for any research about ethnic history. Chapters on Chinese, Japanese, Filipinos, Koreans, and Indochinese; many theme chapters on topics such as family patterns, language maintenance, and religion.)

Ujimoto, K. Victor, and Hirabayashi, Gordon. *Visible Minorities and Multiculturalism: Asians in Canada*. Scarborough, Ontario: Butterworth, 1980.

Wang, L. Ling-chi. "Asian American Studies." *American Quarterly* 33(1981):339-54. (Describes Asian American studies in colleges and universities.)

White, Peter T. "Lands and Peoples of Southeast Asia." *National Geographic* 139(March 1971):295-365.

In addition to these titles, there are 47 books forming a series called *The Asian Experience in North America*. The series is edited by Roger Daniels and published by Arno Press, Three Park Avenue, New York, NY 10016. Write for the free catalog.

Periodicals and other sources

Amerasia Journal. Published twice a year by the Asian American Studies Center at the University of California, Los Angeles, 3232 Campbell Hall, Los Angeles, CA 90024. Winter issue carries annual bibliography of books, articles, and dissertations.

Annals of the American Academy. Vol. 454 for March 1981 was a special issue titled "America as a Multicultural Society."

The Asian American Education Commission of the Los Angeles Unified School District, 450 North Grand Ave., Los Angeles, CA 90012, produces curriculum materials.

The Asia Society, 725 Park Ave., New York, NY 10021, publishes two magazines. *Asia* provides articles of general interest; *Focus* (begun in 1982) is written specifically for teachers.

The Center for South and Southeast Asian Studies, 260 Stephens Hall, University of California, Berkeley, CA 94720, includes an outreach program for schools and public organizations.

The Indochinese Materials Center, U.S. Department of Education, 324 East 11th St., Kansas City, MO 64106, has extensive lists of materials about refugees.

The Japanese American Curriculum Project, P.O. Box 367, San Mateo, CA 94401, has a catalog of books on a variety of topics relating to all Asian Americans.

The National Indochinese Clearinghouse, 3520 Prospect St. NW, Washington, DC 20007, publishes pamphlets, materials lists.

The Social Science Education Consortium, 855 Broadway, Boulder, CO 80302, publishes catalogs and lists Asian American programs as part of its Ethnic Heritage Studies Project.

The Stanford Program on International and Cross-Cultural Education, Lou Henry Hoover Building, Stanford, CA 94305, develops curriculum materials about Chinese and Japanese Americans. Similar work in the midwest takes place in two centers at the University of Michigan: Project on East Asian Studies and Education, 104 Lane Hall, and Center for South and Southeast Asian Studies, 130 Lane Hall, both University of Michigan, Ann Arbor, MI 48109.

The Union of Pan Asian Communities of San Diego County, 1031 25th St., San Diego, CA 92102, publishes various materials.

Visual Communications, 244 South San Pedro, Los Angeles, CA 90012, has photographs and films about Asian Americans.

World Affairs Council, 314 Sutter St., San Francisco, CA, sponsors a school services program focusing on Asian Americans.

There are a number of bookstores that specialize in materials by and about Asians and Asian Americans. They include:

Eastwind Books & Arts, Inc., 1435-A Stockton St., San Francisco, CA 94133

Everybody's, 17 Brenham Pl., San Francisco, CA 94102

Amerasia Bookstore, 322 East 1st St., Los Angeles, CA 90012

David Ishii Bookseller, 212 1st St. South, Seattle, WA 98104

China Books, 2929 24th St., San Francisco, CA 94110. Also stores at 174 W. Randolph, Chicago, IL 60601 and 125 Fifth Ave., New York, NY 10003.

Kinokuniya, the largest bookstore chain in Japan, with U.S. outlets in San Francisco, Los Angeles, and New York City.

Several dozen colleges and universities have Asian or Asian American study programs. The largest programs with the best libraries and most professors are at these institutions:

Brown University

University of California (Berkeley and Los Angeles)

Cornell University

Harvard University

University of Hawaii

University of Illinois

University of Michigan

Northwestern University

Stanford University

University of Washington

University of Wisconsin

Chinese Americans

Chen, Jack. *The Chinese of America*. New York: Harper and Row, 1980.

Daniels, Roger, ed. *Anti-Chinese Violence in North America*. New York: Arno Press, 1979.

Dennis, Phillip A. "The Anti-Chinese Campaigns in Sonora, Mexico." *Ethnohistory* 26(1979):65-80. (One of the very few accounts in English of Chinese in northern Mexico.)

Dicker, Laverne. *The Chinese in San Francisco: A Pictorial History.* New York: Dover Books, 1980.

Fairbanks, John K. *The United States and China.* Cambridge: Harvard University Press, 1979. (A basic scholarly account of historic relationships between the two nations.)

Kingston, Maxine Hong. *Chinamen.* New York: Alfred Knopf, 1980. (Describes her father's and grandfathers' experiences as sojourners.)

Kingston, Maxine Hong. "San Francisco's Chinatown." *American Heritage* 30 (1978):36-47. (Her commentary on historic photographs by Arnold Genthe.)

Kingston, Maxine Hong. *The Woman Warrior.* New York: Vintage Press, 1975. (About her childhood as a Chinese American girl sorting out two cultures.)

Lai, Him Mark. *The Chinese of America, 1785-1980.* San Francisco: The Chinese Culture Foundation, 1980. (Full of fine photographs and other visual materials.)

Mark, Diane Mei Lin, and Chih, Ginger. *A Place Called Chinese America.* Dubuque, Iowa: Kendall Hunt, 1982. (The most comprehensive and best illustrated of recent books about Chinese Americans.)

Marlatt, Daphne, and Itter, Carole, eds. *Opening Doors: Vancouver's East End.* Victoria, British Columbia: Provincial Archives, 1979. (Includes extensive narratives by descendants of early Chinese immigrants to Canada.)

Nee, Victor, and Nee, Brett. *Longtime Californ': A Documentary Study of American Chinatowns.* New York: Random House, 1973.

Spence, Jonathan. *The Gate of Heavenly Peace: The Chinese and Their Revolution, 1895-1980.* New York: Viking Press, 1981. (Tells the story through the experiences of writers and scholars.)

Steiner, Stan. *Fusang: The Chinese Who Built America.* New York: Harper and Row, 1979.

Sung, Betty Lee. *Mountain of Gold:The Story of Chinese in America.* New York: Macmillan, 1972.

Wong, Jade Snow. *Fifth Chinese Daughter.* New York: Harper and Row, 1950. (Autobiography of growing up in San Francisco.)

Japanese Americans

Adachi, Ken. *The Enemy that Never Was: A History of Japanese Canadians.* Toronto, Ontario: McClelland, 1976.

Bonacich, Edna, and Modell, John. *The Economic Basis of Ethnic Solidarity: A Study of Japanese Americans.* Berkeley: University of California Press, 1980.

Broadfoot, Harry. *Years of Sorrow, Years of Shame.* New York: Doubleday, 1977. (Oral histories of Japanese Canadians.)

Conroy, Francis H., ed. *East Across the Pacific.* Santa Barbara, California: Clio Press, 1972.

Daniels, Roger. *The Politics of Prejudice.* Berkeley: University of California Press, 1962.

Hosakawa, Bill. *Nisei: The Quiet Americans.* New York: William Morrow, 1969.

Ichihaski, Yamoto. *Japanese in the United States.* Palo Alto: Stanford University Press, 1932.

Kiefer, Christine. *Changing Culture, Changing Lives: Ethnography of Three Generations of Japanese Americans.* San Francisco: Jossey Bass, 1974.

Kitano, Harry. *Japanese Americans: The Evolution of a Subculture.* New York: Prentice Hall, 1969.

Levine, Gene, and Rhodes, Robert. *The Japanese American Community: A Three Generation Study.* New York: Praeger, 1982.

Montero, Darrel. *Japanese Americans.* Boulder, Colorado: Westview Press, 1980.

Peterson, William. *Japanese Americans: Oppression and Success.* New York: Random House, 1971.

Reischauer, Edwin O. *The Japanese.* Cambridge: Harvard University Press, 1977.

Sone, Monica. *Nisei Daughter.* Boston: Atlantic Monthly Press, 1953. (Autobiography)

Wakatsuki, Yasuo. "Japanese Immigration to the United States, 1866-1924." *Perspectives in American History* 12 (1979).

Weglyn, Michi. *Years of Infamy: The Untold Story of America's Concentration Camps.* New York: William Morrow, 1976. (The most exhaustive study of Executive Order 9066.)

Wilson, Robert, and Hosokawa, Bill. *East to America: A History of the Japanese in the United States.* New York: William Morrow, 1980.

Filipino Americans

Allen, James P. "Recent Immigration from the Philippines and Filipino Communities in the United States." *Geographical Review* 67(1977):195-208.

Buaken, Manuel. *I Have Lived with the American People*. Caldwell, Idaho: Caxton, 1948.

Bulosan, Carlos. *America is in the Heart*. Seattle: University of Washington Press, 1973. (Autobiography by the leading literary figure among Filipino Americans.)

Kim, Hyung-chan, and Mejia, Cynthia C. *Filipinos in America, 1898-1974*. Dobbs Ferry, New York: Oceana Publications, 1974.

Lasker, Bruno. *Filipino Immigration to the Continental United States and Hawaii*. Chicago: University of Chicago Press, 1931. (This book is still the classic account of early Filipino immigration.)

McWilliams, Carey. *Brothers Under the Skin*. Boston: Little, Brown, 1943. (The classic description of California farm workers during the 1930s.)

Melendy, H. Brett. *Asians in America: Filipinos, Koreans, and East Asians*. Boston: Twayne, 1977.

Quinsaat, Jesse. *Letters in Exile: A Reader on the History of Filipinos in America*. Los Angeles: University of California, 1976.

Saito, Shiro. *Filipines Overseas: A Bibliography*. New York: Center for Migration Research, 1977.

Stanley, Peter W. "The Manongs of California." *Harvard Magazine* 83 (May-June 1981): 36-45.

Korean Americans

Bong-youn Choy. *Koreans in America*. Chicago: Nelson-Hall, 1979.

Houchins, Lee, and Houchins, Chang-su. "The Korean Experience in America, 1903-1924." *Pacific Historical Review* 43(1974):548-576.

Hurh, William Moo. *Assimilation of the Korean Minority in the United States*. Philadelphia: Philip Jaisohn Foundation, 1977.

Kim, Hyung-chan. *The Korean Diaspora*. Santa Barbara, California: Clio Press, 1977.

Kim, Warren Y. *Koreans in America*. Seoul: Po Chin Chai Printing, 1971.

Patterson, Wayne, and Kim, Hyung-chan. *The Koreans in America*. Minneapolis: Lerner Publications, 1977.

Refugee administration

Ellis, William. "Hong Kong's Refugee Dilemma." *National Geographic* 156(November 1979):709-732.

Garrett, Wilbur E. "Thailand: Refuge from Terror." *National Geographic* 157(May 1980):633-662.

McClellan, Grant, ed. *Immigrants, Refugees, and U.S. Policy*. New York: H. W. Wilson, 1981.

Stein, Barry, and Tomasi, Sylvano, eds. "Refugees Today." Special issue of *International Migration Review* 15(1981). Bibliography pp. 331-393.

Tepper, Eliot L., ed. *Southeast Asian Exodus from Tradition to Resettlement: Understanding Refugees from Laos, Kampuchea, and Vietnam in Canada*. Ottawa: Canadian Asian Studies Association, 1980. (Distributed in the U.S. by the University of Chicago Press.)

Wain, Barry. *The Refused: The Agony of the Indochina Refugees*. New York: Simon and Schuster, 1982.

Vietnamese Americans

Arden, Harvey. "Troubled Odyssey of Vietnamese Fishermen." *National Geographic* 160(September 1981):378-396. (About the fishing rights controversies in the Gulf of Mexico.)

Kelly, Gail. *From Vietnam to America*. Boulder, Colorado: Westview Press, 1979.

Liu, William T. *Tradition to Nowhere: Vietnam Refugees in America*. New York: Charter Spring, 1979.

Montero, Darrel. *Vietnamese Americans: Patterns of Resettlement and Adaption*. Boulder, Colorado: Westview Press, 1979.

Thuy, Vuong G. *Getting to Know the Vietnamese and their Culture*. New York: Frederick Unger, 1976.

Woodside, A. B. *Community and Revolution in Modern Vietnam*. Boston: Houghton Mifflin, 1976.

Laotian Americans

Garrett, Wilbur E. "The Hmong of Laos: No Place to Run." *National Geographic* 153 (1974).

Graham, David C. *Folk Religion in Southwest China*. Washington: Smithsonian Press, 1967.

Levine, Ken. *Becoming American*. A 45 minute film tracing a Hmong family from Thailand through its first year in Seattle, Washington. Available from Iris films, 720 West Blaine, Seattle, WA 98119.

Lutheran Immigration Services. *The Hmong: Their History and Culture*. Lutheran Immigration Services, 360 Park Ave., New York, NY 10010.

Tambiah, S. J. *Buddhism and the Spirit Cults in Northeast Thailand*. Cambridge: Cambridge University Press, 1970.

Young, Gordon. *The Hill Tribes of Northern Thailand*. Bangkok: Siam Society, 1962.

Overseas Chinese

Alley, R. *Refugees from Vietnam in China*. Beijing: New World Press, 1980.

Center for Applied Linguistics. *Background Information on the Ethnic Chinese Refugees*. Available from Center for Applied Linguistics, 3520 Prospect St. NW, Washington DC 20007.

Grant, Bruce. *The Boat People*. New York: Penguin, 1979.

Willmott, W. E. *The Chinese in Cambodia*. Vancouver: University of British Columbia Press, 1967.

Kampuchean Americans

Allman, T. D. "Cambodia: Nightmare Journey to a Doubtful Dawn." *Asia Magazine* 4(April 1982):8-15.

Garrett, Wilbur E. "The Temples of Angkor: Will they Survive?" *National Geographic* 161(May 1982):548-589.

Vek Huong Tiang. *Ordeal in Cambodia: One Family's Escape from the Khmer Rouge*. San Bernardino, California: Here's Life Publishers, 1980.

White, Peter T. "Kampuchea Awakens from a Nightmare." *National Geographic* 161 (May 1982):590-623.

Index

Appendix Six

France, 141, 176-178, 182, 185, 200, 202, 206-208, 244, 250, 258-259, 260, 266, 276, 279-280, 296
French Indochina: See Indochina
Fresno, California, 31, 53, 73
Fu Manchu, 37
Fusang, 10

Gallup polls, 164, 186
Garment industry, Asians in, 38
Geneva Accords (1954), 179, 182, 208, 259
Geneva Conference (1954), 139, 178-179, 200, 252, 276, 280, 296
Geneva Conference (1979), 266, 276
Gentlemen's Agreement (1907), 58, 64, 84, 90, 91, 112, 120, 138
German Americans, 69, 72
Gold: See Mining
Gold Hill, California, 84
Guam, 185
Gulf of Mexico, 152, 195-198
Gulf of Tonkin Resolution (1964), 182-183, 201
Gum San (Mountain of Gold), 9, 34, 42

Hainan, 223
Haiphong, 202
Haiti, 141
Hanoi (See also North Vietnam), 173, 178, 192, 202, 266
Hawaii, Asians in: Chinese, 12, 14, 36, 259; Japanese, 52, 56; Filipinos, 92-93, 112; Koreans, 118-119, 121, 122, 124; Southeast Asian refugees, 151, 245
Heng Samrin, 277, 285, 294, 299
HIAS, 147-148
Hirabayashi, Gordon, 74, 76
Hirayana Buddhism (See also Buddhism), 222
Hiroshima, 79
Hmong, 144, 145, 150, 154, 156, 163, 206, 208, 209, 211, 222, 224, 225, 230, 232, 236-255, 254
Hmong Family Associations, 248-249
Hoa, 257, 265
Ho Chi Minh, 178, 200, 202, 252

Japan: closed door policy, 47-50; consulate system of, 52, 57, 99; in Korea, 50, 116, 118-122, 138; in Manchuria, 30, 34, 44, 50, 64, 116; in Southeast Asia, 50, 65, 200, 206, 220, 238, 252, 259, 280; map, 49; Meiji Restoration, 50, 64; occupation of Philippines, 97, 104-105, 113; pact with Germany and Italy, 65, 66; war brides, 126; war with Russia, 50, 118

Japanese Exclusion Act: See Immigration Act of 1924

Jewish refugees, 142, 161, 166

John Day, Oregon, 17

Johnson, Lyndon, 182-183, 201-202

Joss house, 19

Kampuchea, Democratic (See also Cambodia), 214, 255, 263-280, 297-299; map, 281

Kampuchean (or Khmer) refugees, 148, 154, 156, 158, 160, 161, 165, 168, 202, 212, 278-299

Kennedy, John, 39, 45, 182, 201

Kent State University, 298

Khao I Dang refugee camp, 284, 285

Khmer Empire, 174, 206, 296

Khmer refugees: See Kampuchean refugees

Khmer Rouge, 280-283, 286, 294, 298, 299

Khmer Serei, 286

Kibei, 74

King, Coretta Scott, 286

Kissinger, Henry, 202, 298

Korea: Christian influence in, 118, 119; division of, 204; history of, 115-124, 179; map, 117; nationalism, 120-123, 138; relations with Japan, 50, 116, 119, 179, 124, 138; Russian occupation of, 124-126

Korean Central Intelligence Agency, 134

Korean National Association, 138

Korean War, 126, 132, 133

Koreatown (Los Angeles), 134-135

Ku Klux Klan, 198

Kuomintang, 32

Kwangtung Province (China), 10, 12

Ky, Nguyen Cao, 180

Tonkin, 173, 178
Topaz, Utah, 73
Truman, Harry, 76, 80, 305
Tule Lake Relocation Center, 71, 73

Uganda, 141
Ullman, Liv, 286
Unaccompanied minors as refugees, 149, 291
UNICEF, 287, 288
Union Pacific Railroad, 21, 27
Union reaction to Asian immigrants, 53, 56-58, 62
United Cannery and Packing House Workers of America, 102
United China War Relief, 34
United Farm Workers Organizing Committee, 92, 99, 106
United Nations (UN), 42, 124, 126, 130, 141, 166, 168, 210, 255,
    287, 294
United Nations High Commissioner for Refugees (UNHCR), 142,
    166, 270
United States Agency for International Development (USAID),
    182, 208, 240, 241, 253, 254
U.S. Catholic Conference, 147
U.S. Census figures: Chinese, 16, 44, 45; Japanese, 54, 58, 84,
    85; Filipino, 91, 106, 113; Korean, 123, 132-133, 139;
    Southeast Asian, 203, 299
U.S. Center for Disease Control, 154, 248
U.S. Immigration and Naturalization Service (INS), 138, 154,
    206, 298
U.S. Special Forces, 182
USSR, 32, 33, 50, 118, 124, 138, 141, 148, 179-181, 254, 259,
    296, 299
Utah, Asians in, 15, 31, 73, 100, 151

Vancouver, British Columbia, 10, 20, 24
Vang Pao, 240-242
Victoria, British Columbia, 24
Vientiane, Laos, 206, 207
Viet Cong, 200, 201, 297
Vietminh, 178, 179, 200, 208, 280

Acknowledgments

Appendix Seven

In October 1975 a Vietnamese boy told his story of the trip from Saigon to the United States. Later he wrote the story down, ending with his last memory of home—his puppy scratching at the gate, whining to go along. Though stories I have listened to since then described more tragic losses, Ky Anh Phan introduced me to what it meant to be a refugee.

Since then many people contributed the encouragement, assistance, and criticism which made this book possible. I owe special thanks to Chuck Galford, Mark Beach, Mike Sweeney, Kathleen Ryan, Ellen Martin, and Ay Choy Sae Lee. Susan Page-York, who edited it, and John Laursen, who designed it, turned this book into what we all wanted it to be.

For advice and guidance I thank Gordon Hirabayashi, Gilbert Hirabayashi, Linda Wing and her students at the Berkeley Unified School District, Galen Beery, Cyble Campbell, Al Cardwell, Dr. Robert Swartout, Jr., Congressman Norman Mineta, Wayne Patterson, Darrel Montero, Greg Oliveros, Sylvestre Pulmano, Vongthonthip Kiat, Khamone Keopraseuth, Louis Flannery, Susan Seyl, Elizabeth Winroth, Sammy Lee, Father Tran Cong Nghi, Father Vincent Minh, George Leong, Ed Sponga, Charlene Day, Elaheh Greenbaum, Darlene Durgan, John Withers, Lucinda Wong, Jean Pullen, Karen Green, Steve Reder, Roger Daniels, Farm Yoon

Sae Lee, Pramaha Boungkong Singsouvanh, Jerry Burns, Dr. David Kim, Tim Collins, Sothirak Pou, Elizabeth Ciz, and Patrick Wong.

Numerous organizations generously provided information. I am grateful for the help of teachers, administrators, and students in the ESL-Bilingual program of Portland Public Schools, Seattle Public Schools, and the Berkeley Unified School District. I also thank members of the Japanese American Citizens League, Hong Kong Christian Service, Church World Services, Sponsors Organized to Assist Refugees (SOAR), United Nations High Commissioner for Refugees, Center for Applied Linguistics, Office of Refugee Resettlement, Indochinese Cultural Center of Portland, Southeast Asian Foxfire Project, Oregon Historical Society, Portland Chinese Benevolent Association, Portland Refugee Forum, and administrators of historical archives up and down the West Coast.

Finally, I salute the people who inspired this book: the sojourners, immigrants, and refugees. Some shared memories as narratives. Others stated opinions about past opportunities and present realities. A few showed photographs of their families and friends. All enhanced my awareness of the rich diversity involved not only in becoming Americans, but also of being Americans. Thank you.

Tricia Knoll

Becoming Americans

Tricia Knoll is a writer living in Portland, Oregon. Ms. Knoll holds degrees with honors from Stanford and Yale Universities. During the 1970s, while teaching high school, she had an increasing number of Southeast Asian refugees in her classrooms.

The production of *Becoming Americans* has been a sustained and rewarding collaboration of five people, including the author. Susan Page-York edited the text. Mark Beach and Kathleen Ryan, co-publishers, compiled and edited the photographs. John Laursen designed the book and executed the page layouts.

The cover was designed and lettered by Elizabeth Anderson. The maps were produced especially for this volume by Al Cardwell at GeoGraphics. The type is Meridien, set by Irish Setter. The paper is Finch offset vellum. The printing and binding have been done by Malloy Lithographing of Ann Arbor, Michigan.